INTEGRATED PRACTICE

The Integrated Musician

A BOOK SERIES CONCEIVED AND EDITED BY PEDRO DE ALCANTARA

As a musician you're part performer, musicologist, linguist, historian, psychologist, athlete, and mathematician. The Integrated Musician is a book series designed to help you develop many of these skills and unify them in a harmonious whole.

Two books underpin the series. *Indirect Procedures: A Musician's Guide to the Alexander Technique* explores concepts of whole-body and body-mind awareness. *Integrated Practice: Coordination, Rhythm & Sound* invites you to use music itself to guide your search for wholeness and psychophysical freedom.

The series will continue with volumes covering more detailed ground for string players, singers, woodwind players, and keyboardists. In the future, the series may grow to include other musical domains as well.

THE INTEGRATED MUSICIAN: A MANIFESTO

We tell stories and listen to them continuously, the better to understand the world and navigate it. Story includes narrative, metaphor, illustration, humor, explanation, analysis, sounds, images, and gestures. The integrated musician is a storyteller, using elements of story while practicing, rehearsing, and performing.

Music is a language, and as such it has its own syntax, orthography, and punctuation. Like all languages, music has a prosody as well—that is, a rhythmic organization. The integrated musician is a master of rhythm in all its dimensions.

What you say and how you say it are never far apart. When you express yourself in an individual manner that is unique to you, your technique too will be individual and unique. The integrated musician invents and reinvents his or her technique.

Your whole body is present in all that you do. There is a circuit of connections from finger to hand, to arm, shoulder, head and neck, and also to back, pelvis, legs, and feet. The integrated musician is a "connected animal."

Creativity, the intellect, and the emotions play a permanent role in daily life as well as in music making. The integrated musician balances out mind and body, structure and improvisation, the rational and the irrational.

Theory and practice can be good friends. To understand tonality and modality, acoustics, historical practice, and other theoretical concepts is to feel and perform music differently. The integrated musician finds pleasure in knowledge.

There is a difference between a creator (Beethoven, for instance) and a reproducer (a performer playing Beethoven today). Meaningful art always is close to the creative source. The integrated musician makes music as a creator, from within, even when performing pieces composed by other people.

Pedro de Alcantara
Paris and New York
April 2010

INTEGRATED PRACTICE

COORDINATION, RHYTHM & SOUND

Pedro de Alcantara

OXFORD
UNIVERSITY PRESS

OXFORD
UNIVERSITY PRESS

Oxford University Press, Inc., publishes works that further
Oxford University's objective of excellence
in research, scholarship, and education.

Oxford   New York

Auckland   Cape Town   Dar es Salaam   Hong Kong   Karachi
Kuala Lumpur   Madrid   Melbourne   Mexico City   Nairobi
New Delhi   Shanghai   Taipei   Toronto

With offices in

Argentina   Austria   Brazil   Chile   Czech Republic   France   Greece
Guatemala   Hungary   Italy   Japan   Poland   Portugal   Singapore
South Korea   Switzerland   Thailand   Turkey   Ukraine   Vietnam

Copyright © 2011 by Oxford University Press, Inc.

Published by Oxford University Press, Inc.
198 Madison Avenue, New York, New York 10016

www.oup.com

Audio and Video clips (🔺) are available online at
www.oup.com/us/integratedpractice

Library of Congress Cataloging-in-Publication Data
Alcantara, Pedro de, 1958–
Integrated practice: coordination, rhythm & sound / Pedro de Alcantara.
p. cm. — (The integrated musician)
Includes bibliographical references and index.
ISBN 978-0-19-531707-7; 978-0-19-531708-4 (pbk.)
1. Musicians—Health and hygiene.   2. Alexander technique.   I. Title.
ML3820.A43 2011
781'.11—dc22   2010017040

To my beloved teacher, Robert D. Levin

ACKNOWLEDGMENTS

In 1997 Oxford University Press published my first book, *Indirect Procedures: A Musician's Guide to the Alexander Technique*. Following its publication, I had the opportunity to coach instrumentalists, singers, and conductors all over the world. The present book is the result of my encounters with these talented and motivated musicians. At the risk of leaving out many cherished friends, I'd like to thank Joel Anderson, Gerald A. Brown, Patrick Cavagnet, François-Xavier Chauchat, Keyvan Chemirani, Immanuel Davis, Kati Debretzeni, Hager Hanana, Käthe Jarka, Frédéric Ligier, Beryl Marshall, Ivo Perelman, Victoria Roth, Hisaichi Shimura, Pedro Couto Soares, and Matt Turnbull. Over the years I've had sustained support from the late Laurel Anderson and her students and colleagues in Switzerland; Lila Brown and Nina Tichman, and their students and colleagues in Germany; the members of the Orchestre National de Lille, the Ensemble Intercontemporain, the Orchestra of the Age of Enlightenment, and the Orchestre Romantique et Révolutionnaire; innumerous musicians who came by my studio in Paris or who met me in my travels; and the worldwide community of Alexander teachers.

My friend João Mourão, a skillful and very patient man, set the music examples. Ulysses Chuang, Florian Cousin, Deirdre Dowling, and Debora Growald contributed to the video files, as did Rebecca and David Tepfer at the Atelier de la Main d'Or in Paris. Nicolas Bilder of Iloz Productions recorded and edited the video files. Gerald A. Brown and Hisaichi Shimura contributed to the audio files, which Jeremy Gerard recorded and edited at Gurari Studios in New York City. AlumniVentures, an initiative of the Yale School of Music, awarded me a generous grant to develop these video and audio materials.

Parts of this book have appeared in different form in the magazines *The Strad* and *Médecine des Arts*.

My editor at the OUP, Suzanne Ryan, has steered this project from conception to birth, giving me sober advice and warm encouragement over the years. Without her watchful guidance, *Integrated Practice* would simply not exist.

Finally, my wife Alexis Niki has long been my de facto cowriter, accompanying me in my creative adventures and defending me fiercely whenever any one of my books threatens to kill me, which is often. That she's my wife and not my widow demonstrates how well she takes care of me, and I can't thank her enough.

PERMISSIONS

Excerpt from "The Planets" in *Poems* by C. S. Lewis, copyright © 1964 by the Executors of the Estate of C. S. Lewis and renewed 1992 by C. S. Lewis Pte. Ltd., reprinted by permission of Houghton Mifflin Harcourt Publishing Company.

Excerpt from "τεθνάκην δ' ολίγω 'πιδεύης φαίνομ' αλαία" in *Collected Poems 1947–1980* by Allen Ginsberg, copyright © 1984. Used by permission of HarperCollins Publishers.

Excerpt from "Moses und Aron" by Arnold Schoenberg: used by permission of Belmont Music Publishers, Los Angeles.

Scherzo from SIX PIECES FOR VIOLONCELLO by Roger Sessions: copyright © 1967 by Edward B. Marks Music Company. Copyright renewed. This arrangement copyright © 2010 by Edward B. Marks Music Company. International Copyright Secured. All Rights Reserved. Used by Permission. Reprinted by Permission of Hal Leonard Corporation.

The photo of a child in chapter 11: used by permission of Catherine de Chevilly and Marianne Violot.

The photo of Arthur Rubinstein in chapter 11: used by permission of Philippe Coqueux/ SPECTO.

Excerpt from *Music of Tibet* in chapter 19: used by permission of Huston Smith.

CALVIN AND HOBBES ©1991 Watterson. Dist. By UNIVERSAL UCLICK. Reprinted with permission. All rights reserved.

The author has made every effort to contact all copyright owners and would be happy to amend these acknowledgments in later editions of the book.

CONTENTS

A COMPANION WEBSITE

www.oup.com/us/integratedpractice

Integrated Practice contains several dozen exercises to improve your coordination, rhythm, and sound. By and large, there are three types of exercises: those that can be studied by all musicians from the outset; those demonstrated at a specific instrument but that can be easily adapted to other instruments, as well as to singing and conducting; and those that seem to be pertinent exclusively to a single instrument, but that contain pedagogical and musical insights of interest to all open-minded musicians.

Oxford has created a website to accompany *Integrated Practice.* The site contains video and audio files in which I demonstrate many of the book's principles and exercises with the help of several other musicians. Recorded examples available online are found throughout the text and are signaled with Oxford's symbol ⬤.

Consult the appendix to grasp the essence of each exercise and to map the exercises' presence in the book and on the dedicated website.

VIDEO CLIPS

Chapter 1, "Words, Sounds, Gestures"

1. Prosodic Patterns I: Walking
2. Prosodic Patterns II: An Overview
3. Prosodic Patterns III: At the Cello

Chapter 5, "Coincidence: Intention and Gesture"

4. Coincidence I: At the Piano
5. Coincidence II: At the Flute

AUDIO CLIPS

Chapter 15, "The Quadrupedal Prosodist: A Piano Lesson"

INTEGRATED PRACTICE

INTRODUCTION

Some years ago I gave a public class on the applications of the Alexander Technique to music making. One of the participants, a boy of thirteen, was a budding pianist whose teacher was concerned about his posture at the piano, and she hoped that I could help him relax a little.

The boy—we'll call him James—sat at the piano and played the exposition from the first movement of Franz Schubert's Sonata in A Major, D.959. It's a substantial work of art, sweeping in construction and intricate in detail. Learning it is an ambitious project for a child of James's age, although such an assignment is appropriate and welcome given the right conditions. Indeed, young people thrive when faced with the most daunting musical challenges, without which they wouldn't be able to fulfill their promise.

From the first few notes onward, James made it clear he could play fast and loud. The volume of a musician's sound doesn't depend directly on the size of his or her body. It's unsurprising to hear a small child with a big sound, or a big person with a small sound. James's sound, though, wasn't exactly big; it was just loud. You can be loud if you bang at an instrument hard enough. A big sound, however—a sound that is resonant, uniform, and yet elastic in its potential for changes of dynamics and color—requires more than brute force. Rather, it entails the total *absence* of brute force, and instead the perfect coordination of the musician's entire body, from head to toe; a virtuosity of contact between the player and his or her instrument; and, most important, the capacity to allow sound to flow out of the instrument.

James's posture at the piano was problematic. Throughout his performance he pulled his shoulders up and in. He flung his head forward and down in order to emphasize a note or accent. After each emphasized note, James pulled his head up and back, submitting his neck to incessant whiplash. James's straining was both visible and audible. His playing, loud and aggressive, was also uneven in rhythm and articulation. There lacked a legato bringing notes together into organic units, or the inflections that would indicate where those units started and where they ended. Random notes received noisy accents. Either James had made unjustifiable interpretive decisions or he had made no interpretive decisions at all, and the accents were accidents of a gawky technique, bumps on the journey up and down the keyboard.

In this sonata, the main theme of the first group—the opening tune, so to speak—is loud and lively. The main theme of the second group, however, is softer and lighter. I thought it'd be useful for James to work on the more introspective passage, so I went to the piano and sounded its first few notes, showing the audience what "tune" we were going to study.

James looked up at the ceiling, as if summoning God's help. With his fingers touching the keyboard lightly, he gave a silent and extremely quick performance from the beginning of the movement all the way up to the tune I had sounded, fast-forwarding a page and a half of music in his head until he reached the point in question. Only then did he start playing.

James's teacher was right to be concerned, but wrong in her diagnosis. In her view, James's "machinery" needed to run more smoothly. In my view, James's fundamental problem consisted in his having been turned into a machine in the first place.

You can conceive of music in two different ways: as a series of physical gestures that create sounds, or as a series of words and phrases that, to be rendered audible, require certain physical gestures. My hypothesis is that James had learned the physical gestures, not the words and phrases—as revealed by his inability to recall an excerpt of text from memory and play it. Instead, he had no choice but to retrieve the gestures in the unbroken sequence he had learned them, a bit like a mouse trained to follow a certain route inside a lab maze, or a computer programmed to spew out data in a fixed order.

As a musician, you take on the mantle of an oracle, an orator, a protagonist in a comedy, an entertainer, and so on. Every role demands that you become an expert storyteller with a deep command of the language. Robert D. Levin explains how music is a dramatic genre:

> All genres of Western art may be characterized as dynamic; that is, they incorporate a definite feeling of motion and energy. In a novel or a play, it is the unfolding of a succession of events that produces dramatic movement. These events must not be random; if they are merely a string of unrelated episodes, there will be no coherence, and no "plot." For the events to be considered a plot—for them to be considered dramatic—there must be a direct relationship between them. This relationship often assumes a relentless logic.... We must define music at the very outset as a dramatic genre.... Not only will large-scale principles of organization be analogous from drama to music; there will also be a wide range of parallels between musical and verbal devices.[1]

Arnold Schoenberg wrote extensively on the linguistic aspects of music. His essay "Brahms the Progressive," collected in the book *Style and Idea*, is full of insights on meter, articulation, phrasing, and so on.

> *Form in Music* serves to bring about comprehensibility through memorability. Evenness, regularity, symmetry, subdivision, repetition, unity, relationship in rhythm and harmony and even logic—none of these elements produces or even contributes to beauty. But all of them contribute to an organization which makes the presentation of the musical idea intelligible.... The language in which musical ideas are expressed in tones parallels the language which expresses feelings or

thoughts in words.... [T]he aforementioned elements of its organization function like the rhyme, the rhythm, the meter, and the subdivision into strophes, sentences, paragraphs, chapters, etc. in poetry and prose.[2]

To Schoenberg's list of parallels between musical and verbal language we may add grammar, spelling, punctuation, diction, and others still. Levin likens a secondary progression to a subordinate clause, and a modulation to a change in subject. A secondary progression borrows chords from a key different from the key of the passage where the progression occurs; a modulation changes the passage's key. Levin's example of a subordinate clause is too delicious not to be quoted.

> My theory teacher gives long assignments.
> My theory teacher, who is a stiff grader, gives long assignments.

Consider the passage below. It's the opening phrase of the piece that James played for me.

EXAMPLE 1. Franz Schubert: Sonata for Piano, D.959 in A Major, first movement

The chords noted by the bracket constitute a secondary progression—a parenthetical reference, briefly stated, much like a subordinate clause that doesn't change the subject of discussion. Levin notes that this "can be conveyed in performance by rhythmic articulation, dynamics, and sometimes even with subtle variations in tempo."[3] This seemingly innocuous remark points to a principle at the heart of *Integrated Practice*: Every linguistic aspect of music can and must be made clear in performance. If a subordinate clause calls for a little bit of inflection from an attentive performer, so do syntax, phrase structure, punctuation, and all else besides.

You might argue that it's unfair to expect a young child to comprehend the intricacies of the musical language. In my experience, however, children of all ages—and, in fact, every musician without exception—can understand that to make music is to tell stories.

For about a year I had an enchanting nine-year-old cello student called Andrea. We spent part of every lesson improvising. Andrea's specialty was making animal sounds. In her hands the cello meowed, barked, and squealed. One day I requested a tune in the "Chinese style." Andrea thought about it, and then played a melody built on the pentatonic scale, which is the foundation of Chinese musical folklore. She had gleaned the relevant information from films, cartoons, and whatnot, and made an educated guess regarding the demands of the "Chinese style."

I'd ask her to play melodies in various keys: C major, G major, and D major. Her improvisations didn't always make sense. One of her parents—her American father or her Mexican mother—always accompanied her to the lessons. Her mother made a remark on one occasion, phrasing it in Spanish-tinted English. Andrea rolled her eyes and exclaimed, "Mother, that is *not* grammatical!" When she next improvised a nonsensical melody, I told her, "You're using the words of D major, but your improvisation is *not* grammatical." Her face lit up in recognition, and afterward she improvised her melodies much more cogently.

Syntax and grammar are crucial, but they're not the be-all and end-all of musical comprehensibility. Perhaps you remember the scene in *Modern Times* where Charlie Chaplin gets a job as a singing waiter. The problem is that the Tramp has a terrible memory for lyrics. His friend the barefoot gamine, played by Paulette Goddard, writes the lyrics down for him on his shirt cuff, which he intends to look at during his performance. But just as he enters the stage and waves his arms exuberantly, the cuff flies off his sleeve. (The scene is posted on YouTube. Use the keywords "Charlie Chaplin Modern Times singing.") The Tramp has no choice but to improvise his lyrics, so he sings in a language that he makes up on the spot:

> *Se bella piu satore, je notre so catore,*
> *Je notre qui cavore, je la qu' la qui, la quai!*
> *Le spinash or le busho, cigaretto totto bello*
> *Ce rakish spagoletto, si la tu, la tu, la tua!*[4]

The scene is hilarious for many reasons. His predicament makes us nervous for him. His gestures and grimaces persuade us that he's singing a lewd song. And the Tramp tricks us into believing that what he sings makes perfect sense, in a language that nobody speaks but everybody understands.

The sense of his song comes not from vocabulary, syntax, or grammar: It comes from its rhythmic construction and the inflections that Chaplin gives it in performance. If he used the absolute same rhythms and inflections but changed all the syllables, we'd still respond to the song and believe that we understood it. In sum, the song makes sense because it's *prosodic*.

Prosody, not syntax or grammar, is the bedrock of musical comprehensibility.

At the keyboard or away from it, James doesn't need to become a more smoothly functioning machine or a more relaxed athlete. He must become a fluent prosodist in the language of music, and his gestures as a pianist must reflect his prosodic ability note for note, phrase for phrase. Then he'll be able to take on the mantle of the orator, the preacher, or the entertainer.

Prosody affects everything that you do as a musician: your coordination, rhythm, and sound, the way you think, speak, sing, play, move, practice, and perform.

"But what *is* prosody?" you ask. "What does it mean to play prosodically or un-prosodically? How could James become a machine without his parents' noticing it?"

I hope to answer these questions, and many others, in *Integrated Practice*.

PART I

RHYTHM

CHAPTER 1

WORDS, SOUNDS, GESTURES

LIFE IS RHYTHM

At rush hour, Times Square subway station in New York City is one of the busiest places on the planet. Ten or twelve subway lines converge here, and a shuttle train connects Times Square with Grand Central Station, another major hub. Thousands of people pass through the station, walking or running upstairs and downstairs, elbowing other people and being elbowed by them. The station has a large hallway where buskers play, sing, and dance for the entertainment of the passersby.

Most people here tonight are in a hurry, trying to make it home after a long day's toil. But you have all the time in the world. You're here to study humanity, to marvel at the richness of individual behavior, and to learn what makes people tick—almost literally, as you'll see. Imagine that you're invisible and untouchable; that you can be anywhere in the station without anyone pushing and trampling you; and that you can look at anyone without being noticed.

An elderly man with a military bearing strides by. His gait reveals a lot about his character, his upbringing, his convictions and suppositions: HUP, two, three, four, HUP, two, three, four...A young girl skips by in the opposite direction. She's the embodiment of youthful insouciance, and her movements are infused with the folk rhythms she danced to in her afternoon class: ta-TUM, tee-TUM, ta-TEE-tee, tee-TUM!

A woman in high heels wobbles through the crowd, bumping into people and almost falling down every three steps: TUM-tee-tee. TUM-tee-tee. TUM-tee-tee. A blind man walks by, his steps lopsided and uncertain. His guide dog, however, is a model of smooth regularity. If you had to ascribe a tempo mark to the dog, you'd say "andante moderato senza rubato, poco forte sempre."

A voice comes over the public announcement system: "Theptwntwozzdld." Blaming the station's poor acoustics and lousy loudspeakers, you despair of ever understanding those useless announcements. But not long afterward another person talks into a microphone somewhere deep inside the station. "The uptown 2 train is delayed. We apologize for the inconvenience." The first speaker had rushed and jumbled her words, letting her voice rise and dip too far, too soon. The second speaker stretched her vowels slightly, put a tiny space between some of the words, and modulated her voice as if declaiming a poem by William Carlos Williams:

The uptown
two train
is delayed.

We apologize
for the in-
convenience.

You find yourself next to two men talking earnestly, and you overhear their conversation. You can't explain how, but you suspect that they, too, are speaking poetry:

"I thought I'd never see my wife again."
"I'm glad the two of you made up and...stuff."
"You bet. Without Irene I'm not myself."

You go down to one of the platforms, just missing the Brooklyn-bound N train. You hear the music it makes: ka-ta-CHAM, ka-ta-CHAM, ka-ta-CHAM, ka-ta-! And you wonder, what happened to the last "CHAM"? The "CHAM" was a downbeat to the ka-ta's upbeat. The last downbeat was amputated, yet you could feel it ever so clearly in your imagination. (You'll find out more about amputated downbeats in chapter 9.)

Climbing the stairs back to the big hallway, you alternate covering one step with the right foot, then two steps at once with the left one, giving a good push with the right foot so that the left can cover the greater distance. It creates a pleasant asymmetrical pattern: short-LONG, short-LONG. Or rather, upbeat-DOWNBEAT, upbeat-DOWNBEAT. Or still, preparation-STRESS, preparation-STRESS, where preparation corresponds to the push with the right foot, and stress the landing on the left foot.

In the hallway, four teenagers dance to a tune coming from a boom box, leaping and gyrating with incredible virtuosity. Their words, sounds, and gestures all coincide in a swirl of rhythm and life. A suburbanite moves to the song's beat, irrepressibly infected by the teenagers' verve. But the poor woman looks perfectly ridiculous. Her head and neck move as if disconnected from her spine, and her timing is off. She's trying to follow the kids' rhythm, but there are two things wrong with it: "trying" and "following," neither of which the kids themselves would ever abide.

Rhythm is present in every single aspect of every scene you have witnessed. It's impossible to define rhythm precisely, but we can make a list of some of its constituting elements. Rhythm is time subdivided. The subdivisions can be regular or irregular, and delimitated or not by markers such as beats and measures. The subdivisions can be organized in groups of varying sizes, and the groups themselves can be organized into a hierarchy. In rhythm there's speed, duration, pacing, and timing. There exist different kinds of rhythmic energy, combined into patterns of infinite variety. The train's ka-ta-CHAM is one such pattern; the HUP-two-three-four of the Army man, a different pattern.

Patterns of preparation, stress, and release infuse speech, song, locomotion, and every human activity. We'll call the "CHAM" of the train's ka-ta-CHAM a *stress*, and the two sounds that precede it *preparation*. The Army man's "HUP" is a *stress* and the two-three-four that follow a *release*. When you climb the steps pushing strongly with one leg and landing firmly on the other, you use a pattern of *preparation* and *stress*.

We'll borrow a few terms from the vocabulary of poetics and call a self-contained rhythmic grouping a *foot*. The pattern of "preparation-STRESS" is an *iambic foot*, the pattern of "STRESS-release" a *trochaic foot*. You can also refer to them simply as an *iamb* and a *trochee*. (The next chapter will develop this vocabulary and put it in context.)

The men you overheard spoke phrases containing five units of "preparation-STRESS." They don't realize it, but they're talking in *iambic pentameter*.

"I THOUGHT | I'd NE- | ver SEE | my WIFE | a-GAIN."
"I'm GLAD | the TWO | of YOU | made UP | and…STUFF."
"You BET. | With-OUT | I-RENE | I'm NOT | my-SELF."

Rhythm is coordination, and coordination is personality; ergo, rhythm is personality. No two individuals have ever had identical rhythms. The rhythms of spoken English are different from those of spoken French. New York patterns are different from Midwestern or Southern ones. Rhythmic patterns of introversion are different from those of extraversion. The former colonel, the young girl, the tottering shopper, the hipsters, the suburbanite, the blind man, the blind man's dog—they all have wholly different rhythms, and therefore wholly different personalities. The only thing they share is the fact that their rhythms reflect and even determine their personality.

Rhythm can contribute to health or to disease. The colonel has an arthritic hip joint in part because of his long-standing habits of posture and gait—in other words, habits of rhythm. The young girl has a rhythm of thought and gesture that gives her all the freedom in the world. Bounding upstairs at great speed becomes effortless and fun once you find the right rhythms to do so. Lose those rhythms, however, and you risk falling down and breaking your neck. The principle applies to everything you do and say—and, logically enough, every note you sing, play, and conduct.

It's such a basic principle that musicians take it for granted, assuming that making music automatically entails some control of rhythm. This is the same attitude that says, "Dancers are so graceful. That's because they are…*dancers*." "Restaurant chefs know their ingredients. What do you expect? They are *chefs* after all." Needless to say, there exist clumpy dancers, chefs who serve undercooked chicken, crazy psychotherapists, sinful priests, and professional musicians whose sense of rhythm is terrible. There exist long-established ensembles that can't "play" together: a string quartet in which the cellist drags the tempo, the second violinist rushes, and the first violinist and the violist pull in opposite directions. There exist famous conductors who wave their arms about in such an unrhythmic fashion that their orchestras and choirs can survive only by ignoring them.

Your musicianly duty is to think, breathe, and live rhythm all day long, developing your mastery of rhythm in speech, locomotion, song and dance, and in your every last gesture.

GO FOR A WALK

To start your work on rhythm, I propose that you walk in seven different ways. This will give you the foundation to understand most of everything else in *Integrated Practice*. Walk by yourself or enlist a friend to keep you company and increase the fun.

🌓 This exercise is illustrated in video clip #1, "Prosodic Patterns I: Walking."

Start by walking in an ordinary manner, up and down the block in front of your house or along the corridors of your music school. Wherever you are, walk for a minute without further thought.

Now, as you walk, say out loud Hamlet's famous words:

To BE | or NOT | to BE …

In this fragment, every two syllables belong together in an iambic pattern of "preparation-STRESS." As you walk, make each spoken syllable coincide with a step. Step more lightly on the lowercase words and more heavily on the capitalized words, using the lighter steps to launch the heavier ones. Practice on a continuum from exaggeration to subtlety:

1. Walk in an exaggerated manner, saying the words out loud and making the difference between preparation and stress obvious to yourself and to anyone watching you.
2. Walk in a normal manner, saying the words out loud.
3. Walk in a normal manner, silently thinking the words.
4. Walk in a normal manner, not thinking the words anymore, but remembering what they felt like in your brain, your throat, and your steps.

As an intermediate step toward mastery, exaggeration in its playful mode is useful. The ultimate goal of all our exercises, however, is to help you internalize information, so that the mere intention arising from your creativity carries the energies you need to turn the intention into gesture or sound. Subtlety is our goal, exaggeration a casual means toward it.

To begin with, use your right foot for the stresses: left-RIGHT, left-RIGHT. After a few rounds, change feet: right-LEFT, right-LEFT. Then switch back and forth between the two patterns.

Now walk with a trochaic pattern of "STRESS-release." You can use another line of Shakespeare, this one said by King Lear:

NE-ver, | NE-ver, | NE-ver, | NE-ver, | NE-ver!

If you prefer, use your own words. The English language abounds in trochaic words:

FA-ther, | MO-ther, | BRO-ther, | SIS-ter, | NEIGH-bor.
IN-dex, | PIN-kie, | EL-bow, | SHOUL-der, | PEL-vis.
SAL-mon, | TU-na, | HAD-dock, | SNAP-per, | FLOUN-der.

Start with the pattern RIGHT-left, using all variations as before. Then switch to LEFT-right. Alternate between the two, taking ten or twelve steps in one pattern before shifting to the other.

So far we have studied four walking patterns:

1. Iamb, stressing the right foot.
2. Iamb, stressing the left foot.
3. Trochee, stressing the right foot.
4. Trochee, stressing the left foot.

Now use three-step patterns. A three-syllable word with a stress on the first one, followed by a release of tension in the second and third syllables, is called a *dactylic foot* (or a *dactyl*): WASH-ing-ton, JEF-fer-son, HA-milt-on, TEN-der-ly, BEAU-ti-ful.

A three-syllable word of which the first syllable is a preparation, the second a stress, and the third a release is called an *amphibrachic foot* (or an *amphibrach*): ba-NA-na, ma-GEN-ta, bal-LIS-tic, car-NA-tion, fra-TER-nal.

A three-syllable word or set of words of which the first two are preparations and the final one a stress is called an *anapestic foot* (or an *anapest*). Few three-syllable words in English are stand-alone anapests. Some people would count a word like "interrupt" as an anapest, while others would consider that its first syllable has a secondary stress. Better illustrations of anapestic feet are three short words that belong together: "don't be MEAN," "by my SIDE," or, as the English poet Samuel Taylor Coleridge famously illustrated in a poem about anapests, "with a LEAP | and a BOUND."

Start by using a dactyl. Walk while saying "WASH-ing-ton" out loud, making the step on the first syllable heavier than your next two steps. Go through all the variations from exaggeration to subtlety. Then use an amphibrach such as "ba-NA-na." Follow it by an anapest such as "I am HERE."

When you walk to a two-syllable pattern, your stressed step always falls on the same foot. When you walk to a three-syllable pattern, the stresses alternate between feet:

Dactyl	RIGHT-left-right | LEFT-right-left
Amphibrach	Right-LEFT-right | left-RIGHT-left
Anapest	Right-left-RIGHT | left-right-LEFT

Normally one tends to walk in a more or less unconscious pattern of two steps, putting stresses on one's dominant foot. The dominant foot, stronger by birth, gains further strength on account of one's tendency to put weight on it. Over the years this exaggerates the body's innate asymmetry, sometimes causing muscular and skeletal problems. Walking in patterns of three counters the asymmetry to some degree, since both feet receive weight in alternation. Patterns of three can also have a wonderfully propulsive quality. Once you enter into the patterns' rhythms, you may find yourself walking faster and farther with less muscular effort.

Different people react differently to each pattern. If you've always walked with a trochaic pattern favoring your dominant foot ("STRESS-release"), an unfamiliar pattern such as the amphibrach ("preparation-STRESS-release") might feel foreign. Unconscious rhythmic patterns of movement are so integral to our sense of self and our emotional identity that conscious and nonhabitual patterns can be downright threatening! Difficult as it may be, you need to suspend emotional, moral, and aesthetic judgments while learning new concepts and exercises. Practice these patterns many times, and immerse yourself in their sensations, without rushing to judgment.

We now have seven walking patterns. Patterns of two steps can be stressed on either foot; patterns of three steps automatically alternate the stresses between feet.

1. Iamb: left, RIGHT.
2. Iamb: right, LEFT.
3. Trochee: RIGHT, left.
4. Trochee: LEFT, right.
5. Dactyl.
6. Amphibrach.
7. Anapest.

There exist other possible patterns: two equally stressed steps or two equally unstressed ones; three-step patterns with more than one stress; four- and five-step patterns; and as many other patterns as your imagination cares to create. These seven patterns, however, are enough for our purposes. The information you acquire from practicing them is so rich you'll spend years applying it to your music making. And many other patterns, in music and in daily life, often turn out to be straightforward variations on these basic patterns.

Once you notice how you walk habitually with a fixed prosodic pattern, you may safely assume that you do many other things with a habitual pattern that escapes your awareness. To take but one example, a string player's simplest gesture consists in playing two notes in succession, down-bow, up-bow. For the majority of string players, their habitual pattern is like most people's walking—that is, trochaic, with the down-bow invariably sounding a stress and the up-bow sounding a release. If the music itself is written in iambic units but the player forces upon it an unconscious trochaic gesture, a struggle breaks out, much like two dancers not in step. The pains and aches typical of a performing musician result in part from the repeated accumulation of rhythmically inadequate gestures in singing, playing, and conducting. To become integrated and healthy, then, you need to sense the patterns of preparation, stress, and release contained in your scores, and to let these patterns inform and animate your gestures, which then become varied and adaptable rather than habitual and fixed.

LIVE AND BREATHE RHYTHM

We'll take the rhythmic information we've gathered so far and organize it in different media, so that you can learn the same information as words, sounds, gestures, numbers, and so on. The idea is for you to make your study of rhythm as broad, deep, and playful as possible.

🔊 This exercise is illustrated in video clip #2, "Prosodic Patterns II: An Overview."

The iambic pattern consists of two gestures, syllables, or steps of which the first is a *preparation*, the second a *stress*.

- A linguistic example is "to BE | or NOT | to BE."
- Musically, think of it as "upbeat, DOWNBEAT."
- As a gesture in space (in dance and locomotion, for instance), consider it "a journey toward a DESTINATION."
- When conducting it, your arm moves "up, DOWN."
- If you count beats numerically and assign the number 1 to the "DOWNBEAT," then a series of iambs goes "two-ONE, two-ONE, two-ONE."
- An iambic children's song you probably know well is "Heigh Ho, Heigh Ho" (from *Snow White and the Seven Dwarfs*).

The trochaic unit consists of two gestures, syllables, or steps of which the first is a *stress*, the second a *release*.

- Linguistic examples are "MO-ther, FA-ther, SIB-ling."
- Musically, think of it as "DOWNBEAT, offbeat."
- Spatially, in locomotion and in dance, think of it as "PUSH and let go."
- When conducting it, your arm moves "DOWN, up."
- Counting numerically, a series of trochees goes "ONE-two, ONE-two, ONE-two."
- A trochaic children's song you probably know well is "Twinkle, Twinkle Little Star."

Table 1.1, "Two-Unit Feet in Multiple Media," helps you organize this information. Use the same procedure to organize the dactylic, amphibrachic, and anapestic units, as illustrated in table 1.2, "Three-Unit Feet in Multiple Media."

It's not enough to memorize the tables. You need to feel these energies with your whole being, and I propose that you practice them in many different ways.

1) Walk in the manner we studied. Given how much you walk in your daily life, before long you'll become an expert prosodist through walking alone.

2) Speak. Say lists of iambic or trochaic words out loud. Listen to other people talking and detect iambic sequences, trochaic words, ear-catching dactyls and amphibrachs. Declaim published poems or invent your own. All you need is an attentive ear and the willingness to take a few risks.

The iambic pattern goes "ta-DUM, ta-DUM, ta-DUM." Repeat these two syllables for a while, and iambic words will naturally come to you.

> You WILL | in-VENT | a PRET- | ty VERSE.
> It's NOT | as HARD | as PEO- | ple THINK.

The trochaic pattern goes "DUM-ta, DUM-ta, DUM-ta."

> TEA-cher, | ASK me | SOME-thing | SIM-pler.
> PO-ems | MAKE me | RA-ther | NER-vous.

TABLE 1.1 Two-Unit Feet in Multiple Media

Media	Iambic Foot	Trochaic Foot
Language	to BE |or NOT|to BE	NE-ver|NE-ver|NE-ver
Rhythmic energies	preparation-STRESS	STRESS-release
Beat structure	upbeat-DOWNBEAT	DOWNBEAT-offbeat
Children's songs and ditties	Heigh-HO,|heigh-HO,|it's OFF|to WORK|I GO|	TWIN-kle,|TWIN-kle|LIT-tle|STAR
Conducting gestures	up-DOWN	DOWN-up
Movement in space	grow to a DESTINATION	PUSH and let go
Numbers	two-ONE, two-ONE, two-ONE	ONE-two, ONE-two, ONE-two

TABLE 1.2 Three-Unit Feet in Multiple Media

Media	Dactylic Foot	Amphibrachic Foot	Anapestic Foot
Language	WA-shing-ton, JEF-fer-son	ma-GEN-ta, ba-NA-na	come and SIT | by my SIDE
Rhythmic energies	STRESS-release-release	Preparation-STRESS-release	Preparation-preparation-STRESS
Beat structure	DOWNBEAT-offbeat-offbeat	Upbeat-DOWNBEAT-offbeat	Upbeat-upbeat-DOWNBEAT
Children's songs and ditties	PUS-sy cat,|PUS-sy cat,|WHERE have you|BEEN?	My BON-nie|lies O-ver|the O-cean	This old MAN|he played ONE
Conducting gestures	DOWN-right-up	Up-DOWN-right	Right-up-DOWN
Movement in space	PUSH and let go	Grow to a DESTINATION and let go	Grow and grow to a DESTINATION
Numbers	ONE-two-three, ONE-two-three	Three-ONE-two, three-ONE-two	two-three-ONE, two-three-ONE

3) Scat. In jazz, scatting means singing improvised patterns using nonsense or onomatopoeic syllables in imitation of an instrument. Scatting can be simple or elaborate. To start, improvise a little iambic ditty, then a trochaic one.

ba-DEE ba-DOO bee-DOH ba-*DAH*!
BA-dah BOO-dee, BA-dee DAH-dee.

In chapter 6 you'll learn how to use scatting to discover the rhythmic core of everything you sing, play, and conduct.

4) Take your instrument and play scales and improvisations, paying particular attention to the behavior of your head and neck (for reasons that will become clear in due course).

🔊 This exercise is illustrated in video clip #3, "Prosodic Patterns III: At the Cello."

5) Sit at a piano and play patterns at the keyboard. With a single mallet strike, a timpanist can transform an entire orchestra's performance, charging it with direction and energy. You can do something similar with a banging fist.

🔊 The banging fist is further discussed in the section "Movement, Rhythm, and Personality" in chapter 13. It's illustrated in video clip #48, "Anti-Nodding Strategy."

6) At the piano or on a tabletop, tap a three-note pattern with three fingers, for instance, the right hand's thumb, index finger, and middle finger. Use an amphibrachic pattern such as the word "banana," where each syllable has a different prosodic weight:

ba-NA-na
preparation, STRESS, release

Tap it metronomically several times in a row, sensing how each finger's prosodic role changes from line to line. Speak the syllables out loud if you wish.

ba-NA-na
thumb, index, middle
ba-NA-na
index, thumb, index
ba-NA-na
middle, index, thumb
ba-NA-na
index, middle, index
ba-NA-na
thumb, index, middle.

You can be good at the game by birth or by acquired reflex from practicing it. But you can't be a good instrumentalist if you aren't good at the game!

7) Clap, whistle, play the tambourine, open and close squeaky doors, throw a yo-yo, and do everything in your life while pondering rhythm. Every action in your daily life lends itself to this study. And every action, however banal, can be improved thanks to it.

We'll develop these rhythmic skills throughout the book, but first we need to study a little poetry better to understand the linguistic aspects of music.

CHAPTER 2

PROSODY, OR THE SECRETS OF RHYTHM

RHYTHM IS MEANING AND EMOTION

You're sitting at a diner having a cup of coffee when a couple barges in, gabbing in a language you don't recognize. Almost despite yourself, you respond in some way to what the couple is saying. You might not understand them, and you might even completely *mis*understand them, but you react nevertheless.

Your immediate apprehension of something you hear isn't through your intellect but your senses. When it comes to language, you respond first not to vocabulary and grammar but to the sounds and vibrations a speaker issues, and to the rhythmic elements that underpin the speaker's discourse.

The primacy of rhythm applies to all languages, including the language of music. It applies both to compositions and performances. It's not possible for a poem or a composition to be any good if it has rotten rhythms, and it's not possible for a speaker or musician to give a good performance without a good sense of rhythm.

The study of rhythm in written and spoken language—and in particular the rhythm of poetry—is called *prosody*. The term has arrived to us through Latin (in which *prosodia* means "the accent of a syllable") from classical Greek (in which *prosōidia* means "a song with accompaniment," from *pros* "toward, in addition to" and *ōidē* "song"). Ezra Pound (1885–1972) wrote a provocative little book about prosody, titled *ABC of Reading*. From it we extract a useful kernel:

> The author's conviction on this day of New Year is that music begins to atrophy when it departs too far from the dance; that poetry begins to atrophy when it gets too far from music; but this must not be taken as implying that all good music is dance music or all poetry lyric. Bach and Mozart are never too far from physical movement.[1]

The conductor William Christie, an expert on the French Baroque, was asked in an interview to explain how linguistic concepts applied to French instrumental music:

[A]ll dances have texts—imaginary texts in some cases. Any allemande, any courante, any dance form (with a very few exceptions) is essentially a dance with specific numbers of syllables per line; one could say that instrumental dances are always accompanied by imaginary texts. Indeed, all good instrumental styles have the voice as their model. Almost everything has a verbal basis.[2]

Behind music and dance, then, there lies a verbal and linguistic basis, of which rhythm is the most important element. By unlocking the secrets of rhythm, prosody helps us understand the vital unity of language, music, and movement—or words, sounds, and gestures.

Poetry is enhanced spoken language. Or, to put it differently, poetry is the organization, condensation, and compression of spoken language into something potentially more powerful and durable. This issue is of interest to all musicians. Do you want your music making to have the condensation and power of structured poetry? Or do you believe that a composition or performance that's too structured sounds phony? Is it possible to find a balance between structure and freedom?

Understanding the basics of poetic prosody will help you answer these questions. Start in the old-fashioned manner: by reciting a poem.

INTEGRATION, SEPARATION, DIRECTION

Here are a few lines from an anonymous, naive poem. Read them out loud.

> There is a lady sweet and kind,
> Was never face so pleased my mind;
> I did but see her passing by,
> And yet I love her till I die.
>
> Her gesture, motion, and her smiles,
> Her wit, her voice my heart beguiles,
> Beguiles my heart, I know not why,
> And yet I love her till I die.

By instinct or by acquired reflex, you're likely to seize the poem's inner rhythm (or to be seized by it) and make it audible in your reading. The poem's rhythm is unvarying, consisting of four iambic feet:

> There IS | a LA- | dy SWEET | and KIND,
> Was NE- | ver FACE | so PLEASED | my MIND.

Your ears also seize a sequence of vowel sounds repeated in both lines: the "e" of there/never, the "a" of lady/face, the "ee" of sweet/pleased, and the "i" of kind/mind.

Together, these two elements—rhythm and rhyme—create a grid for the poem, a skeleton of sorts in which some elements are varied and others fixed. (We study grids in depth in the next chapter.) A poem's skeleton is similar to a human being's: Certain parts belong together (like vertebrae on a spine) while other parts are articulated (like the upper arm and the forearm, separated by the elbow). When we analyze a poem's skeleton, we ask ourselves the following questions: "Who belongs with whom? What letters belong together in a syllable, and what syllables belong together in a word? How much space ought there to be between words so that we sense where a word ends and another begins? Where does each word or line point to?" To answer these questions, you need the tools of *integration*, *separation*, and *direction*.

We start by integrating letters into syllables, a skill so primary we take it for granted, although we shouldn't. (We look at in the section "Graphic Aspects of Language" later in the chapter.) Then we integrate syllables into feet, feet into lines, and lines into a group called a *verse* or *stanza*. Our illustrative poem has two syllables per feet, four feet per line, and four lines per stanza.

A foot can be a complete word, two or more short words together, parts of a long word, or parts of separate words brought together. The words "There IS" belong together and form a foot. The syllables "a LA-" also form a foot. We want our poems and songs to have strong, driving rhythms, and if these require a word to get split up among different feet, so be it. The urge to create a lilting line of verse also leads the poet to say "Was never face so pleased my mind," instead of "Never has a face so pleased my mind."

Separation follows integration. Imagine if you could never bend your wrist or your knee again: Your life would become extremely awkward. The lack of articulation in written and spoken language, and in music, is similarly awkward. After integrating disparate elements into groups of different sizes, we must separate the groups to some degree, inserting a little time and space between words and sentences in spoken and written language or between notes and phrases in music making. The amount of articulation and separation is highly variable: It may be infinitesimal in between individual words or notes, and considerable in between lines and paragraphs.

Each unit in a poem—be it a foot, a line, or a stanza—has a certain direction or energy, manifested as degrees of tension and relaxation. In the iambic feet of our illustrative poem, the first syllable serves as an upbeat to the second, thereby giving each group a sense of forward motion:

> There is a lady sweet and kind,
> ta-DUM, ta-DUM, ta-DUM, ta-DUM.

Imagine a poem containing the line "Mother, father, brother, sister." Its direction and energy would be quite different:

> Mother, father, brother, sister,
> DUM-ta, DUM-ta, DUM-ta, DUM-ta.

As we saw in the previous chapter, there also exist three-syllable feet with energies and directions of their own:

WASH-ing-ton	DUM-ta-ta	dactylic
come on DOWN!	ta-ta-DUM	anapestic
ba-NA-na	ta-DUM-ta	amphibrachic

Lines, stanzas, and whole poems are also suffused with direction. Look at the second stanza of our poem again. It feels as if we're driven to the end of each line, the last word being a sort of exclamation mark for the whole line:

Her gesture ... motion ... and her SMILES
Her wit ... her voice ... my heart BEGUILES.

The first two lines belong together in a *couplet*, in which the second line has a bit more driving power than the first one:

Her gesture, motion, and her smiles ...
Her wit, her voice my heart BEGUILES.

The second syllable of each foot is more charged than the first; the last word of each line is more charged than the preceding words; the second line of a couplet is more charged than the first; and the second couplet is more charged than the first, ending with an emotional climax:

I love her TILL I DIE!

In this poem all elements share these propulsive energies and point toward a common destination. In other poems, the layers of direction might interact in complex ways. You can have a tense line inside a relaxed couplet, for instance, or a series of rushing lines leading to a sudden placid climax. Musical compositions are exactly like poems in that they, too, have multiple layers of direction. Notes, measures, phrases, and sections are all charged with varying types and degrees of energy, and the way these energies interact give a composition its emotion and meaning.

In sum, to analyze a text prosodically means to find out which elements of the text belong together, how the groups so formed are articulated, and how all elements and groups are suffused with direction. Since poetry, music, and dance spring from the same source, the prosodic tools of integration, separation, and direction apply to all levels of music analysis and performance, as well as coordination and movement. We'll study these concepts throughout the book.

A PROSODY FOR EACH LANGUAGE

Prosody underpins all languages. Each language, however, has its own individual prosody according to the way the language is spoken. Languages evolve, and so do their prosodies; the poetic prosody of medieval English is quite different from that of modern English. The subject is too vast for us to cover it in depth. Here we touch upon five basic poetic prosodies (illustrating how different languages necessarily have different prosodies) and one instance of nonpoetic prosody (illustrating how prosody affects everything you say).

1. ACCENTUAL-SYLLABIC VERSE

Stress plays an important role in English. When you say the word "im-POR-tant," the second syllable has a clearly audible stress or accent. But in French, the same word might be pronounced "IM-por-tant," "im-por-TANT," or "IM-POR-TANT," depending on the speaker's personality or the mood of the moment. This doesn't mean that stress doesn't play a role in French. It's more accurate to say that French allows for fluctuating stresses, while the stresses of English are for the most part fixed.

Because stress is such a central aspect of spoken English, it's natural that its poetic prosody, too, focuses on stress. The little poem that started our exploration of prosody has an unvarying number of stresses per line—four. It also has an unvarying number of syllables—eight.

> There is a lady sweet and kind,
> ta-DUM, ta-DUM, ta-DUM, ta-DUM,
> one-TWO, three-FOUR, five-SIX, seven-EIGHT.

Verse that counts the number of both syllables and stresses is called *accentual-syllabic* (accent here being synonymous with stress). Many kinds of accentual-syllabic lines exist, and they receive technical names based on the type of feet they employ (iambic, trochaic, dactylic, and so on) and the number of feet per verse (tetrameter, pentameter, hexameter, and so on).

Mathematically, we could imagine an immense number of combinations of feet and lines. In practice, the nature of the language itself limits the number of poetically usable feet. Some feet work much better than others, and the number of feet per verse also tends to stay within a limited range. A tremendous number of English poems, for instance, have been written in iambic pentameter, which for some prosodists represents the idealized rhythm and length of an utterance in English. You might remember a few instances of iambic pentameter from the previous chapter. Look at them again, just to appreciate how natural the iambic pentameter sounds in English.

> "I thought I'd never see my wife again."
> "I'm glad the two of you made up and ... stuff."
> "You bet. Without Irene I'm not myself."

2. ACCENTUAL VERSE

Different languages and epochs have favored different poetic qualities. For instance, Old English, spoken and written from about 500 A.D. to about 1100 A.D., was a heavily stressed Germanic language. Stress carried the language, so to speak, and it was natural for poems in Old English to be written in a form that fixed the number of stresses but not the number of syllables. This is called *accentual verse*.

Its standard lines had four stresses divided by a *caesura*, a slight separation that had grammatical as well as rhythmic weight. The poems in accentual prosody used a lot of *alliteration*, the repetition of a letter or sound at the beginning of adjacent or connected words, such as "mother's milk."

Poets have always enjoyed exploring forms from foreign cultures and times, pouring the wine of their spoken languages into the poetic vessels of alien languages. Some of the resulting poems may be disastrously inorganic, others attractive on account of their very strangeness. C. S. Lewis (1898–1963), the author of *The Chronicles of Narnia*, wrote poems in modern English using the accentual prosody of Old English. Notice the four stresses per line, the alliterations, and the caesuras in the form of commas, semicolons, and dashes.

> ... A haughty god
> MARS mercenary, makes there his camp
> And flies his flag; flaunts laughingly
> The graceless beauty, grey-eyed and keen,
> —Blond insolence—of his blithe visage
> Which is hard and happy....[3]
> ("Mars & Prince Caspian," *The Planets*)

Let's eliminate the words from the poem and retain only the stresses and punctuation. It might go something like this:

> ... Ka BANG-ka BANG
> BANG BANG-ka-ka-ka, ka BANG ka BANG
> Ka BANG ka BANG; BANG BANG-ka-ka
> Ka BANG-ka BANG-ka, BANG-ka ka BANG,
> —BANG BANG-ka-ka—ka ka BANG BANG-ka
> Ka ka BANG ka BANG-ka....

Many poets and songwriters start their composing primarily through rhythm; when they find a song's driving rhythms, its words or notes follow almost as if by magic. George Enescu (1881–1955), the great Romanian composer, violinist, and conductor, encapsulated the importance of rhythm in the compositional process:

> Often enough one believes that a poet's job ... is to translate into verse a well-defined, predetermined idea, when in fact his main effort is to invent rhythms, sound colors, and moods in order to attract words that will succumb to them, as if falling into traps. A poem's sense arises from its sonority and accords with it. To write a poem is not an intellectual action but a sensorial one, which I compare willingly with the work of a sorcerer. A musician composes like a poet: he, too, looks for his words tentatively, he forces the best ones to come out of hiding, he seduces them by a kind of incantation.[4]

The driving force of rhythm helps not only the poet and the composer, but the performer as well. Stripping a poem of its words and looking exclusively at its rhythms gives you a sense of what drives the poem. You can do the same thing to the compositions you're studying, then "ride the force" in performance much as the composer did in composition. Chapter 6 develops this concept in practice.

3. QUANTITATIVE VERSE

In the poetry of classical Latin and Greek, the most important prosodic element was the length of vowels. Using an example from English, "sit" has a short vowel and "seat" a long one; "pot" is short, "post" is long. A Greek poet might have written a line of poetry with the following pattern:

Seat sit |seat sit |seat sit sit |seat sit |seat sit.

In the jargon of poetics, verse that concerns itself with vowel length is called *quantitative*. Classical poems used elaborate combinations of short and long vowels in lines with fixed numbers of syllables. The structure of the lines had an element of freedom. Here and there the poet added a syllable, called an *anceps*, that was short or long as she wished. Sappho, who lived in the sixth century B.C., favored the following form, now called a Sapphic stanza:

Long-short-long-free | long-short-short-long | short-long-free
Long-short-long-free | long-short-short-long | short-long-free
Long-short-long-free | long-short-short-long | short-long-free
Long-short-short | long-free

Much like C. S. Lewis's writing accentual verse, modern poets have had a go at composing Sapphic stanzas. As with all such efforts, a compromise arises, since the form isn't exactly native to the language; you have to bend the form to suit the language, or bend the language to suit the form. The very bending, however, can create marvelous poetry. Here's a Sapphic stanza from a poem by Allen Ginsberg (1926–1997):

Heavy limbed I sat in a chair and watched him
sleep naked all night afraid to kiss his mouth
tender dying waited for sun rise years a-
      go in Manhattan[5]
("τεθνάκην δ ολίγω πιδεύης φαίνο αλαία")

In classical prosody, a two-syllable foot in which the vowels were "short long" was called *iambic*, and "long short" *trochaic*. These are the same names that we've been using for rhythmic units that measure stress, not vowel length. The same names mean different things depending on context! If you've studied Latin or Greek in school, you might remember the words "iambic," "trochaic," and "dactylic," for instance, and you might believe that you know exactly what they mean. If your mind doesn't catch up to the ambiguity in the vocabulary, you risk misunderstanding basic prosodic principles.

The French composer Olivier Messiaen (1908–1992) drew inspiration from classical prosody and composed many pieces using units of long and short notes in complex combinations. Regular meter, where the downbeat of any measure has an implicit stress, isn't dissimilar to a clock ticking and tocking. Messiaen used quantitative prosody (together with many other rhythmic elements) to avoid the overly measured time of stressed downbeats. Some of his compositions create a feeling of displaced time or even timelessness. Example 2.1 is an excerpt from his piece "Quatour pour la fin du temps." Note the absence of time signature and the irregular note groupings and length of measures. The phrase is scored unison for violin, clarinet, cello, and piano.

EXAMPLE 2.1. Olivier Messiaen: "Quatuor pour la fin du temps"

4. SYLLABIC VERSE

Modern languages that aren't heavily stressed, such as Portuguese, French, and Japanese, lend themselves to poems in which the prized regular element is the number of syllables rather than stresses per line. This is called *syllabic verse*. I grew up in Brazil, and my mother tongue is Portuguese. As a schoolchild I had to learn how to count syllables in poetry. Various sound effects create counting uncertainties. If a word ends with a vowel sound and the next word also starts with a vowel sound, the two vowel sounds amalgamate into a single syllable. If the last syllable in a line of verse is unstressed, you don't count it. (This also shows that stress does play a role in Portuguese, as it does in French.) Here are some of the opening lines from the epic poem *Os Lusíadas*. Composed by Luís de Camões (ca. 1524–1580), the poem relates the exploits of Portuguese seafarers as they subjugate Africa and India.

> As armas e os barões assinalados
> Que por mares nunca dantes navegados
> ...
> Cantando espalharei por toda a parte
> Se a tanto me ajudar engenho e arte.[6]
> > (*Os Lusíadas*, Canto I)

The lines are decasyllabic—that is, they each contain ten syllables. In the first line, two syllables are amalgamated on account of the adjacent vowels ("e + os") and the very last syllable isn't counted because it's unstressed.

> As | ar-| mas | e/os | ba- | rões | as- | si- | na- | la (-dos) ...

Besides the strict verse length, the poem also follows a strict rhyming scheme, ABA-BABCC. These prosodic strictures might choke a different language to death, but they're absolutely organic to Portuguese, making *Os Lusíadas* a very musical composition.

Prosody arises from the language itself, from how it's spoken and sung by the native speakers. Your task as a musician isn't to impose a prosodic scheme onto every composition, but to sense each composition's singular, inner prosody so that you can "speak" it like a native speaker.

5. FREE VERSE

Poetry takes spoken language and condenses and structures it. The very process that gives poetry its power, however, carries risks and dangers. A bad poem can be more offensive to the ear than an ordinary verbal utterance. Many poets in modern times have rebelled against structured poetic forms and have sought to write poems in *free verse* (a term that encompasses many varieties of poetry). Like musicians who embrace the no-rules or antirules improvisatory aesthetics of free jazz, these poets write poems that disregard any formal grids involving meter or rhyme.

Allen Ginsberg, speaking about one of his early influences, William Carlos Williams (1883–1963), relates how he realized that Williams "was trying to adapt his poetry rhythms out of the actual talk-rhythms he heard rather than metronome or sing-song archaic literary rhythms." Ginsberg built upon his insight:

> I took out little four-or-five line fragments that were absolutely accurate to somebody's speak-talk-thinking and rearranged them in lines, according to the breath, according to how you'd break it up if you were actually to talk it out, and then I sent 'em over to Williams. He sent me back a note, almost immediately, and he said "These are it! Do you have any more of these?"[7]

In his compositions, Arnold Schoenberg evolved from a prosody based on symmetry and repetition to one that approximated what Ginsberg called "somebody's speak-talk-thinking." In other words, over the years Schoenberg's musical prosody came to resemble free verse, as if tending away from poetry and toward prose. He advocated that "great art must proceed to precision and brevity."[8] A musician ought to lend to every sentence "the full pregnancy of meaning of a maxim, of a proverb, of an aphorism. This is what musical prose should be—a direct and straightforward presentation of ideas, without any patchwork, without mere padding and empty repetitions."[9]

Look at example 2.2, in which Schoenberg seems to be writing free verse. Notice the changing time signatures, the rhythmic irregularities within bars, and the varied articulations. Play, sing, whistle, or scat it, and you might recognize the similarity of its rhythms to everyday "speak-talk-thinking."

Sometimes you come across a text that looks, reads, sounds, and feels like a poem without conforming to any of the standard prosodies. The Bible's structure of chapter and verse is not dissimilar to a poetic grid of line and stanza. Like all good poetry, the King James Bible uses enhanced, condensed language:

1 In the beginning God created the heaven and the earth.
2 And the earth was without form, and void; and darkness was upon the face of the deep. And the Spirit of God moved upon the face of the waters.

EXAMPLE 2.2. Arnold Schoenberg: "Moses und Aron," Act 1, Scene 2

3 And God said, Let there be light: and there was light.

4 And God saw the light, that it was good: and God divided the light from the darkness.

5 And God called the light Day, and the darkness he called Night. And the
evening and the morning were the first day.

(Gen. 1:1–5)

The Bible doesn't fit a narrow definition of poetry, and yet we can't deny how poetic it is. It may be convenient to call it free verse.

The discourse of the American poet Walt Whitman (1819–1892) occasionally feels like a profane preacher's. On the one hand, he uses some of the free-verse cadences of the King James Bible and a tone of voice tending toward the exalted. On the other hand, he employs ordinary American words, sometimes discreetly praising homosexual love. Poets who hewed closely to the idealized iambic pentameter found Whitman's poetry shocking, but his prosody flows logically from his temperament, his land, and his times.

A song of the rolling earth, and of words according,
Were you thinking that those were the words, those upright lines? those curves,
angles, dots?
No, those are not the words, the substantial words are in the ground and sea,
They are in the air, they are in you.

Were you thinking that those were the words, those delicious sounds out of your
friends' mouths?
No, the real words are more delicious than they.[10]

("A Song of the Rolling Earth," Leaves of Grass)

6. THE PROSODY OF EVERYDAY SPEECH

It's easy to think that prosody is all about convention, tradition, rules, and regulations. These have their role to play, but prosody "works" when it helps you connect rhythm and language, time and place, intention and gesture, form and content, mind and heart.

Prosody operates across all of speech, including the simplest everyday utterances. Linguists who study ordinary speech define prosody in a different way from poets, but the two meanings of the word are complementary rather than conflicting.

> In linguistics, prosody … is the rhythm, stress, and intonation of speech. Prosody may reflect various features of the speaker or the utterance: the emotional state of a speaker; whether an utterance is a statement, a question, or a command; whether the speaker is being ironic or sarcastic; emphasis, contrast, and focus; or other elements of language that may not be encoded by grammar or choice of vocabulary.[11]

Figure 2.1 encapsulates the essence of prosody in ordinary speech. It gives you clues on how to perform a recitativo by Rossini, a Beethoven scherzo, or a Webern miniature—and, in fact, every piece in which you can take a conversational approach.

PROSODY FOR THE INTEGRATED MUSICIAN

The poets of antiquity systematized their prosody into a complex system of feet and lines. Two-syllable feet included the familiar trochee and iamb, plus the *spondee* ("long long") and *pyrrhic* ("short short"). Three-syllable feet included the dactyl, anapest, and amphibrach, plus several others with names such as *bacchic* and *molossus*. Four-syllable feet included the *ionic*, *epitrite*, and *paeon*, among others. Each foot had a different usage, some being more suited to heroic poetry, others for satire or love songs.

English prosodists borrowed the classical terminology, but used it to refer to stress rather than vowel length. Some prosodists speak of "stressed" and "unstressed" syllables; others prefer "strong" and "weak" syllables; others still speak of "accented" and "unaccented" syllables. Some theorists have adapted the entire list of classical feet to English prosody; others have retained the handful of feet most common in English and chucked the rest. There are theorists who reject the classical terminology altogether, considering that neither the terms nor the concepts apply to English. We'll ignore the fights among the theorists, take a few terms from classical prosody, and show how they're used by many people today, with a couple of examples for each foot. The adjectival form is often used as a noun; you can say "a trochaic, an iambic" instead of "a trochee, an iamb." The information is displayed in Table 2.1, "Five Basic Feet."

TABLE 2.1 **Five Basic Feet**

Name	Rhythmic Qualities	Example
Trochee, trochaic	strong weak	MO-ther, FA-ther
Iamb, iambic	weak strong	to BE | or NOT | to BE
Dactyl, dactylic	strong weak weak	WA-shing-ton, JEF-fer-son
Anapest, anapestic	weak weak strong	come and SIT | by my SIDE
Amphibrach, amphibrachic	weak strong weak	ba-NA-na, ma-GEN-ta

A text or a composition is a sequence of highly varied energetic impulses. Prosody is important because it helps you sense, understand, and utilize these energies. I believe that discerning two energies and calling them "strong" and "weak" doesn't quite account for all the types of energy that exist, how different they are from one another, and how they relate in language, music, dance, and daily life. I propose that we "play" (broadly speaking) not with two energies, but with the three we learned in the previous chapter: preparation, stress, and release, each existing in infinite varieties and degrees of intensity. I propose that we borrow traditional names from classical and English prosody, concentrating on five basic combinations of rhythmic energy. I propose that we take for granted that there exist many more combinations than these five. Finally, I propose that we pay more attention to the energies themselves than to the system of names we give them. Over time, you can broaden and deepen your knowledge of prosody and its technical vocabulary. For now, all you have to do is learn the names of the basic patterns outlined in table 2.2, "Three Prosodic Systems."

TABLE 2.2 **Three Prosodic Systems**

Name	Classical Prosody	English Prosody	Integrated Musician
Trochaic	long short	strong weak	STRESS release
Iambic	short long	weak strong	preparation STRESS
Dactylic	long short short	strong weak weak	STRESS release release
Anapestic	short short long	weak weak strong	prep. prep. STRESS
Amphibrachic	short long short	weak strong weak	prep. STRESS release

In addition to the five basic feet, it's useful to learn the meaning of the words *spondee* (adj. *spondaic*) and *pyrrhic* (adj. also *pyrrhic*) since they come up often in prosodic studies. In classical prosody, a spondee was "long long" and a pyrrhic was "short short." In English prosody, a spondee is "strong strong" and a pyrrhic "weak weak." As a musician, consider the spondee "stress stress" and the pyrrhic "release release."

THE GRAPHIC ASPECTS OF LANGUAGE

For rhythm to exert its power, its components need to be organized and articulated—that is, visible in print and audible in sound. Look at the following paragraph:

wehadntseeneachotherinmorethantwentyyearsonceuponatimewewereascloseastwinsisters
butwehadmadethemistakeoffallinginlovewiththesamemanoneofusmarriedhimtheotherdrif
tedawayinacloudofresentmentregretunspokensadnessourmeetingwasaccidentalunprepare
dorperhapsitwasiwhowasunpreparedtoseeheragainyoulookgreatidontthinksomyvoicecam
eoutharsherthanimeantitoursilencewasheavywithanemotionicouldntnamewestoodforamo
menthowsfineiwantedtoknowiwasafraidtoknowihavetogoitwasgoodseeingyousheturnedan
dwalkedawayinahurrysuddenlyithitmeihadneverforgivenherforstealingmylove

It's extremely difficult (though not impossible) to read and understand it. Before rhythm
and prosody can bring the text alive, we need to separate letters and integrate them into
words.

> we hadnt seen each other in more than twenty years once upon a time we were as close
> as twin sisters but we had made the mistake of falling in love with the same man one of
> us married him the other drifted away in a cloud of resentment regret unspoken
> sadness our meeting was accidental unprepared or perhaps it was i who was unprepared
> to see her again you look great i dont think so my voice came out harsher than i meant
> it our silence was heavy with an emotion i couldnt name we stood for a moment hows
> fine i wanted to know i was afraid to know i have to go it was good seeing you she turned
> and walked away in a hurry suddenly it hit me i had never forgiven her for stealing my
> love

It's a big improvement, but reading it remains uncomfortable. Let's add capitals and
punctuation marks.

> We hadn't seen each other in more than twenty years. Once upon a time we were as close
> as twin sisters. But we had made the mistake of falling in love with the same man. One of
> us married him; the other drifted away in a cloud of resentment, regret, unspoken sadness.
> Our meeting was accidental, unprepared—or perhaps it was I who was unprepared to see
> her again. "You look great." "I don't think so." My voice came out harsher than I meant it.
> Our silence was heavy with an emotion I couldn't name. We stood for a moment.
> "How's—" "Fine." I wanted to know, I was afraid to know. "I have to go." "It was good
> seeing you." She turned and walked away in a hurry. Suddenly it hit me. I had never
> forgiven her for stealing my love.

From this version we get the text's meaning, but not its full emotional impact. Let's add
indents and increase the degree of separation between phrases, creating paragraphs of
varying lengths.

> We hadn't seen each other in more than twenty years. Once upon a time we were as close
> as twin sisters. But we had made the mistake of falling in love with the same man. One of
> us married him; the other drifted away in a cloud of resentment, regret, unspoken sadness.
>
> Our meeting was accidental, unprepared—or perhaps it was I who was unprepared to
> see her again.
>
> "You look great."

"I don't think so." My voice came out harsher than I meant it. Our silence was heavy with an emotion I couldn't name.

We stood for a moment.

"How's—"

"Fine."

I wanted to know, I was afraid to know. "I have to go."

"It was good seeing you." She turned and walked away in a hurry.

Suddenly it hit me. I had never forgiven her for stealing my love.

Here's a partial list of the visual elements that contribute to clarity and meaning in written language.

1. Punctuation marks such as commas, colons, semicolons, periods, exclamation and question marks, ellipses, hyphens, "em" and "en" dashes, and apostrophes.
2. Typesetting features such as *italics*, **bold**, and <u>underlining</u>.
3. The use of CAPITALS and lowercase in various combinations: ALL CAPITALS, all lowercase, Mixed, iNVERTED.
4. Signs that indicate integration and separation: parentheses and brackets such as ( ), { }, [ ], and < >.
5. Spatial features such as margins, layout, indents, and blank spaces between letters, words, phrases, paragraphs, and pages.

It took millennia for punctuation to develop. Ancient texts, for instance, didn't have spaces between words, and readers had to provide their own separations as they read the text. Punctuation mixes subjective and objective elements. Two individuals from the same background make different punctuation choices according to their personalities. Mainstream British punctuation is quite different from mainstream American punctuation. There exist punctuation marks in French, Spanish, and German that don't even exist in English!

Differences in national and personal styles don't change four fundamental facts:

1. Without punctuation, a written text becomes much harder to read, whether silently or out loud.
2. Punctuation helps a great deal, but it doesn't guarantee readability.
3. To change the way a text is punctuated is to change both its meaning and its emotional impact.
4. Every punctuation system is a compromise by definition. Each system is a different compromise, with its strengths and weaknesses.

Punctuating a musical text is similar. The amount of punctuation varies from era to era, from composer to composer, from piece to piece, and from edition to edition. Baroque scores are almost wholly unpunctuated, and reading them requires creativity and musicological knowledge. Johann Sebastian Bach writes a cantata for his in-house musicians. The players and singers know Bach's personal habits, the conventions of the era, and the prevailing aesthetics (which changed every few years). Bach leaves his scores unpunctuated

EXAMPLE 2.3. J. S. Bach: Sonata for Solo Violin, BWV 1001 in G Minor, Presto

on purpose, trusting his musicians to follow established practice and expecting them to add their own variations and improvisations. Three hundred years later, how are we meant to read and speak Bach's unpunctuated scores? Example 2.3 is from a piece for solo violin that we'll study thoroughly in chapter 10.

If the composer doesn't punctuate a score, you may be tempted to assume that you can play it *without* punctuation, or that the composer has given you implicit permission to use *any* punctuation. Both assumptions are foolish, although you may one day run into a composer who delights in the interpreters' whims and who gives you permission to punctuate it willy-nilly if you so wish.

Musical notation has evolved tremendously over the centuries and continues to do so today. Yet it'll never be able to become an all-encompassing, reliable system covering every aspect of music. Arnold Schoenberg wrote at length about the imperfection of musical notation, which during his lifetime was much more elaborate than during Bach's:

> In tempo and its modifications; in dynamics, in accents and phrasing, in coloration—in all these fields we are still far from able to indicate perfectly what it is we want. For example, we use the same sign to indicate phrasing and legato. ... We have not yet even thought of indicating in any way how a tone is to end, and yet a great deal depends on just that; nor do we possess a sign for gradation, suspension and displacement of accent.[12]

We'll make a study of musical punctuation throughout the next chapters.

NEW GRAPHIC TOOLS

Punctuation and other features of written language can guide an oral reading, but they can't guarantee that the reading will be clear, beautiful, or even correct. Written English, for instance, doesn't indicate whether syllables are stressed or not. Consider the following words: "Present. Minute. Record. Content." Only in context will you know how to pronounce them: "I had a minute to act. I added a minute amount of cyanide to her martini." Table 2.3, "The Role of Stress in Meaning," clarifies the double sense of the words above.

In some languages, the use of *diacritics* lessens the difficulty of knowing how to pronounce, stress, or inflect a written word. A diacritic is a mark above or below a printed letter, normally indicating that it must be pronounced or stressed differently from an unmarked letter. In Portuguese, for instance, the name "Alcântara" takes a circumflex on

TABLE 2.3 The Role of Stress in Meaning

Trochaic		Iambic	
PRE•sent	*n* gift	pre•SENT	*v* to introduce
MI•nute	*n* 60 seconds	mi•NUTE	*adj* tiny
RE•cord	*n* document	re•CORD	*v* to write down
CON•tent	*n* substance	con•TENT	*adj* happy

the second vowel, indicating that the syllable is stressed: "al-KAHN-tah-rah." In the study of English poetry, diacritics are used to show stressed and unstressed syllables: "móthĕr." For the most part, however, everyday English doesn't use diacritics, though some publications use them for a few words such as "coördination," indicating that the two o's don't belong together as they would in "boot."

In music, some graphic signs play the role of diacritics. For instance, the sign > shows an accent above a note or chord. Musical diacritics are far from unequivocal; musicologists have fought bitterly about the meaning of dots and wedges in Mozart. In some ways the ambiguity inherent in musical scores is a good thing. It allows room for the expression of individuality and requires a degree of initiative and responsibility from everyone: What do these notes and signs mean to you? How are you going to transform them into sound? How do you justify your choices?

To clarify your interpretive decisions, I propose that you use a few graphic signs regarding integration, separation, and direction.

1. For integration, use curly brackets, which are also called *braces*: {}. Most of the time the brackets will lie horizontally under notes or measures.
2. For separation, use dotted lines. Most of the time the dotted lines will lie vertically between notes or measures.
3. For direction, use arrows or, alternatively, the letters P for preparation, S for stress, and R for release. The letters can play the role of diacritics much like the circumflex in the original "Alcântara." It may be helpful to use a capital S but lowercase p and r.

We'll illustrate the principle with our little poem first, then with a couple of music excerpts. Example 2.4 is the poem's first stanza, and it uses braces, dotted lines, and arrows in a straightforward manner. Example 2.5 is an iconic tune you'll recognize easily. It shows how you can use arrows or letters at will. Example 2.6 shows how you can annotate multiple layers of rhythmic activity. On one level, every eighth note is like a syllable in a word, and the passage contains many four-note groupings similar to four-syllable words. On another level, more or less hidden from sight, the passage contains three-unit patterns much like three-syllable words, but moving at a much slower pace.

Writing something on a score inevitably transforms it. Look at these two sentences:

I've never been so insulted in my life.
I've never been so insulted in my Life.

EXAMPLE 2.4. "There Is a Lady . . ."

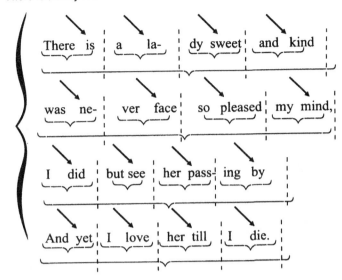

EXAMPLE 2.5. Wolfgang Amadeus Mozart: Symphony #40, K. 550 in G Minor, first movement

With a single change in annotation, the sentence's tone changes a fair amount. When you write anything over a passage—a fingering, a breath mark, a diminuendo—you change the passage's emotion. It doesn't matter if the change is tiny or huge; what matters is that a change inevitably happens. Your eyes, mind, and ears risk incorporating your markings so thoroughly that you may forget that the score existed in a different state before you intervened. Keep an unmarked copy of every score you study, and mark photocopies or duplicate scores instead. This allows you to go back to the unmarked score and look at it with fresh eyes. It may be a good idea to annotate a study score thoroughly, and then perform the piece using an unmarked score.

Use more signs when you are in the earlier stages of learning the system, fewer or none when you have digested and internalized the basic information the signs convey. Use more signs for complex passages, fewer for simpler ones. If a pattern repeats itself many times in a row, mark a few instances of the pattern, not all of them. Once you pinpoint a tricky crossroads in a passage, use as many signs you need at the crossroads in order to clarify it, and leave the territory before and after it unmarked or lightly marked. Mark your scores in pencil, not pen: You'll need to erase signs if you make a mistake, if you change your mind over time, or if you internalize the information and don't need the crutches of the annotations anymore.

You can look at someone's face as a single, organic entity, and react accordingly. Or you can zoom in on a detail like the nostrils or the eyelashes . . . and react accordingly.

EXAMPLE 2.6. J. S. Bach: Toccata, BWV 914 in E Minor

Prosodic analysis works in the same way. You can focus on two notes and their relationship—trochaic or iambic, heavily stressed or not, one soft, the other loud, and so on—or you can see an eight-bar phrase as a unified structure in which the relationship between any two notes plays a relatively minor role. In order to learn the basics correctly, however, you may need to spend a fair amount of time sensing and figuring out exactly how two little notes fit together.

Before long we'll look into specific aspects of musical prosody and the prosody of gesture. First we need to study the Grid, or the organizational principle that underlies all human endeavor.

CHAPTER 3

THE GRID

A Life Principle

STRUCTURE AND FLOW

What do hopscotch, American football, and Arnold Schoenberg have in common?
Two words explain everything: The Grid.

From birth to death, every day all day long, our existence depends on an organizing principle composed of interlocking lines and numbers. The lines, straight or curved, may be visible like grooves on a sidewalk or invisible like the meridians of Chinese medicine. The numbers may be overt like the twelve tones of Schoenberg's method of composition, or deeply hidden like the forty-six chromosomes in the nucleus of a human cell. Together, the lines and numbers constitute a grid—the crucial framework behind every human activity and endeavor.

Hopscotch, football, and twelve-tone music wouldn't exist without their underlying grids. Fundamental as it may be, however, the grid alone doesn't amount to much more than an abstraction. The grid becomes a life principle when energy flows through it and in opposition to it.

The word *grid* means different things depending on context. Overlaid on a map, a grid is a system of evenly spaced lines that cross one another at right angles, forming squares or rectangles. The lines are numbered or lettered, making it possible to create an index of locations on the map according to their coordinates. The grid increases the amount of information you can draw from the map. Thanks to it you can read the map better, and eventually navigate the world that the map represents.

A grid is also a network of power stations, towers, cables, and pipes that distributes electrical power over a territory. Without the grid, electricity wouldn't be able to travel around the city and give it light and heat. Without electricity, the grid would be inert. In other words, the grid alone is useless, just as electricity alone is useless. It's their meeting and opposing each other that makes them useful.

The system of parallel lines painted on a field for playing American football is called the grid or *gridiron*. Football itself is informally called the gridiron—an indication of how important the grid is to the game! The starting position of cars on a racecourse is also called the grid.

The map, the system of cables and power stations, the lines on the football field, and the positions of cars at the start of a race are dictionary definitions of the word *grid*. As I see it, all these grids are manifestations of a larger concept that we might call the Grid, with a capital G.

The Grid is the structure underpinning any system—a relatively rigid framework built of simple geometrical and mathematical elements that interact with one another as numbers, lines, curves, and angles, delineating space and time. It may be visible or invisible, audible or inaudible, tangible or intangible. The Grid is organized and predictable, but the energies that oppose it are fluid and unpredictable. Thanks to opposition, the Grid condenses and multiplies the energies that flow through it.

GRIDS IN DAILY LIFE

A set of bookshelves is a grid. In a library, a whole wall may be given over to a collection of identically shaped books, in which case there is a sort of coincidence between the grid and what occupies it. But elsewhere—in your home, for instance—you might organize your books against the grid, counterpointing the grid's predictability with a jagged mini-skyline of books of different sizes, shapes, and colors.

The three-act structure of many plays and films is a grid. A 110-page screenplay that is the blueprint for a conventional Hollywood action movie has recognizable dividers: on page 10, the *inciting incident*, a dramatic event that pulls the hero into the action; on page 30, the *first-act turning point*, in which the story kicks into high gear; and so on throughout the screenplay, the *midpoint* at page 60, the *second-act turning point* at page 90, the *crisis, climax, and resolution* in the last few pages.

The grid creates expectations: The moviegoing public expects the hero to behave in a certain way after the inciting incident, and in a different way after the crisis and climax. The job of the filmmaker is to manipulate expectations and then thwart them, or perhaps fulfill them in original ways. Character arcs, plots and subplots, and the rise and fall of dramatic tension all play with the grid or against it. The movie, then, is an interplay between expectations and realities, formulas and surprises, conventions and inventions. The dynamic pull between these forces makes or breaks the movie.

Children delight in the grid of the sidewalk. You can step exclusively on the squares, avoiding the lines and grooves that separate the squares; or you can step on the lines quite on purpose. But if you decide to avoid stepping on the lines and your foot lands on one by accident, your whole destiny might change, up to your wedding day and beyond!

The human body is a series of interlocking grids including the skeleton, the muscle system, the nervous system, and the meridians of Chinese medicine, among others. Life is a play against the grid—the opposition between the inescapable limits of biological grids and our desire to overcome these innate limitations. The capillary system connecting arteries and veins, for instance, is a grid. Without this particular grid, there can be no life; but without the flow of blood pushing *against* the grid, there can be no life either!

A chessboard is a two-colored grid of sixty-four squares: eight times eight, or two to the power of six. There's so much latent mathematics in the chessboard that you could spend a lifetime just pondering the possible relationships and operations within it. The chess pieces' hierarchy is a function of how much power they have to move against the grid. Rooks move up and down, bishops diagonally, the queen both ways. The queen, then, is worth as much as a rock and a bishop. The entire game is completely dependent on the grid and the pieces' capacity to move against it.

The urban street grid has existed for as long as there have been cities. In antiquity the Romans, the Greeks, and the Chinese all built cities using grids. Some of the grid's modern manifestations are particularly interesting—New York City, for instance, or Chicago or Los Angeles. The street grid organizes aspects of urban life such as traffic flow, garbage collection, and mail delivery. Most city grids combine strict geometrical patterns with not-so-strict corners, diagonals, and dead ends—partly on account of a city's geographical features, partly because the human element in city planning is inevitably unpredictable. In a great American city like New York, the highly organized grid is the background for an unpredictable, asymmetrical skyline—buildings of many shapes and sizes, sometimes at right angles to the grid, sometimes not. The variety of buildings plays against the predictable grid, and the end result is endlessly stimulating. In a not-so-great American city, the grid itself lacks interest, being much too even, and the buildings and parks within the grid don't create enough opposition to the grid. Everyone is too well behaved, the grid as well as the stuff in it.

The calendar is a grid of days, weeks, and months. The numbers seven (days in a week) and twelve (months in a year) are pregnant with meaning. So are the numbers thirteen (full moons in a year), fifty-two (weeks in a year), and sixty (seconds to the minute, minutes to the hour). Behind the calendar's mathematical arrangement there lie the cycles of the sun and moon, astronomic events that carry tremendous physical and metaphysical power.

We grow up having internalized the calendar-as-grid. We follow the days and weeks intuitively, and we keep track of certain obligations and events without thinking about them. But we also externalize the calendar-as-grid through the use of watches and clocks, calendars, agendas, and lists. It's impossible to have a wholly internalized calendar, amounting to an absolutely reliable inner feeling for the passage of time in all its dimensions. And it's undesirable to have a wholly externalized calendar, becoming overly dependent on lists and clocks to organize your daily life.

POETIC GRIDS

Written and spoken languages all have their grids. The alphabet itself is a grid of sorts; so is the conjugation of verbs with its interplay of rules and exceptions. Poetry being "enhanced language," logically enough it has "enhanced grids," or poetic forms. These are of interest to musicians since they share many similarities with musical forms. I propose to cover three grids: the haiku, the limerick, and the sonnet. My main intention is to show you that grids themselves play a role in meaning and emotion.

1. THE HAIKU

Our daily life is suffused with mathematics (numbers) and numerology (the often ungraspable psychological and even mystical meaning of numbers). We could say that number alone is a kind of energy. We feel that three is sacred, as in the Holy Trinity; seven is lucky, thirteen unlucky. Musicians are so used to playing sonatas and symphonies in three or four movements that a piece in two movements, or five, carries the interest and energy of its being an exception to the norm. When it comes to time signatures, average musicians know their twos, threes, and fours, but five and seven are a different matter. Two, three, four, and six are "friendly." Five and seven raise the red flag!

The haiku is a spare poetic form originating in Japan, comprised of three lines of five, seven, and five syllables. A haiku would be a completely different form if it had four lines rather than three; or if the syllable count was the same on every line; or if the syllable count were six, eight, and six syllables rather than five, seven, and five. (Truth be told, Japanese poets vary the syllable count a little bit if the poem justifies it.)

Traditionally, a haiku makes a metaphorical reference to an aspect of nature and the seasons in order to address timeless human behaviors and foibles. This is how William Packard explains it:

> Every traditional haiku uses a *kigo*, or season word, to specify whether the poem is of winter, spring, summer, or autumn mood. Traditional haiku will also be characterized by *renso*, or loose association of disparate images, and contain an elliptical leap from the second to the third line which simulates sudden Zen *satori* or enlightenment, illumination of the true nature of reality.[1]

The first line makes a statement; the second line seems to make an unrelated statement; the third line says something surprising and unexpected, showing that the previous lines were in fact closely related. A proper haiku, then, is a rather dynamic and complex form. Its mathematical components are restrictive, imposing limits and obligations: You must fit all your words and everything you want to say into this unyielding vessel. While the grid is fixed, the poem's words are fluid, speaking of the seasons, the sun and the moon, wind and rain, lakes, rivers, trees, falling leaves...all with a metaphorical and psychological dimension.

According to this broader definition of a haiku, the following poem can't be considered a haiku even though it has the required number of syllables:

Terrible headache
Whenever she comes to town.
Yep. Mother-in-law.

This one, though, might pass muster:

Season of the witch.
I love my wife, but—oh, doom.
Here comes her mother.

2. THE LIMERICK

Arising from folk tradition, a limerick has five lines of varied and jagged lengths. Lines 1, 2, and 5 have seven to ten syllables and rhyme with one another; lines 3 and 4 have five to seven syllables and rhyme with each other. Many of the syllables in a limerick form into anapestic feet: ta-ta-DUM. Sequences of anapests in English contain a rollicking energy difficult to restrain; anapests carry humor and wit by their very nature. A limerick's rhyme scheme is AABBA, with unexpected or even forced rhymes. Traditionally, the first line makes a reference to a person or a locale. Table 3.1, "The Limerick Grid," shows an abstract limerick.

In construction, sound, and meaning, the limerick is coarse by definition. Traditional limericks are obscene, or at the very least full of double entendres. Hearing a limerick, a child might not understand it altogether and yet laugh at its sounds, while an adult might blush at what it hints at. The passage of time has lessened the tradition of obscenity, and today there exist limericks as pure as the driven snow. Limericks are poetic jokes, told out loud. For this reason they circulate widely, and it's easy to lose track of a limerick's authorship. Table 3.2, "The Limerick against the Grid," illustrates a limerick side by side with its abstract grid. Most feet in the example are anapestic. Can you spot the exceptions?

Asymmetry, tortured rhymes, the deliberate distortion of the stresses and grammar of everyday language, words and lines repeated at unexpected times: many formal aspects of the limerick might be called "perverted prosody," and for that very reason the poetic form lends itself to expressing provocative or obscene thoughts. It'd be difficult to use it to express exalted sentiments, to speak of God, love, or mourning.

Form is meaning. Compare one of Anton Webern's epigrammatic pieces lasting thirty seconds or less, with Richard Wagner's eighteen-hour *Ring* cycle. Can they really convey

TABLE 3.1 **The Limerick Grid**

Line #	Abstract Anapestic Verse	Rhyme
1	ta-ta-DUM ta-ta-DUM ta-ta-DUM	A
2	ta-ta-DUM ta-ta-DUM ta-ta-DUM	A
3	ta-ta-DUM ta-ta-DUM	B
4	ta-ta-DUM ta-ta-DUM	B
5	ta-ta-DUM ta-ta-DUM ta-ta-DUM	A

TABLE 3.2 **The Limerick against the Grid**

Line #	Abstract Anapestic Verse	Rhyme	Limerick
1	ta-ta-DUM ta-ta-DUM ta-ta-DUM	A	There was a young lady of Niger
2	ta-ta-DUM ta-ta-DUM ta-ta-DUM	A	Who smiled as she rode on a tiger.
3	ta-ta-DUM ta-ta-DUM	B	They returned from the ride
4	ta-ta-DUM ta-ta-DUM	B	With the lady inside
5	ta-ta-DUM ta-ta-DUM ta-ta-DUM	A	And the smile on the face of the tiger.

similar messages? Once you embrace the principle that form is meaning, you can collaborate with the form and allow it to work for you. If you inhabit the form, you don't need to strain, to fight, to huff and puff, to emote. Instead, the energies in your performance will come from the opposition between the fixed grid and the fluid forces that run against the grid.

3. THE SONNET

The sonnet is a rich poetic form that arose in Italy in the 1200s and that now exists in multiple variations across languages and cultures. The Italian poet Petrarch (1304–1374) developed an enduring structure of fourteen lines subdivided into an *octave* (two *quatrains* or stanzas of four lines) and a *sestet* (another quatrain, followed by a couplet), with the rhyme scheme ABAB CDCD EFEF GG. In the Petrarchan form, the octave stated some sort of metaphysical or emotional problem, and the sestet proposed a solution. The subject matter tended to be courtly love, with the poet using the first person ("I love her, but she doesn't love me"). This tradition lasted centuries, but in time the form came to embrace many other subjects.

Shakespeare's sonnets use a slightly different form. Instead of an octave and a sestet, they employ four quatrains and finish with a couplet that offers some sort of conclusion or moral for the poem. You can visualize the grids of Petrarchan and Shakespearean sonnets in this way:

Petrarch   {(4 + 4) (3 + 3)}
Shakespeare   {(4 + 4 + 4) (2)}

In English, poets write their traditional sonnets in iambic pentameter: five iambic feet per line, for a total of ten syllables per line. Poets give themselves the freedom to amputate a syllable from the count or add one; as long as five stresses remain, lines with nine syllables (one unstressed syllable amputated) or eleven syllables (one unstressed syllable added) don't break the game's rules.

A sonnet's grid is so different from a haiku's or a limerick's that its contents must also be different. Form is meaning—there's no escaping this truth! Readers and listeners expect that every foot in a sonnet written within the English tradition will be iambic. A good sonnet, however, follows the grid to some degree and deviates from it to another degree. Precisely because the grid creates expectations, deviations generate a kind of friction that increases the poem's interest. The poet might sprinkle a few trochaic feet ("TUM-da") here and there, or an anapest ("ta-ta-DUM"). Great poets are masters of expectation and deception, carefully setting up expectations better to deceive and delight their readers.

Table 3.3, "The Sonnet against the Grid," shows Shakespeare's Sonnet 18 side by side with its abstract grid. See if you can catch where Shakespeare chose rhythms that push against the grid, and where he submitted his pen to the grid's tyranny—for instance, by compressing a word ("oft'") better to fit the grid.

TABLE 3.3 A Shakespeare Sonnet against the Grid

Line #	Abstract Iambic Pentameter	Rhyme	Sonnet 18
1	ta-DUM ta-DUM ta-DUM ta-DUM ta-DUM	A	Shall I compare thee to a Summer's day?
2	ta-DUM ta-DUM ta-DUM ta-DUM ta-DUM	B	Thou art more lovely and more temperate:
3	ta-DUM ta-DUM ta-DUM ta-DUM ta-DUM	A	Rough winds do shake the darling buds of May,
4	ta-DUM ta-DUM ta-DUM ta-DUM ta-DUM	B	And Summer's lease hath all too short a date:
5	ta-DUM ta-DUM ta-DUM ta-DUM ta-DUM	C	Sometimes too hot the eye of heav'n shines,
6	ta-DUM ta-DUM ta-DUM ta-DUM ta-DUM	D	And oft' is his gold complexion dimm'd;
7	ta-DUM ta-DUM ta-DUM ta-DUM ta-DUM	C	And every fair from fair sometime declines,
8	ta-DUM ta-DUM ta-DUM ta-DUM ta-DUM	D	By chance or nature's changing course untrimm'd.
9	ta-DUM ta-DUM ta-DUM ta-DUM ta-DUM	E	But thy eternal Summer shall not fade
10	ta-DUM ta-DUM ta-DUM ta-DUM ta-DUM	F	Nor lose possession of that fair thou owest;
11	ta-DUM ta-DUM ta-DUM ta-DUM ta-DUM	E	Nor shall Death brag thou wanderest in his shade,
12	ta-DUM ta-DUM ta-DUM ta-DUM ta-DUM	F	When in eternal lines to time thou growest:
13	ta-DUM ta-DUM ta-DUM ta-DUM ta-DUM	G	So long as men can breathe, or eyes can see,
14	ta-DUM ta-DUM ta-DUM ta-DUM ta-DUM	G	So long lives this, and this gives life to thee.

GRIDS IN MUSIC

The musical cosmos abounds with grids. The piano keyboard is a grid, set in a pattern laden with numerical implications. For each octave, there are seven white keys and five black ones. The octave is divided into two symmetrical tetrachords: C-D-E-F, G-A-B-C; tone-tone-semitone, tone-tone-semitone. Let's agree that the thumb is different from the other fingers; the pianist's ten fingers, then, are organized (from the left little finger to the right little finger) as $\{(4 + 1) (1 + 4)\}$. In the vast majority of passages ever played at the piano, the hands' mathematics don't coincide with the keyboard's—and that's a good thing, since it creates a dynamic opposition between the keyboard's implacable grid and the hands' capacity for variety and invention.

In twelve-tone music, a complex grid is built from a simple row. Like all grids, it contains multiple mathematical elements: the twelve tones of the row itself, the four variants of a row that are permitted in the system (the prime, the inversion, the retrograde, and the retrograde-inversion), the twelve possible transpositions of each row and its variants, and so on. And, like all grids, it carries its own meaning, its own emotional charge: Anything you compose inside the twelve-tone grid will be inevitably different from anything you compose inside the tonal grid.

The chords of tonal music form a complex grid based on the interval of the third. Each third can be major, minor, diminished, augmented, doubly diminished, or doubly augmented. Take a major third, stack a minor third above it, and you have a major triad. Three thirds stacked together create a seventh chord; four thirds create a ninth chord. (If you like puzzles, look at the Forlane from Maurice Ravel's "Le Tombeau de Couperin" and try to figure out all the seventh and ninth chords he uses!) The key of C major uses a subset of the total grid. In a tune in C major, which arises out of the C-major grid, an F-sharp is in opposition to the grid. But in a tune in G major, it's an F-natural that opposes the grid.

The thirds play important roles in music, but the foundational grid of tonal music is the circle of fifths. It consists of twelve fifths arrayed in a circle like the hours on a clock, moving up clockwise and down counterclockwise. Starting on C, the fifths go up to G, D, A, and so on, until we arrive back at C; or down to F, B-flat, E-flat, and so on, until we again arrive back at the starting point. The basic elements couldn't be simpler, and yet the circle of fifths gives rise to the entirety of tonal music, organizing consonance, dissonance, structural relationships, and so on. Beethoven is different from Vivaldi because he opposes the grid of the circle of fifths in a different way. As tonal music developed, composers explored ever more complex oppositions to the grid until the oppositions overcame the grid and gave rise to atonality.

THE METRIC GRID

In this book we'll make an in-depth study of the metric grid. Subsequently you can use the insights and tools you'll learn from it to explore the grids of twelve-tone music, counterpoint, modal music, tonal music, bebop, and so on.

Let's define the metric grid as "a pulse, plus a time signature, plus a certain number of measures." An example is the pulse of a quarter note per second (that is, the metronome set at 60), with the time signature of $\frac{4}{4}$, over thirty-two measures subdivided in eight four-bar phrases.

The metric grid is ubiquitous throughout tonal music, but also in atonal, polytonal, modal, twelve-tone, serial, folk, jazz, and world music. In truth, all of human life is deeply touched by the metric grid. Primeval activities such as breathing, circulation, lovemaking, and dancing follow rhythmic patterns that can be easily inserted into a metric grid—as do lesser activities such as brushing teeth, ironing, and beating eggs.

Before we turn our attention to the metric grid, let's summarize the main characteristics of the Grid as a life principle, since they'll guide us in the chapters that follow.

1. There exists a life principle called the Grid, with capital G.

The Grid functions as a relatively rigid construction against which fluid energies push and flow. It underpins all human endeavors and, more broadly, the workings of the universe. The Grid is the archetypal model for all grids, an entity that the metaphysically inclined might liken to a deity. You can attune yourself to the Grid, sense and understand it, and organize your life in opposition to it. For the sake of argument, suppose you disagree with me about the very existence of the Grid. You'd still learn a lot of useful, practical things from studying grids without a capital G.

2. Grids have multiple dimensions.

A grid contains any or all of these components: visual, auditory, mathematical, geographical, historical, geometrical, topographical, hierarchical, aesthetic, emotional, and biological. This list isn't exhaustive.

3. All grids are built from simple components such as numbers and lines.

The chessboard is simple. Each chess piece is simple. The rules of the game are simple. Together, these elements are complex. You can deal better with complexity when you understand the simplicity that underpins it. When you practice and study, keep going back to the fundamentals—the numbers and lines that create the grid. They'll help you "play the game" better.

4. Every grid carries its own meaning and emotion.

Consciously or unconsciously, we respond to abstract mathematical relationships and to numbers themselves. We consider a thirteen-line grid to be different from a twelve-line one, a square grid to be different from a round one, and a symmetrical grid to be different from an asymmetrical one. Perfect symmetry charges the grid with certain emotions and meanings; asymmetry charges the grid with different emotions and meanings. Either way, each grid has a "personality."

5. A grid becomes dynamic when human life flows against it.

Grids capture and enhance natural forces. From early childhood onward, we all think about grids, observe them, live in them, and use our inner resources to push against the grids' pull. Knowledge of the grid increases the pleasure of opposing it.

6. We combine intellect and intuition when we learn and use any grid.

Your knowledge of the multiplication table, which is a mathematical grid, allows you to conduct quick operations mentally. You reckon "three times three" effortlessly, by acquired reflex. To acquire it, you used analysis, memory, intuition, and imagination. If you try to study the metric grid with analytical processes only, you'll find the grid boring and threatening. Bring your creativity to the party and you'll not only have more fun, you'll learn the materials more quickly and more deeply.

7. We can and must internalize each grid to some degree.

Most of us have internalized a large number of grids over the years: the calendar, our neighborhoods' street grid, the multiplication table. Internalized grids make your life easier and healthier, while overly externalized grids make your life complicated and unhealthy. When it comes to the metric grid, externalizing it costs you a lot of energy, interfering with your ability to create oppositions with the grid.

In the next chapter we'll study the metric grid in depth. Following it we'll practice two prosodic skills that make it easier for you to learn and internalize the metric grid: the exercises of Coincidence (chapter 5) and Rhythmic Solfège (chapter 6). Then we'll look at metronomic precision and rubato (chapter 7), two opposing rhythmic forces that charge the metric grid with different kinds of energy. We'll look at practice strategies for studying the superbar structure, or the "measures of measures" that give the metric grid its largest dimension (chapter 8). Finally, we'll look at a number of musical excerpts to see how composers handle the grid: Johannes Brahms (chapter 9) and J. S. Bach (chapter 10). Part II, "Coordination," might at first appear unrelated to the Grid, but in fact coordination itself is a matter of opposing lively energies to relatively rigid grids. Part III, "Sound," will relate indirectly to the Grid because the harmonic series (the subject of chapters 16 and 17) will show us that the circle of fifths—the foundational grid of tonal music—is borne of the vibrations of a *single note*!

CHAPTER 4

THE METRIC GRID

MATHEMATICS FOR THE INTEGRATED MUSICIAN

Every endeavor in our lives contains a mathematical dimension. You can't play cards without knowing a little about probabilities. You might be a lousy poker player who loses every game, but you'd still understand that a hand of four aces is more infrequent and more valuable than three aces. You can't play snooker without knowing algebra and geometry, whether your knowledge is analytical or intuitive. If a menu offers a choice of three appetizers, five main courses, and three desserts, you can't order dinner without using combinatorial analysis.

You might flinch if I asked you how much is two to the power of three, but you probably wouldn't mind if I asked you how many great-grandparents you have. And yet the question is the same. "Two parents, four grandparents, eight great-grandparents. Two to the power of three equals eight." Numbers don't pose any difficulty for most people as long as the mathematical operations aren't abstract.

When you walk, your "inner animal" senses and experiences what it is like to have two legs and two arms, and to take steps in sequences of two. To that physical reality your analytical brain gives names and graphic signs: "two," "2," "bipedal," "bilateral." When you start with the feeling of something concrete and later add a name and a structure to it, the inner animal and the brain get along so well that they become inseparable. (The inner animal merits its own section in chapter 14.)

You can't make music without "making mathematics." The metric grid contains mathematical components such as time signatures, subdivisions of note values, length of phrases, and combinations of prosodic energies. Let feeling, playfulness, and your innate linguistic abilities guide you, and you won't be afraid of the grid even if you're phobic about math. "How many thirty-second notes are there in a $\frac{3}{4}$ bar?" The question has mathematical, kinesthetic, and linguistic answers. You can probably sing and dance most of the analytical information in this chapter!

We start our study of the grid by looking at the bar line, which isn't the simple matter it appears to the naked eye.

THE BAR LINE, FRIEND OR FOE?

Faced with the blank page upon which we'll write a musical text, we put up stakes delineating units of space. The stakes are bar lines (example 4.1).

EXAMPLE 4.1. Bar lines as stakes in space

| | | | |

We fill the spaces with beats or pulses. Now the bar lines delineate units of both space and time (example 4.2).

EXAMPLE 4.2. Bar lines enclosing subdivisions of time

We transform these beats into specific note values, choosing quarter notes for the sake of convenience. A quarter note is pregnant with meaning: It contains two eighth notes, four sixteenths, three eighth-note triplets, and other mathematical possibilities. A beat and a note are two different concepts, but in example 4.3 every note lasts one beat, and to every beat there corresponds a note. Whenever two concepts coincide, there exists the risk of ambiguity, as we'll see throughout the chapter.

EXAMPLE 4.3. Beats

Choosing two quarter notes per bar grants us the right to write down a time signature: ${}^2_4$ (example 4.4). We could have acted the other way around, choosing a time signature first and then writing in the note values. One decision is kinesthetic ("I want to dance a sequence of two steps") and the other mathematical ("I want to dwell in the world of 2, the duple and binary world"), but as you now know, these two decisions are intimately related. In this context, a time signature plays a double role: as a spatial sign much like a bar line, delineating a territory on the page; and as a mathematical sign indicating the meter of every bar that follows it.

EXAMPLE 4.4. The time signature

Some bar lines say, "We hold a self-contained group of notes, of which the first is stronger than all the others."

| (A b c d) | (A b c d) | (A b c d) | (A b c d) |

Other bar lines might say, "We mark the destination for a group of notes. The destination stands to our right, but the group departs from our left."

| (b c d | A) (b c d | A) (b c d | A) (b c d | A)

Maybe the bar lines say, "We help your eyes travel across the page. We don't dictate how notes are grouped together."

| (A b c) (d | A b) (c d | A) (b c d) | (A b c d) |

Some bar lines are intruders. In Bach's time, musicians shared the assumption that time signatures were fixed over a movement or section. If a phrase was jagged and asymmetrical, the time signature (with its corresponding bar lines) didn't change to accommodate it. Bach might compose something equivalent to this:

| A b c d | A b c d | e f A b | c d e f | A b c d |

Igor Stravinsky would bar that same phrase differently:

| A b c d | A b c d e f | A b c d e f | A b c d |

Bar lines can be normal, abnormal, neutral, prescriptive, essential, superfluous, and even downright harmful. There's no convenient way of indicating, in ordinary music notation, all the possible roles of a bar line.

A bar line is a little bit of *data*. You interpret the data and decide what role the bar line plays in a passage. Now the data has become *information*. If you use it in performance, it becomes *knowledge*. You play many pieces over time, and your knowledge matures into *wisdom* and *insight*. What happens when you misinterpret data? The whole chain from data and information to knowledge and wisdom is corrupted.

Look at example 4.5. It uses four distinct signs to indicate degrees and types of togetherness.

1. The bar lines, delineating space and time, gather groups of six eighth notes.
2. Stems bring together every three eighth notes.
3. The single long slur brings all notes and bars into a unified phrase.
4. The braces indicate an anapestic note grouping on a local level.

EXAMPLE 4.5. Stems and other graphic indications

Each sign is a bit of data, and like all data you need to interpret it in order to understand it and put it into practical use. The stems, for instance, are visually helpful but potentially misleading. Compare these three versions of the same phone number:

12125559267
121 255 592 67
+1 (212) 555–9267

The first version is hard to read, memorize, and dial. The second is easier to read in the abstract, but the separations between digits don't respect the number's logic. The third version is the clearest. It uses a variety of graphic tools to spell out the information and render it legible: the + sign, blank spaces, parentheses, and a hyphen. The + sign indicates a long-distance access code, variable from country to country. It's followed by the country code for the US, the city code for New York, and a subdivided seven-digit phone number.

The stems grouping eighth notes together in example 4.5 are like the second version of the phone number: The groupings aren't necessarily logical from a prosodic point of view. Stems sometimes *coincide* with the prosody, but they don't actually *indicate* prosody.

Because of the ambiguities of bar lines and stems, you may find it useful to write a dotted line right next to a bar line, and a brace underneath a group of notes that is fully contained within the bar (example 4.6). If we juxtapose two sequences, the first trochaic, the second iambic, you'll see how useful it is to have braces and dotted lines at your disposal. The initials stand for preparation, stress, and release.

EXAMPLE 4.6. Braces and dotted lines in prosodic analysis

TIME SIGNATURES

Time signatures contain two numbers. They tells us what kind of beat the bar uses, and how many beats are there per bar.

Ordinary signatures in the average musician's repertoire have two, three, or four beats. If the signature has two beats, it's called *duple time*; three beats, *triple time*; and four beats, *quadruple time*. A fast piece can be played as if it has only one beat per bar even if its time signature indicates otherwise. Then we say the piece is in *single time*.

Ordinary beats are the eighth, the quarter, and the half note (and, less frequently, the sixteenth). If the beat is a plain eighth, quarter, or half note, the measure is called *simple*; if the beat is a dotted eighth, quarter, or half note, the measure is called *compound*. Table 4.1,

TABLE 4.1 **Basic Time Signatures**

	Duple				Triple				Quadruple			
Simple	2/2	2/4	2/8	2/16	3/2	3/4	3/8	2/16	4/2	4/4	4/8	4/16
Compound	6/2	6/4	6/8	6/16	9/2	9/4	9/8	9/16	12/2	12/4	12/8	12/16

"Basic Time Signatures," shows all possible combinations, some of which are used more infrequently than others.

Mentally catalog pieces written in each time signature, until you recognize time signatures as friendly entities with distinct personalities. "Frère Jacques" is in 2/4, "La Marseillèse" is in 4/4, "Happy Birthday" is in 3/4, "Silent Night" is in 6/8. You "walk" 4/4 rather differently from how you "walk" 6/8. You couldn't waltz in duple time, and you might find it hard to do a funeral march in triple time. If you open a score by Brahms and its meter is in triple time, you anticipate that sooner or later Brahms will include one or more hemiolas in a passage. A set of six equal elements can be organized as two groups of three or three groups of two. A hemiola is the juxtaposition or the alternation of these groupings:

    1 2 3 1 2 3
    1 2 1 2 1 2

In a piece in 6/8, for instance, a hemiola is like a brief switch to 3/4; in a piece in 6/4, a hemiola is a switch to 3/2.

In your music making, you're likely to run into time signatures other than those shown in table 4.1: quintuple time, for instance (such as 5/4 and 5/8), or additive meters (such as $\frac{3+2+3}{8}$, with three metric stresses spread asymmetrically over the bar). Unfamiliar time signatures most often are variations and deviations from the simpler time signatures. The more comfortable you are with basic principles, the easier you'll learn their variations and deviations.

Your inner animal knows how to respond to rhythm and how to gather and dispense rhythmic energies. If you grow up listening exclusively to music in binary and ternary patterns, you don't encounter fives and sevens until you're an adult whose inner animal has been suppressed. Then you try to learn fives and sevens by counting mathematically, as a civilized adult—and it's very hard going! Counting is effective only when your inner animal's muscular and verbal instincts guide it. If you can "feel something," you can count it.

FEELING, SPEAKING, COUNTING

To illustrate how to learn new rhythmic patterns without counting, we'll use a five-unit pattern with two stresses. This could be the basis for a 5/4 or 5/8 bar, or for a quintuplet inside an ordinary bar. Speak the following lines out loud:

"Guess who's coming to dinner: Clinton!"
"Clinton who?"
"*Hillary* Clinton."

You clarify what you mean by emphasizing the first word, of which the first syllable is stressed. You do so without thinking, with a spontaneous energy charged with your authentic emotions—be they pro-Clinton or anti-Clinton.

HIL-la-ry CLIN-ton.

Having connected with the spontaneous energy that drives your speech, retain the prosodic feeling of what you said and substitute nonsense or scatting syllables:

HIL-la-ry CLIN-ton, **TA**-tee-tee Ta-tee.

Give each syllable the same length—an eighth note, for instance—and assign the sequence a tempo such as allegro moderato.

⅝ **TA**-tee-tee Ta-tee | **TA**-tee-tee Ta-tee |

Instead of syllables, now use physical actions such as snapping your fingers or playing single notes on the piano. Take a pencil and tap it three times on a tabletop, then move the pencil a little and tap twice on a different spot. This allows you to marry hand motion, eyes, ears, and linguistic intention over time and space.

TAP-tap-tap
TAP-tap

Thanks to this procedure, fives stop being such a foreign music. When you encounter the pattern in a score—by Béla Bartók, for instance—the inner animal, trained by your conscious intelligence, will help you read and perform the passage comfortably (example 4.7).

EXAMPLE 4.7. A basic unit in ⅝

Now read out loud the lines below:

"Guess who's coming to dinner: Hillary!"
"Hillary who?"
"Hillary *Clinton*."

In every piece you perform, there'll be different layers of prosodic energy, from groups of notes to bars to phrases. "Hillary" is dactylic; "Clinton" is trochaic. Put together, the two words create a larger unit with a variable prosody according to how you say it. "*Hillary* Clinton" has a trochaic feel to it, since the first stress is heavier. "Hillary *Clinton*" has an iambic feel, since the second stress is heavier (example 4.8).

EXAMPLE 4.8. Layers of prosodic energy

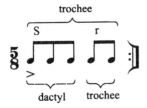 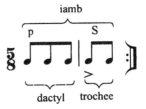

THE SUPERBAR STRUCTURE

What do "Happy Birthday," "Oh! Susanna," and "The Star-Spangled Banner" have in common?

The best way to find out is by singing them in succession. Their lyrics certainly aren't similar. They don't share a key either; it'd be happenstance if you sang them all in C major. "Happy Birthday" and "The Star-Spangled Banner" are in $\frac{3}{4}$, but "Oh! Susanna" is in $\frac{2}{4}$, so they don't share a time signature. But if you conduct the songs, or if you stomp your foot at the downbeats of every measure, you'll see that all three songs have similar phrase structures. Their notes and lyrics coalesce into units of four bars, and every two of these four-bar units coalesce into self-contained phrases of eight bars. The whole of "Happy Birthday," in fact, consists of eight bars subdivided into two equal halves.

The four bars that belong together in a phrase are so organically linked that they have their own rhythmic propulsion. Sing "Oh! Susanna" and try to stop after the third bar. What happens? Something inside yourself compels you to go on and finish if not the song, the four bars that belong together in a phrase. The first bar drives you to the second, the second to the third, and the third to the fourth. In the case of a song you know, this may be due in part to the pull of familiarity and memory. But in any one piece, including ones you hear for the first time in your life, bars that belong together in a phrase will produce a similar effect: you'll want them to "go on" to what you feel is their logical, inevitable end.

In our ears, minds, and bodies, we perceive a rhythmic structure that goes beyond individual bars to embrace all four bars at once. In this structure, the downbeat of each bar becomes a beat inside a larger structure. Four bars of $\frac{2}{4}$ in "Oh! Susanna" become one bar of $\frac{8}{4}$; four bars of $\frac{3}{4}$ in "Happy Birthday" become one bar of $\frac{12}{4}$. This "measure of measures" is called a *superbar*. (In Latin, "super" means "above, over, on top of, beyond, besides, in addition to.")

In short, the three songs of our example share a common superbar structure. The superbar structure gives the metric grid its large-scale organization, much like paragraphs gather sentences together in a written text.

THE PREVALENCE OF FOUR-BAR PHRASES

Most children's songs use the four-bar phrase, often in groups of two phrases integrated into an eight-bar whole. Test this by singing "Twinkle Twinkle Little Star" and "Mary Had a Little Lamb." Pedagogical materials such as Suzuki manuals, the "Notebook for Anna Madgalena Bach," and Robert Schumann's "Album für die Jugend" contain more four- and eight-bar phrases than any other length. So do hymns in every church denomination, the blues, anything played by a marching band, and most everything that we receive aurally, from the cradle onward.

There are many reasons for the phenomenon.

1. A four-bar phrase can usually be sung in a single breath from beginning to end. This lends the phrase a nearly biological dimension: it "fits," so to speak, with our instinctive functioning. Needless to say, a song may have inflections and pauses within a four-bar phrase where we can take breaths, and sometimes the very meaning of what we sing is improved if we take more frequent breaths. The biological component of the four-bar phrase, however, is present whether or not we choose to take breaths inside the phrase.

2. A four-bar phrase is a packet of organized information, like a shopping list with elements all to be found on the same supermarket isle. Not only do we understand it readily, we memorize it easily too.

3. In structure and length, a four-bar phrase simulates many types of spoken sentences. Its meaning can be self-contained and easy to understand, digest, and memorize.

   a. In structure and length, a four-bar phrase
   b. simulates many types of spoken sentences.
   c. Its meaning can be self-contained
   d. and easy to understand, digest, and memorize.

4. The mathematical strength of the four-bar phrase comes in part from the multiple structures it can contain and generate: the eight-bar, sixteen-bar, and thirty-two-bar structures, as well as the two-bar subdivisions often featured inside a four-bar unit. The numbers underpinning the organization of everything we do are powerful in themselves. Examples are the calendar of seconds, minutes, hours, days, weeks, and months, in which the numbers sixty, twenty-four, twelve, and seven are pregnant with meaning; or our anatomical features of two arms and two legs with five fingers or toes on each extremity, the four chambers of the heart, the seven orifices of the head, and so on. Number has an undeniable mystical component, as illustrated by the seven capital sins, the twelve apostles, and the Holy Trinity. Four is a symbol of stability and wholeness, as exemplified by the four cardinal points. In other words, a quasi-mystical power resides within the number four itself, and we respond to it in ways our reason alone can't comprehend.

5. The four-bar phrase is a perfect motor for our hips and feet: It leads us into dance, taking us readily from (a) here to (b) *there*, and from (c) there back (d) *here*. When we studied prosody in chapter 2, Ezra Pound and William Christie helped us understand that music, dance, and poetry spring from the same source. Every dance has a text, every text has a dance, and music is the bridge between the two—a bridge most easily crossed along the four-bar phrase.

In short, the four-bar phrase represents an ideal from the point of view of musical linguistics. Generally speaking, the music you study, perform, and listen to corresponds to this ideal; approaches, teases, and flirts with the ideal, only to diverge from it; or desperately tries to free itself from the tyranny of the ideal and either succeeds or fails. Even when you dwell in a domain where not one phrase is four bars long (for instance, the world of free jazz improvisation), the four-bar phrase is inescapable because the world at large is populated by it. The free jazz improviser can't ever "forget" the four-bar phrase for very long, so deeply ingrained it is in ordinary life.

The idealized superbar structure in tonal music is called a *period*. It consists of a four-bar section called the *antecedent*, followed by another four-bar section called the *consequent*. The antecedent ends in a half cadence—that is, on the dominant chord, which represents musical tension. The consequent ends in a perfect cadence—a tidy resolution to the tonic chord, which represents musical release. It has often been said that the antecedent states a question, and the consequent answers it. In fact it has been said so often that many musicians now consider it a tired cliché and reject it outright. A cliché, however, sometimes encapsulates a useful truth. Take note of the question-and-answer aspect of many superbar structures, while remaining alert to the rich variety of musical phrases that don't follow the question-and-answer format.

Here are two instances of the archetypical period. Example 4.9 is the beginning of "Oh! Susanna." Example 4.10 is the opening phrase of Joseph Haydn's Sonata for Piano in D Major, Hob. XVI: 37.

We can summarize the archetypical period's superbar structure with the schema in example 4.11, in which H signifies a half cadence, P a perfect cadence, I the tonic chord, and V the dominant.

Historically, a majority of four-bar phrases follow a double-trochaic pattern: the downbeat of the first measure is a primary stress, the second one a release; the third measure is a secondary stress, the fourth a release. Our two examples of a complete period both appear to obey the double-trochaic pattern.

We'll study superbar structures in greater detail in chapter 8.

EXAMPLE 4.9. Stephen Foster: "Oh! Susanna"

EXAMPLE 4.10. Joseph Haydn: Sonata for Piano, Hob. XVI: 37 in D Major, first movement

EXAMPLE 4.11. The periodic phrase structure

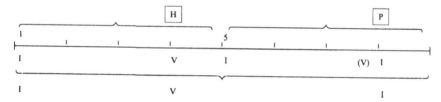

MUSICAL ENERGIES AND THE METRIC GRID

In tonal and metric music—that is, most of Classical music written between 1600 and 1900—four types of accents or energies coexist in every composition. To sense and understand each accent and how they collaborate will help you sight-read, learn, memorize, and perform your pieces. You can also adapt much of what you'll learn in this section to non-tonal and non-metric music.

1. METRIC ACCENTS

The very construction of a measure of music indicates that different notes inside the measure have different qualities or energies, which we'll call *metric accents*. Notes within a bar rank in relative metric importance. The downbeat has greater weight than other beats and receives a *primary* metric accent. Depending on how the piece is composed, other notes may have secondary, tertiary, and even smaller stresses. In a $\frac{4}{4}$ bar with four quarter notes, the third quarter note receives a secondary metric accent. If the bar has running eighth notes, those falling on the strong beats of 1, 2, 3, and 4 will be more accented than those on the offbeats. The same principle applies to running sixteenth and thirty-second notes, where every other note might be a tiny little bit more important than its immediate neighbors, receiving a quaternary accent (example 4.12).

EXAMPLE 4.12. Layers of metric stresses

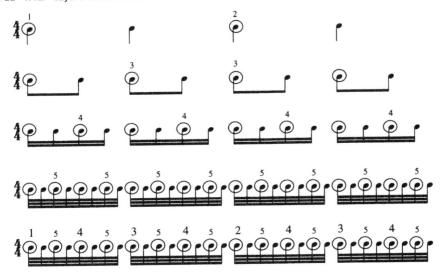

EXAMPLE 4.13. Ludwig van Beethoven: Variations for Piano and Cello on a theme by Mozart, WoO 46 in E-flat Major

In most pieces in your repertoire, the smallest levels of metric accents have no importance. Sooner or later, however, you'll encounter a composition where the appreciation of layered metric accent is essential. In example 4.13, the thirty-second and sixty-fourth notes are difficult to read and place correctly, but sensing which notes within the various groups receive metric stresses—however infinitesimal—will help you organize the whole passage.

Mathematical calculations won't give the passage its swing and flow. Using your head, neck, and other body parts as metronomes will hinder your sound production, your dexterity, and even your rhythmic precision. It's by sensing the passage's linguistic construction and its propulsive prosodic pulls that you can best perform it.

2. AGOGIC ACCENTS

Amidst a sequence of running eighth notes, a quarter note would be conspicuous, calling attention to itself simply on account of its length. The energy of a longer note within a passage is called an *agogic accent*. A four-bar phrase may have any number of agogic accents within it, depending on its construction. It's possible for every third or fourth note in a composition to have an agogic accent.

Metric and agogic accents don't necessarily coincide. In example 4.14, the primary metric accent falls on a note that is comparatively short.

EXAMPLE 4.14. Camille Saint-Saëns: Concerto for Cello and Orchestra, opus 33 in A Minor, first movement

The agogic accents risk usurping the role of the metric accents, and the player might unwittingly "rewrite the passage," much to its detriment (example 4.15).

EXAMPLE 4.15. Camille Saint-Saëns: Agogic accents usurping the role of metric accents

To perform is to make choices. Experiment with the degrees of weight you give to each note. Make your varied versions exaggerated first, then subtle. Ask a friend to listen to your experiments and report on their results. Does the passage sound more compelling when you favor the metric accents, when you favor the agogic ones, or when you vary their interaction?

3. TONAL ACCENTS

All other things being equal (length, volume, articulation, and so on), a high note carries more tension than a low one, and our ears are drawn to it for acoustic and psychological reasons. In any passage where a note is higher than its neighbors, the higher note will receive a *melodic* or *tonal accent* (and here the word "tonal" refers to tone or sound, not tonality). A note lower than its neighbors receives a *reverse tonal accent*. Tonal accents are a form of energy implicit in the composition, which you can make explicit in performance. Needless to say, tonal accents compete for attention with metric and agogic accents. High notes, much as long notes and downbeats, "want to be heard."

Many passages reach a melodic climax or tonal accent some notes before the passage's last downbeat or metric accent. As a performer, will you bring all your energies to a peak at the melodic climax and start relaxing after it, or will you hold off the relaxation until you reach the subsequent downbeat? Loosely speaking, to peak at the melodic climax creates a sort of trochaic impetus: "REACH A PEAK and relax into the downbeat." To sustain your energies until the following downbeat creates an iambic impetus: "Grow past the melodic climax and REACH A PEAK." Constant experimentation is the only way for you to discover how best to connect with each phrase you perform.

4. DYNAMIC ACCENTS

Compare these two sentences:

In every bet there is a fool and a thief.
In every bet there is a fool and a *thief*.

The italics spice up the sentence and change its emotion to some degree. In music we call this form of extrinsic energy a *dynamic accent*. It requires an extra typographical indication equivalent to italics, such as *sforzando, subito forte, fp*, wedges, dots, and so on.

Different composers use the same marking to mean different things; a *fp* in Mozart doesn't have the same musical logic as a *fp* in Brahms. Beethoven sprinkles his compositions with an extravagant number of dynamic accents. How to play them? Example 4.16 is from the "Diabelli" theme, a piece we'll study in greater detail in chapter 15.

Some performers take dynamic accents as invitations to let rip, executing each accent as a shout of sorts. Musicologists affirm that the prevailing aesthetics in Beethoven's time required the downbeats to be always sounded more strongly than other beats in the bar. Some speculate that Beethoven's dynamic accents simply say, "Don't let these notes here sound too much weaker than the downbeats, as you normally would." In this case, dynamic accents aren't invitations for you to let rip, but for you to balance the weight between downbeats and nondownbeats. Vary your accents' resonance, intensity, and

EXAMPLE 4.16. Ludwig van Beethoven: Variations on a Theme by Anton Diabelli, opus 120 in C Major

color. Perform strong dynamic accents without scrunching your neck and shoulders. Then choose to let rip . . . or not.

THE FOUR ACCENTS AND THE GRID

If you bring the metric grid alive in an intelligent and playful manner, agogic, dynamic, and tonal accents gain in emotion and power.

The beginning of Maurice Ravel's "Valses Nobles et Sentimentales" illustrates the accents to perfection (example 4.17). The downbeats of every bar receive metric accents, and beats 2 and 3 receive agogic accents. The third beat receives both tonal and dynamic accents. But a waltz requires a strong downbeat to propel the dancer forward, so the pianist ought to highlight the metric accents instead of letting them be overwhelmed by all the other accents.

EXAMPLE 4.17. Maurice Ravel: "Valses Nobles et Sentimentales" for Piano

Example 4.18 schematizes the four accents. Like all schema, it's an oversimplification that you may one day find insufficient and ambiguous. To study all the accents and their interaction, choose a passage from your repertoire. Write a simplified version of the metric grid underneath it, so that you can visualize all the primary and secondary metric accents. Note the agogic, dynamic, tonal, and reverse tonal accents, and see how they collaborate with the metric accents or fight with them. Example 4.19 is the opening phrase of Robert Schumann's Concerto for Cello and Orchestra, opus 129 in A minor. Not coincidentally, it's eight bars long.

The passage has a wealth of agogic accents, most of which don't coincide with metric accents. There are two dynamic accents, one of which on an offbeat that is also an agogic accent. In the cello part, the downbeat (that is, the primary metric accent) goes missing altogether on two occasions. Now look at the cello part in context with the orchestral accompaniment, which adds offbeats and syncopations to the mix (example 4.20). As you'll see, Schumann composed his concerto by creating a fight between the grid-affirming metric accents—which in this composition are mostly implicit, rather than explicit—and the grid-defying agogic, tonal, and dynamic accents. If you don't sense the grid's presence despite the lack of strong downbeats you won't fully appreciate the composition's significance.

EXAMPLE 4.18. Metric, agogic, tonal, and dynamic accents

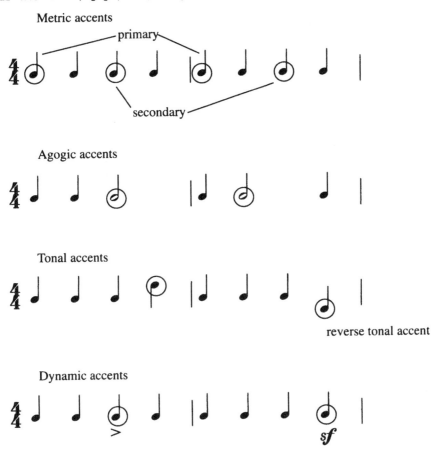

EXAMPLE 4.19. Robert Schumann: Concerto for Cello and Orchestra, opus 129 in A Minor

EXAMPLE 4.20. Robert Schumann: Concerto for Cello and Orchestra, opus 129 in A Minor

OPPOSING THE GRID

The metric grid of bar lines, time signatures, and phrase lengths tends to go unnoticed. Your eyes get drawn in by what has been laid out over and above the grid—notes, chords, dynamics, and so on—and the physicality of playing or singing "the right notes" becomes all-consuming.

This is a pity. Music lives and dies in opposition to the grid. Knowing how to sense the grid and how to oppose it will help you in every possible way: technical, musical, physical, psychological, and professional.

Example 4.21 is a first-violin passage from an orchestral work by Johannes Brahms: the Variations on a Theme by Haydn, opus 56a in B-flat major, also known as the "St. Anthony Variations." I added grids of eighth notes and dotted quarter notes underneath it.

The passage is often requested in orchestral auditions. Fast notes with a bouncy bow stroke spell coordinative problems. The passage's true difficulty, however, is not

mechanical but linguistic. By definition, the metric grid is regular, symmetrical, and predictable, but what Brahms composed is irregular, asymmetrical, and unpredictable. The challenge is to balance out these forces in a way that is musically coherent and technically reliable. Without coherence there can be no reliability.

The passage is in $\frac{6}{8}$ (example 4.22). In a normative bar of $\frac{6}{8}$, the first eighth note receives a primary metric accent, the fourth eighth note a secondary accent. The six eighth notes coalesce into two dactylic feet. Since the first dactyl has a heavier accent than the second, the bar has an overall trochaic impetus.

In this passage Brahms commits at least six subversive acts:

1. He writes phrases of five bars, not four. The theme itself uses phrases of five bars, so the variation "obeys" the theme. But the theme itself is "disobedient," since the normative musical phrase is four bars long.
2. He uses dynamic accents on normally unaccented beats: the sforzando-piano in the first bar and the sforzandi on bars 3 and 4.
3. He doesn't get the violin to sound the downbeats on bars 4 and 5, where the note that normally sounds the downbeat is tied over from the bar before; and he actively undermines the downbeat by writing a decrescendo into it.

EXAMPLE 4.22. The $\frac{6}{8}$ grid

4. He writes a hemiola in bar 5—that is, he superposes a bar of $\frac{3}{4}$ onto a bar of $\frac{6}{8}$. Then he syncopates the hemiola!
5. He writes a pianissimo subito in bar 7, which again sabotages the downbeat.
6. He amputates the metric accents in bars 9 and 10, where the violin plays offbeats exclusively.

Sensing the metric grid and learning how to oppose it will help you solve technical problems more efficiently than working on physical coordination alone. Chapter 9 develops this subject to the full.

RELEARNING AND INTERNALIZING THE GRID

Consider your language skills in your native tongue. It's a certainty that, every day, you make mistakes in speech and in writing. This shows that you can't ever assume you've learned enough about a basic subject with simple fundamentals but complex applications; or that, once you acquire basic knowledge, you'll always remember it dependably and use it correctly.

Most musicians have inadequate knowledge of the grid and the wealth of ways of playing against it, partly from having learned it badly to begin with, and partly from supposing it's too simple a concept to merit study.

Every failed ear-training test, every embarrassing moment in front of the theory class, and every nasty look you received from a conductor contribute to how you feel about the metric grid. If you want to revisit the grid and learn it anew, your first task is to wipe the emotional blackboard clean and approach the metric grid with a curious mind and a playful attitude. Then you'll find it easy to explore it in depth over the months and years.

Many musicians externalize the grid by nodding, lifting and dropping their elbows, swaying their pelvis, and tapping their feet or toes. In and of itself, using body parts as a metronome isn't harmful, but it becomes so when the gestures exist as compensations for an insufficiently clear grasp of rhythm and when they have a disconnecting effect upon the body. This will become clearer after you study coordination in chapters 11–15.

It may seem obligatory for a conductor to externalize the metric grid for the benefit of the orchestral players or choir singers, but even conductors can and must internalize the grid to some degree. Nothing is more exciting in an orchestral concert than when a conductor stops conducting altogether and trusts the musicians to sense, collectively, where the music is going. A conductor who knows how to do this has completely internalized the metric grid, which becomes invisible yet ever-present.

The chapters that follow will continue our exploration of the metric grid, with an emphasis on the practicalities of internalizing the grid and learning to oppose it.

CHAPTER 5

COINCIDENCE

Intention and Gesture

RIGHT HERE, RIGHT NOW!

Being an integrated musician means using all your capacities in a coordinated manner, in which your thinking becomes connected to your gestures, your body to your instrument, your technique to your musicianship, and your sound to your rhythm. It isn't enough for you to develop various capacities separately; they must come together moment by moment, microsecond by microsecond. The exercise I call Coincidence is a sort of meditation on the nature of the moment, the "right *here*, right *now!*"

🎬 This exercise is illustrated in three video clips: #4, "Coincidence I: At the Piano," #5, "Coincidence II: At the Flute," and #36, "Practice Routines III: Coincidence."

Say something out loud. At this point it doesn't matter what you say: read a paragraph from the newspaper, or list your siblings' names and ages. As you speak, snap your fingers and make the snapping coincide with some of the syllables in your discourse. You can snap to the prosodic stresses of what you are saying; snap every syllable; snap a few syllables at random; or say the same sentence a few times and snap different combinations of syllables each time.

Here's a sample sentence in three variations, with the snapped syllables in uppercase:

It's not important WHAT you say,
but HOW you mark the things you say.
It's NOT important what you SAY,
but how you MARK the things you say.
It's NOT im-POR-tant WHAT you SAY,
but HOW you MARK the THINGS you SAY.

Snapping your fingers is only one way of marking the text. Instead you can clap your hands, tap a tabletop with your fingertips, stomp your foot, or walk in place and make the stressed syllables coincide with your steps.

The purpose of the exercise is for you to obtain a total coincidence—in time and space—of linguistic intention, vocal performance, and physical gesture. We tend to believe that the following sequence of events take place:

1. The brain thinks a word or sentence;
2. the brain commands the body (including the lungs, the vocal folds, the lips, tongue, and jaw) to make the sounds of the words and sentences;
3. the brain further commands the fingers to tap, or the hands to clap, or the feet to stomp.

In ideal coordination, the entire sequence becomes so integrated as to be a single multidimensional event, rather than separate events happening quickly one after the other. When you get the hang of Coincidence, you might suddenly feel that the hands, fingers, or feet seem to be "speaking" the word, not under the command of the brain but on their own initiative.

Use every verbal and vocal variation in practicing the exercise. Start with simple phrases that you compose beforehand, saying them several times in a row until you find the "right *here*, right *now*!" of them. Engage in dialogue with a partner, answering his or her questions and snapping (or clapping or stomping) as if it were the most natural thing in everyday conversation. If you speak more than one language, perform the exercise in your second and third tongues. Tell jokes and snap. Declaim poetry and snap.

FROM WORDS TO MUSIC

Sit at a piano. Say a few words, and use one or more fingers to tap notes on the keyboard in total coincidence with chosen syllables in your words. The exercise doesn't require any knowledge of piano technique, and is equally useful to pianists and nonpianists. Try playing a note per syllable for a whole paragraph of speech; or play a note for the occasional syllable. The important thing is to obtain a total coincidence of intention and gesture, so that the thought, the syllable, the finger, and the note all become part of a single entity, moving at the same speed, at the same rate, at the same time.

Now play a few notes on the piano without saying anything out loud. Improvise a short little melody, play a children's song, or play any excerpt from the literature. You might feel as if your fingers are "thinking words and saying them." Without your paying any attention to the mechanical aspects of technique, your fingers' physical behavior has become altered by the linguistic intention that animates it.

If you're not a pianist, now switch to your actual instrument. Hold it in playing position and speak a few words, while fingering, articulating, or plucking random notes at the same time. Always speaking, pluck notes with one hand only; with both hands in alternation; or with both hands together. Now take a piece of music from your repertoire and say its rhythms out loud, using random syllables such as "tah, teh, toh," and so on. At the same time that you "say" the piece rhythmically, finger it at the instrument. Finally, play the piece normally, directing your linguistic energies to the playing alone.

Singers can do a sort of reverse version of the exercise. Sing a little phrase; tap, snap, or clap the syllables in the phrase that receive prosodic stresses; then sing it again, and make it seem as if the syllables in the song are tapping, snapping, and clapping the emphases.

Fred Astaire talks with his feet. Visit YouTube and study clips from his movies. Watch him waltz and tap-dance and you might feel that his feet are more than just dexterous in movement: They're smart, witty, and charming in what they say and how they say it. (Every good dancer does the same thing. As William Christie said in chapter 2, all dances have texts. This means that to dance is to speak.) Organists, pianists, harpists, and drummers all must use their feet in making music. Their feet, much like their fingers and hands, must become good speakers. It's useful for an organist, for instance, to sit at the organ and, while saying a text out loud, tap notes with the feet at the pedal; then saying the pedal line of a piece of music while tapping with the feet; then playing the pedal line while mentally thinking only the spoken sounds, until the feet become completely integrated with the rest of the body, mind, and heart.

Train your feet to become prosodists even if you don't use them when you make music—if you're an orchestral musician, for instance, or a singer in a choir. Good coordination is a reservoir of energies and capabilities at your disposal whether you use them or not. The more capabilities you have in reserve, the freer you become.

RISKS AND DANGERS

As simple as it sounds in description, the exercise of Coincidence can be surprisingly difficult to master. Hands (or fingers or feet) fall a little ahead or a little behind the stressed word; you "forget" to mark words or to speak while snapping; you lose the spontaneity of your speech. Coincidence requires the coordination of separate parts of the brain, one part normally overseeing speech, another part normally overseeing physical gestures. The exercise leads to a temporary brain meltdown in some people, and to an immediate integration of different capabilities in others.

If you become self-conscious about your speech and your gestures, let go of the exercise for a moment and either speak or snap, instead of trying to do both at the same time. Then choose a simple sentence: "Good morning!" Say it several times in a row, varying its inflections freely. Now speak deliberately, choosing to snap a single syllable: "Good *mor*-ning!" Stay with the exercise's simpler version for as long as you need to become comfortable. Then loosen the reins and see what happens.

Some people nod with their heads and necks in an attempt (usually futile) to help the coincidence of speech and snapping. Perform the exercise with a number of different partners, and sooner or later you'll see the phenomenon of the "snapping neck" in one or more of your partners. Your partners will observe you in turn, and they'll tell you whether or not you're misusing your head and neck. Some people overengage their shoulders when speaking, raising and contracting them. Others also sway their pelvis forward and backward unconsciously, causing the lower back to hollow. We'll study problems of coordination and their solutions in chapters 11–15.

The skill of Coincidence prepares you for Rhythmic Solfège, one of the most important exercises in the book. We turn our attention to it now.

CHAPTER 6

RHYTHMIC SOLFÈGE

In Rhythmic Solfège you learn to extract and concentrate the rhythmic core of a passage or piece, the better to ride its driving force in performance. The exercise helps you organize beat, measure, subdivision, and prosodic impetus. Above all, Rhythmic Solfège gives you tools to internalize the metric grid, so that in singing, playing, and conducting you can dedicate your efforts to opposing the grid rather than externalizing it.

SNAPPING BEATS

Rhythmic Solfège requires that you assume a balanced standing position, like a dancer poised to launch a showstopper upon an unsuspecting audience. All is there, latent in you: the bursts of improvisation, the leaps and twists, the derring-do. The exercise doesn't require that you *do* any of it, only that you stand as if ready to do so. Part II (chapters 11–15) covers coordination in detail and will help you discover your latent dancer, acrobat, and martial artist. Start your practice of Rhythmic Solfège right now, and revisit it once you've made improvements to your overall coordination.

Having assumed a poised standing position, snap the fingers of your right hand (middle finger against thumb) in a steady beat at moderate speed.

🌑 This exercise is illustrated in video clip #6, "Rhythmic Solfège I: Beat."

No two people snap in exactly the same way. With a little imagination you can develop the ability to snap in a dozen different styles, varying both the gesture and the sound you make. The snap itself, for instance, can be loud or soft, round or pointy, happy, angry, flippant, and so on.

Explore the coordination of your arm as you snap. Here are some pointers.

1) Lightly suspended in the air (at about breast height), mobile but not floppy, the upper arm moves up and down a few inches to accompany your snapping. The shoulder stays connected to the back and hardly moves.

2) Turning your palm down while your arm is raised is called *pronation*; turning it up, *supination*. We study pronation and supination in chapters 12 and 15. Test how

it feels to snap with your arm in pronation, in supination, and while passing from one to the other.

3) Snap your fingers while moving the wrist in any direction: left, right, up, down, and in circles clock- and counterclockwise. Now snap *without* moving the wrist, instead keeping it in a state of latent mobility.

4) Imagine that you place an object down on a table, then pick it off the table. The two gestures are physically similar, but their direction in space is different: one gesture goes from up to down, the other from down to up. You can direct your snap similarly: as a gesture going from up to DOWN (snap!), or from down to UP (snap!).

Having explored every possible combination of arm gestures, now snap in the following manner: head, neck, back, and legs firm, moving little or not at all; upper arm gently suspended in midair; elbow lightly bent, with the forearm in pronation; wrist firm, though retaining its latent mobility; arm bouncing slightly upward following the snap. This is an elegant gesture that conveys flow, impetus, and rebound. It lends itself to conducting all types of measures.

By itself, the snap is a little burst of energy. When it coincides with your speech's prosodic stresses, it becomes a marker of linguistic intention. In Rhythmic Solfège it becomes a pulse or beat as well. Put on a CD and snap to it, starting with the relative simplicity of Mozart and Haydn and progressing to the complexity of Charlie Parker and Duke Ellington. Find the piece's underlying beat and snap to it. Then snap an offbeat instead of a beat. Change tracks and see how quickly you get the feel for the new song's beat. Can you snap subdivisions to the main beat? Can you snap duplets against Duke Ellington's triplets? After you make friends with jazz, snap to salsa, in which the bass-line progressions don't coincide with the downbeats.

When you become able to sense a piece's beat and snap to it (or off it, as the case may be), you'll be able to give yourself a beat for any piece you perform by thinking through its melodies or bass lines. You'll also be able to give other people the indication of a beat: a colleague in a chamber ensemble, for instance, or the accompanist who asks you what tempo you want for a particular song.

CONDUCTING MEASURES

If you're able to stand with perfect poise and snap your fingers with no effort, then you're ready for the next challenge: conducting a variety of measures.

⏺ This exercise is illustrated in video clip #7, "Rhythmic Solfège II: Measure."

To conduct a measure of two beats (such as $\frac{2}{4}$ or $\frac{6}{8}$), your arm moves "down, up." To conduct a measure of three beats (such as $\frac{3}{4}$ or $\frac{9}{8}$) your arm moves "down, right, up." For a measure of four beats (such as $\frac{4}{4}$ or $\frac{12}{8}$), your arm moves "down, left, right, up." The following schema uses time signatures based on quarters for ease of reference and is a reminder only of the geographical placing of each beat. You shouldn't interpret it as an invitation to move your arm in a pointy, arrow-like manner. The conducting gestures I advocate are fluid curves, as demonstrated in the corresponding video clip.

$$\binom{2}{4}\Uparrow 2 \qquad \binom{3}{4}\Uparrow 3 \qquad\qquad \binom{4}{4} \qquad \Uparrow 4$$
$$\Leftarrow 2 \qquad 3\Rightarrow$$
$$\Downarrow 1 \qquad\qquad \Downarrow 1 \quad 2\Rightarrow \qquad\qquad \Downarrow 1$$

Stand erect, snap a steady beat, and conduct a $\frac{4}{4}$ measure in the conventional manner: down, left, right, up. Your arm gestures ought to be curved, not linear; light, not heavy; flowing, not plodding. Every beat ought to contain the energies that prepare the following beat. As it snaps the first beat, for instance, the hand rebounds a little bit and the arm rides the rebound toward the second beat. Similarly for the other beats: every arrival prepares the following departure.

Imagine that you're conducting a choir of shortsighted amateur singers preparing a fund-raiser with few rehearsals. Your gestures have to be big (so that they are visible to all), clear (to compensate for your singers' lack of experience, and your lack of rehearsal time), and musically compelling (to ensure a successful fund-raiser). Your shortsighted singers must be able to tell exactly where you're going next. Your beats, which are specific points in time and space, must look different from your rebounds, which prepare the travel from point to point.

Stand in front of a wall or mirror. Poise your right arm for conducting, with the fingertips lightly touching the wall. Now conduct a $\frac{4}{4}$ measure, keeping your fingers in constant light contact with the wall. In this way, all beats happen on the same plane, equalizing their spatial character and energy. When you conduct normally, imagine that you touch an invisible wall in front of you, the better to keep all beats on the same plane.

Now that you know the basic $\frac{4}{4}$ gesture, vary its speed and amplitude. Make it tiny and slow, tiny and fast, big and slow, big and fast, and everything in between. Train yourself to make these changes without using movements of head, neck, shoulders, pelvis, or legs.

Measures of two and three beats are more or less shortened versions of the four-beat measure, and you can learn them easily once you get the hang of a four-beat measure. Refer to the relevant video clip for further guidance. A measure of five beats is often subdivided into two measures, of two and three beats or vice versa, but there's a good way of organizing five beats in space without breaking up the measure:

$$\Uparrow 5$$
$$\Leftarrow 2 \quad \Rightarrow 3 \quad 4\Rightarrow$$
$$\Downarrow 1$$

CONDUCTING SUBDIVISIONS

Visualize a slow piece written in $\frac{4}{4}$, full of thirty-second and sixty-fourth notes in intricate combinations. So many things happen within each beat that you may want or need to subdivide your conducting of the $\frac{4}{4}$ measure. The art of subdividing beats within measures must become an integral part of your rhythmic mastery.

🎬 This exercise is illustrated in video clip #8, "Rhythmic Solfège III: Subdivisions."

Start by working on standard measures, subdividing each beat in two. Geographically, a subdivided $\frac{2}{4}$ bar goes "down, down, up, up." Signal the first beat by a snap on the downbeat, then keep your hand in the vicinity of the downbeat and snap the subdivision or offbeat. Move your hand up, snap the second beat, keep the hand in the immediate vicinity, and snap the offbeat. The geography of a two-beat measure subdivided in three goes "down, down, down, up, up, up." (This is a good way to conduct the time signatures of $\frac{6}{8}$ and $\frac{6}{4}$.) To subdivide in four, go "down, down, down, down, up, up, up, up."

The subdividing snaps must balance out two requirements that sometimes fight each other. All subdivisions need to happen in the vicinity of the beat, otherwise a subdivision might look confusingly like a new beat. This is your "geographical requirement." But each snap ought to have some bounce to it, otherwise the gesture is dry and unmusical. This is your "energetic requirement." Let the hand bounce a little for each subdivision, but don't let it travel in space more than an inch or two.

Subdivide a three-beat measure in twos, threes, and fours. Then do the same for four- and five-beat measures. Once you get the hang of subdividing a beat, the mathematics and the geography involved are simple and easy. The real complexity comes when you start infusing your measures and subdivisions with prosodic qualities.

CONDUCTING THE PROSODIC IMPETUS

Much as you can walk with an iambic or trochaic impetus, you can conduct every time signature with a variety of prosodic thrusts.

🌑 This exercise is illustrated in video clip #9, "Rhythmic Solfège IV: Prosodic Impetus."

Start with a two-beat measure such as $\frac{2}{4}$. You can conduct it with an iambic impetus or a trochaic one. (You can also try the pyrrhic and spondaic impetuses. Reread the section "Prosody for the Integrated Musician" in chapter 2 to remind yourself of what the words "pyrrhic" and "spondaic" mean.) The iambic unit is "preparation-STRESS." The arm rises UP following your first snap, thereby indicating the preparation or upbeat. Then the arm travels DOWN onto the second snap, indicating the stress or downbeat. In an iambic gesture, you lift the object off the table first, then you put it down again:

⇑2 (preparation)   ⇓1(STRESS)

The trochaic unit is "STRESS-release." The arm travels DOWN until you snap the stress or downbeat. Then it travels UP until you snap the release or offbeat. In a trochaic gesture, you put the object down first, then you lift it off the table:

⇓1(STRESS)   ⇑2(release)

Your gestures must be clear enough for your shortsighted choir of talented but untrained amateurs to sense whether you intend an iambic or a trochaic impetus. A good way to clarify your prosodic intentions is to alternate gestures with pauses. Conduct an iambic foot of upbeat and downbeat, or preparation and STRESS:

⇑2 | ⇓1

Keeping your arm poised, stop conducting and mentally count the next two beats as iambically organized silences:

(think) | (THINK)

Alternate between "doing" and "thinking," and your conducting gestures will benefit from your "iambically charged thinking":

⇑2 | ⇓1 (think) | (THINK) ⇑2 | ⇓1 (think) | (THINK) ⇑2 | ⇓1 (think) | (THINK)

Then conduct two iambic units followed by a single silent unit:

⇑2 | ⇓1 ⇑2 | ⇓1 (think) | (THINK) ⇑2 | ⇓1 ⇑2 | ⇓1 (think) | (THINK)

Then insert fewer and fewer thinking units, until you can conduct a reliable iambic impetus. Learn the trochaic version in the same way:

⇓1 ⇑2 | (THINK) (think) | ⇓1 ⇑2 | (THINK) (think) | ⇓1 ⇑2 (THINK) (think)

The basic prosodic thrusts in three-beat measures are dactylic, anapestic, and amphibrachic. Conduct a three-beat measure that is visibly dactylic. Indicate its prosodic impetus with the actual gesture of the arm, not by misusing your head and neck. Now conduct the same measure with an anapestic impetus. To make it truly different from the dactylic one, your gesture needs to show an inflection between the downbeat and the second beat, which starts a new anapestic unit—otherwise your shortsighted singers will think that your second beat is the release that follows the stress in a dactylic unit. The inflection is marked as a comma:

Dactyl: **1** 2 3, | **1** 2 3, | **1** 2 3
          S r r, | **S** r r, | **S** r r
Anapest: 2 3 | **1**, 2 3 | **1**, 2 3 | **1**
          p p | **S**, p p | **S**, p p | **S**

You can organize measures of four beats in a similar way. Suppose you want to conduct a sequence built on the pattern {4 | 1 2 3}, or {p | **S** r r}. The first requirement is for you to hold your decision clearly in your mind. Once you start conducting, it's terribly easy to "forget" what you've decided to do and get involved in the struggle of trying to do it. The second requirement is for you to show a little separation between the 3 that ends one sequence and the 4 that starts the next one. The separation makes it clear that the 4 is a preparation or upbeat; if you neglect it, the 4 will look like a release instead.

4 | **1** 2 3, 4 | **1** 2 3, 4 | **1** 2 3, 4 | **1** 2 3
p | **S** r r, p | **S** r r, p | **S** r r, p | **S** r r

RHYTHMIC SOLFÈGE

Certain words and expressions bypass the dictionary and speak directly to us through rhythm and sound alone: "Ba-da-*BING*!" "Yadda yadda." "Yackety yak." "Ding-a-ling." "Yabadabadoo!"

In these expressions, the power of rhythm and sound is displayed naked, as it were: the expressions are nothing *but* rhythm and sound. Fred Flintstone's cry for joy rides on a rhythmic rocket, with triple stresses blasting toward a climax in an embellished anapest:

YA-ba | DA-ba | **DOO!**

Grammar, usage, and additional "civilized" aspects of language sometimes veil the power of rhythm. In music, a similar phenomenon occurs: rhythm can be naked or clothed. Rhythmic Solfège is the art of denuding the musical language of everything but rhythm, the better for it to exert its primeval driving power.

Compare the rhythmic impact of these two imaginary songs:

ta-ta-ta-ta-ta-ta-ta-ta-ta
ta-ta-TA-ta-ta-TA-ta-ta-TA

In the first one, every syllable plays the same role; in the second, every third syllable asserts itself more strongly, changing the meaning of the song.

Now compare again:

ta-ta-TA-ta-ta-TA-ta-ta-TA
tee-tee-TA-tee-tee-TA-tee-tee-TA

The degree of differentiation between syllables rises, and so does their meaning. The syllable "tee" indicates preparation, "TA" a stress. Let's take the technique further, varying the sounds to indicate finer distinctions.

tee-tah-TOH-tee-tah-TOH-tee-tah-TOH

This little song "speaks" with a life of its own, showing that rhythm alone—with the help of a few consonants and vowels—drives language and gives it meaning and emotion.

In Rhythmic Solfège you speak a line of music out loud, replacing its notes with syllables such as "tee," "tah," and "toh" while snapping the beat and conducting the measure, vocally using a narrow melodic range. Stripped of melody and harmony, the line of music must live on rhythm and prosody alone.

⏺ This exercise is illustrated in video clip #10, "Rhythmic Solfège V: A Demonstration." Beat, measure, subdivision, and impetus are demonstrated together in video clip #11, "Rhythmic Solfège VI: An Overview."

The exercise is akin to scatting. In scat, jazz singers use nonsense words and syllables to approximate the lines played by instrumentalists, making it seem that they are "playing" an instrumental solo with their voices. Great scat singers have included Cab Calloway, Louis Armstrong, Dizzy Gillespie, and most notably Ella Fitzgerald. Percussionists in Africa, India, and elsewhere have long assigned syllables to characteristic rhythmic patterns, partly to learn and memorize these patterns and partly to imbue them with the layer of meaning and direction that language provides. For that reason, sometimes percussionists scat in unison with their playing, both in practice and in performance.

Imagine that you host a weekly TV show in which you do musical dictation for the millions. You half-say, half-chant an eight-bar song that your listeners write down and send in for fabulous prizes given out by your sponsor. Your eager listeners don't mind hard assignments, as long as you're absolutely unambiguous in how you vocalize them. But if you're unclear about the beat and measure; about note values, rests, dots, and slurs; about where, why, and how you breathe; and about the rhythmic energies of preparation, stress, and release, then your listeners raise a stink and boycott your show, imperiling your livelihood. Your manner of speech must therefore be crystal-clear, precise, and attractive.

Stand still, in an attitude of perfect latency. Snap your fingers at a quarter per second. Wave your right arm in a two-beat trochaic pattern. Then say the line below out loud, using a handful of syllables of your choosing, such as "tah," "teh," "tee," and "toh" (example 6.1).

The line is simple, but to say it perfectly is not so simple. You need to coordinate your whole body, from head to toe. Your snapping must be effortlessly reliable, and the measure well drawn and prosodically charged. Your scatting must be precise and easily understood. Your whole performance ought to be so compelling that your audience would agree to forgo melody, harmony, counterpoint, instrumentation, and everything else in music; your rhythm alone would sate their musical hunger.

If you believe that the example 6.1 is too easy to merit study, display your Rhythmic Solfège skills on example 6.2, from the Allemande of J. S. Bach's Sixth Suite for Solo Cello, BWV 1012.

EXAMPLE 6.1. Joseph Haydn: Sonata for Piano, Hob. XVI: 27 in G Major, last movement (adapted)

EXAMPLE 6.2. J. S. Bach: Sixth Suite for Solo Cello, BWV 1012 in D Major, Allemande

Can you do it perfectly? Better still, can you do it perfectly at sight? That should be your aim, with every piece you study and perform. To get there, you'll need a fair amount of practice.

Rhythmic Solfège helps you clarify the metric grid and embody it, but it'll achieve its proper goals only when you internalize it. After you say a passage in Rhythmic Solfège a few times, play it or sing it as written, keeping the metric grid wholly inside you. The energized rhythm will "carry" the melody, the passagework, the trills, slides, chords and so on.

◑ This exercise is illustrated in video clip #12, "Rhythmic Solfège VII: At the Flute."

ADVANCED RHYTHMIC SOLFÈGE

In advanced Rhythmic Solfège you learn to change meters, beats, and metronome markings, use accelerando and ritardandi, and add fermatas and other rhythmic details. Example 6.3 is an excerpt from Ernest Bloch's "Schelomo: A Hebraic Rhapsody" for Cello and Orchestra. The meter changes several times between $\frac{3}{4}$ and $\frac{4}{4}$. Can you snap a steady beat, conduct the changing measures, and scat the line of music without losing your head?

From here onward, you have several choices to further explore Rhythmic Solfège:

1. Conquer each rhythmic challenge as it presents itself to you in your daily practice, applying Rhythmic Solfège to every piece you study and perform.
2. Go to the challenges instead of waiting until they come to you. Gather scores in many styles and spend time every day working through their rhythmic difficulties. Example 6.4 is by Roger Sessions (1896–1985). It offers a glimpse of the sort of rugged territory you can explore and conquer with Rhythmic Solfège.
3. Use a step-by-step method with the help of pedagogical tools such as Georges Dandelot's "Étude du Rythme" in five volumes (which you can order from online sheet music stores). Starting with the simplest possible formulations, Dandelot's method covers all time signatures and all basic rhythmic elements: amputated

EXAMPLE 6.3. Ernest Bloch: "Schelomo: A Hebraic Rhapsody" for Cello and Orchestra

EXAMPLE 6.4. Roger Sessions: Six Pieces for Solo Cello, Scherzo

downbeats, triplets, syncopations, hemiolas, and so on. Rather than excerpts from actual compositions, Dandelot uses abstract lines of music that some people find unattractive. If you become a disciplined prosodist, however, the interest of any phrase lies not in the phrase itself, but in what you do with it.

The next two chapters give you tools to improve and broaden your Rhythmic Solfège. We'll look at the metronome and rubato first, then at ways of practicing the superbar structures we encountered when we studied the metric grid.

CHAPTER 7

THE METRONOME AND THE RUBATO

MAKING FRIENDS WITH THE METRONOME

Like all human endeavors, music is a game of order and disorder, rigidity and flexibility, structure and improvisation. All aspects of music depend on this interplay, which is dynamic by definition: There's more life when order and disorder oppose each other than when order, or disorder, exists alone. Metronomic precision and rubato are primary opposing forces in music, and the integrated musician balances one against the other.

The metronome is an agent of order. Many musicians consider it tyrannical and avoid using it. In truth, the metronome becomes good or bad depending on what you do with it. In some situations a metronome is essential—for instance, when trying to determine tempi indicated by a composer on a score. Even if you decide to choose tempi at odds with the composer's indications, it's useful to know what the composer's ideas are to begin with.

Looking at themselves in a mirror, many people can't see their posture's asymmetries or the blotches on their skin. Other people see nothing *but* the blotches, making themselves blind to the larger picture. It's possible, however, to use a mirror to discover things about yourself and change them if needed. The metronome is a similar aid to self-awareness, but to benefit from it, you need to listen to both yourself and the metronome soberly—much as you need to look at yourself in the mirror with dispassionate eyes.

Turn the metronome on to any speed and listen to it for fifteen seconds, without an emotional, intellectual, or kinesthetic reaction. Despite yourself, you're likely to get annoyed at the metronome and turn it off, or to start fidgeting while the metronome clicks away. Keep your cool and do nothing for a while. Then prove to yourself that you're adaptable: Accept the metronome's tyranny by choice and play or sing a few notes to its beat.

Now choose a short, self-contained excerpt from your repertoire, with a clearly defined cutoff point: two bars, for instance. Play the excerpt with the metronome. You'll start it in good faith, listening carefully to the metronome. Before you know it, however, you'll have gone beyond the cutoff point you chose yourself, and by then you won't be listening to the metronome anymore. The "desire to do" trumps the "decision to pay attention."

Every time you fail to stop at your cutoff point, take a few steps back in this series of exercises and listen to the metronome without doing anything else.

Use the metronome's steadiness to organize technical aspects of your performance. To play well with a metronome, you need to internalize the ticks and make them your own, until you *become* the metronome. If you try to follow the metronome, you're likely to fall behind it. If you try to anticipate it, you're likely to rush ahead of it.

After you become adept at performing short passages in strict collaboration with the metronome, then start lengthening your passages until you become able to listen to the metronome whenever you choose to, and for however long. The metronome won't be a tyrant anymore, but a friend instead.

TEMPO RUBATO

In almost every context, ideal performance contains a degree of rubato. The original term, *tempo rubato*, means "stolen time" in Italian, hinting that when you use rubato you "steal time" from one or more notes or bars, potentially to give it to other notes and bars elsewhere in the phrase. Rubato is a big subject that merits deep study, but here we'll settle for a short overview.

Rubato enhances the meaning and emotion of a musical text. It corresponds, in music, to variations of timing that we all use in speech. We hesitate on a word, for instance, only to become insistent on the next word; we go from timidity to assurance, and back to timidity again; we affirm, we exclaim, we beg and plead, and each utterance must be timed in an individual way according to its emotional drive. Because rubato is inherently unpredictable, it's nearly impossible for you to give two identical performances of a composition in which you use rubato. And because rubato is so personal, it allows you to distinguish yourself from all other performers and to develop and affirm your musical identity. For these reasons and many others, rubato is a master musician's most prized quality.

There are three main types of rubato. In the first one, the underlying beat or pulse stays steady while other elements in the composition are performed with a freer rhythm. An example is a double-bass player in a jazz group playing his or her notes in a metronomic manner while the trumpeter stretches his or her solo, sometimes arriving at the metric stresses ahead of the beat, sometimes behind it. Another example is a pianist keeping a metronomic bass line with the left hand while stretching the melody in different directions with the right hand. This form of rubato is present in folk traditions, in jazz, in dance halls, and many other settings. Its power comes from the opposition between fixity and freedom, between what is steady and predictable (such as the pianist's left hand) and what is changeable and unpredictable (such as the pianist's right hand).

One of the iconic recordings in jazz history, "Kind of Blue" was issued in 1958 and has since been cherished and celebrated as a great musical achievement. It marked one of the first times in which jazz musicians played modal (as opposed to tonal) music. It contains five tracks, of which the last is titled "Flamenco Sketches." In the original release, "Flamenco Sketches" lasts nine minutes and twenty-six seconds. Another recorded take has since been issued. It lasts nine minutes and thirty-two seconds. In other words, the longer version is 1 percent longer than the shorter one, a negligible difference. It means that the bassist, Paul Chambers, found his tempo and his beat and kept to it absolutely throughout the piece, much like a metronome. But the soloists (Miles Davis, trumpet; Julian "Cannonball" Adderley, alto sax; John Coltrane, tenor sax; and Bill Evans, piano) improvised freely against this steady beat.

In the second type of rubato, the beat itself shifts, getting faster or slower within the bar, from bar to bar, or from phrase to phrase. In effect, this rubato is a combination or alternation of accelerandi and ritardandi. One tends to associate this type of rubato with Romantic composers, but it's a mistake to think that only Romantic composers use it, or that Romantic composers use it to the exclusion of other types of rubato. Pianists and musicologists have long tried to determine how Chopin himself performed his music. Did he keep a steady beat with the left hand and let his right hand roam widely, or did he speed up and slow down the beat itself? Evidence (in the form of testimonials from his piano students, for instance) exists to support both views.

In the third type of rubato, the first beat of a bar is metronomically predictable, but not the beats that follow. An example is the Viennese waltz, in which the first beat is regular, but the second beat sometimes arrives slightly earlier than the metronome and the third beat slightly later. Balkan dance music uses the same type of rubato, often in measures of five beats. For Western ears accustomed to regularity, it can be difficult to "feel the beat" when a Serbian brass band is in free flow, but in fact the first beat is reliably metronomic while the rest of the bar is stretchy and jagged.

Together with these three types of rubato there are two basic effects or "personalities" in rubato (as I see it). For the sake of convenience, I'll call them a rubato of tension and a rubato of relaxation. The rubato of tension sustains the drama in a phrase and puts the listeners into a state of expectation: What will happen *next*? The rubato of relaxation gives the performer time and space to highlight lyrically beautiful things in a phrase. It tends to drag down a performance, and when done poorly it takes the listeners' attention away from the tension in the music and toward the performer's display of sound or emotion. The archetypical example is a singer dragging an upward run and lingering for too long on a high note.

A RUBATO EXPERIMENT

Gather a few recordings of a composition that requires rubato in performance, plus the score of the piece in question. There are thousands of such pieces, but if you're short of ideas I propose you buy recordings of Claude Debussy's "Preludes," and listen to "La Fille aux Cheveux de Lin." You can download its score from the Internet.

In my library I have recordings by the Frenchman Samson François, the Chilean Claudio Arrau, and the German Walter Gieseking, but any three recordings will do for the exercise. YouTube has multiple versions, including arrangements for violin and piano, for guitar, and for voice. Listen to the performances while looking at the score. If you ignore all other characteristics from each performance—sound quality, engineering, dynamics, the instrument played—you'd still be able to identify each performer by rubato alone.

Conduct the piece while listening to it and following its score. To the best of your ability, anticipate the placing of each beat according to your feeling for what the performer is trying to achieve. The exercise is a bit artificial, since normally you conduct the musical event instead of being conducted by it. Nevertheless, you may come to see that certain types of rubato are easier than others to anticipate, follow, and conduct. In some contexts, a rubato should be so free and unpredictable that no one ought to be able to box the performance into a metric grid. In other contexts, such as in "La Fille aux Cheveux de Lin," an organic rubato ought to be sufficiently logical for you to be able to conduct it, however much it deviates from the metronome.

Notes belong together in words, sentences, and paragraphs. If you ignore a musical passage's linguistic construction, your rubato is likely to be inorganic and incomprehensible. If you sense and internalize the prosodic logic of a passage, however, you may be able to perform it with a very flexible rubato, stretching or shrinking a group of notes that belong together, and stretching or shrinking the spaces in between groups—all while respecting the groupings themselves.

DESIRABLE IMPRECISION

At the risk of oversimplifying things, we could say that a musician's education goes through four phases:

1. Undesirable imprecision.
2. Undesirable precision.
3. Desirable precision.
4. Desirable imprecision.

Precision and imprecision affect all aspects of music making: sound, intonation, rhythm, and everything else. For the sake of convenience, here we concentrate on rhythmic issues. Undesirable imprecision is the sort of disorganized playing or singing in which a musician makes changes of tempo to account for technical difficulties, dragging and rushing the piece without being aware of doing so. This happens because of habit, gaps in knowledge, and the inability or the unwillingness to step back from the intensity of the moment and become an observer as well as a doer. (To study this topic, read the section "Faulty Sensory Awareness and Habit" in chapter 11 and the section "Actor, Receptor, Witness" in chapter 19.) Regardless of its causes, you must tackle undesirable imprecision if you suffer from it. An obligatory step is to acquire some degree of metronomic precision.

The quest for precision isn't free from risks and dangers. There is such a thing as "undesirable precision," a form of music making in which all technical and interpretive aspects sound perfectly even and yet the overall effect is lifeless. There used to be a way of playing Baroque compositions, for instance, in which the metronome ruled. Tempo and phrasing were utterly predictable in performance, and musicians dismissed even first-class Baroque compositions as "sewing-machine music." Undesirable precision isn't limited to bad performances of Baroque music. It's widespread as a goal in itself, the be-all and end-all for many musicians and music teachers—although they don't think of their goal as "undesirable precision" but "ideal evenness."

For some musicians, undesirable precision is an intermediate step in the journey from undesirable to desirable imprecision. You need to be able to sing and play with absolute precision by choice, before you can sing and play with expressive imprecision also by choice. It's possible to achieve "desirable precision," a form of smooth, steady playing or singing that doesn't have the intense beauty of the best rubato but that has its own aesthetic merits. Young children sometimes play their tunes with a complete simplicity of phrasing that is unencumbered and limpid. They may be too inexperienced to understand the concept of rubato, but they're sufficiently alert to produce something attractive and touching in its simple precision.

Needless to say, adults too can make music according to the principle of "desirable precision." If you keep in mind that every sound you make has a linguistic dimension, and that any sequence of sounds has the potential to tell a story, then you can work on the precision of your playing and singing without turning yourself into a sewing machine.

The last step in your evolution is desirable imprecision—in other words, making music with a well-proportioned, organic, meaningful rubato.

ORGANIC (IM)PRECISION THROUGH RHYTHMIC SUBDIVISIONS

Most musicians take the precision of their long notes for granted, assuming that their intuitive feel for the notes' length is accurate. Ask a partner to sing or play a scale in $\frac{4}{4}$, andante con moto, with an unchanging rhythmic pattern: in every bar, a dotted half followed by a quarter. Use a mental metronome to check the length of the long note, counting silently as your partner performs. How accurate is your partner's dotted half? Most likely your partner will rush it, though there are also musicians who drag it, and others who rush some notes, drag others, and play others still in strict time. Now trade places with your partner, and sing or play the scale in question. You might be absolutely sure that you're playing accurately, but most likely your partner will tell you otherwise.

You can solve this problem by employing your voice as a new kind of metronome.

🔊 This exercise is demonstrated (at the cello) in video clip #13, "Rhythmic Subdivisions I: The Basics."

1) At the piano, play a scale in $\frac{4}{4}$, one whole note per bar, one octave or more as you wish (example 7.1). While playing, say "pam pam pam" out loud for beats 2, 3, and 4.

EXAMPLE 7.1. Scale in whole notes, with vocalized subdivisions

Vary the energy of the initial consonant, from caressing to explosive. Vary the vowel's quality, making it open, closed, flat, round, and so on. Vary the length of the final "em" sound, humming and vibrating it. Organize your subdivisions prosodically. If you think iambically, the first "pam" you say is an upbeat to the second one, and the third "pam" an upbeat to the beginning of the next long note.

2) Change the scale's rhythm to a dotted half followed by a quarter (example 7.2). Your voice needs to say only the second and third beats, since you actively play the first and fourth beats. You can choose to say "pam" on either the second or third beat only. This creates a different energy from saying it on both beats.

EXAMPLE 7.2. Scale in a dotted pattern, with vocalized subdivisions

3) On the same scale, say a "pam" for every eighth note in the scale, apart from those notes you actively sound at the first and fourth quarter (example 7.3). Stretch and contract the eighth notes, making some slower, others fast. In this controlled context, you'll "feel and know" when an eighth note becomes too short or too long.

EXAMPLE 7.3. Vocalized eighth-note subdivisions

4) Improvise subdivisions in quarter notes, eighth notes, and shorter note values in varied patterns of crescendo, diminuendo, accelerando, and ritardando (example 7.4). The subdivisions create an informed rubato, since they help you keep track of the proportion of all parts relative to the whole.

EXAMPLE 7.4. Varied vocalized subdivisions

Apply the knowledge you have gathered in your scales to a composition in your repertoire, adapting the following guidelines to your individual practicing style:

1. Use your voice to mark those things in the composition that are hidden, implicit, or latent. Vocalize the subdivisions of long notes; pauses and silences; and downbeats that aren't stated outright, either because of a rest or because the upbeat is slurred over the downbeat.
2. Use the subdivisions to anticipate rhythmic changes within the line. For instance, suppose a bar in $\frac{2}{2}$ starts with a half note, followed by six eighth-note triplets. As you play the half note, you vocalize the triplets that will follow it.
3. Use your voice, not movements of your head and neck, to create all effects in the exercise.
4. Use your voice in a lively manner, not a mechanical one. The voice instructs your legato and sostenuto, enlivens long notes, energizes sluggish passages, and infuses all the gestures of your instrumental technique with a linguistic charge.
5. Once you get good at vocalizing subdivisions, internalize them and use not your voice but thought and sensation alone.

This exercise is illustrated in video clip #14, "Rhythmic Subdivisions II: An Application." Bonus video clip: #15, "Rhythmic Subdivisions III: At the Piano."

Example 7.5 is the opening phrase from Luigi Boccherini's Sonata in A Major for Cello and Piano, as illustrated in video clip #14. The score includes the original cello line; the vocalized subdivisions; and a metronome-like line underneath it to help you see how the subdivisions fit into the grid.

EXAMPLE 7.5. Luigi Boccherini: Sonata for Cello and Piano in A Major, first movement

THE FIVE METRONOMES

You can develop an organic mix of precision and rubato by practicing with five types of metronome: the mechanical metronome itself; the foot; Rhythmic Solfège; vocal rhythmic subdivisions; and the "latent metronome." We'll study the procedure using a passage from Gabriel Fauré's Romance for Cello and Piano, opus 69 in A major (example 7.6).

EXAMPLE 7.6. Gabriel Fauré: Romance for Cello and Piano, opus 69 in A Major

This exercise is illustrated in video clips #16, "The Five Metronomes I: 1, 2, 3," and #17, "The Five Metronomes II: 4, 5, Plus."

THE MECHANICAL METRONOME

Choose a metronome with different types of clicks for the beat, the running subdivisions, and the measures' downbeats. The Romance is in $\frac{4}{4}$. In this piece you'll have the pulse as a quarter note = 76; the downbeat as a different-sounding click every four quarters; and running eighth-note subdivisions throughout. Spend time just listening to the metronome, without trying to play at the same time. The triple layer of rhythmic energy (downbeat, running beats, running subdivisions) has a certain charm to it, even if the clicking of the metronome is nothing but an electronic sound.

A piece performed calmly doesn't lose its expressivity and beauty, and it may even gain in both respects. Play the piece in a sort of low-emotion version that allows you to partner the metronome, as if making chamber music with it. Play a few notes or bars; stop playing; wait a while; and start again. Since the metronome is sounding both the pulse *and* the measure's downbeat, before you resume playing you need to wait until the metronome sounds the right beat.

Sense those points in the phrase where the metronome seems to force you to stretch or contract your sense of time—in other words, points where you're at odds with the metronome. It takes humility to accept that the metronome is right and you're wrong. When the time comes for you to play using expressive rubato, the metronome will be "wrong" and you, right. For now, however, the metronome has the last word.

An unusual rhythmic pattern is repeated several times starting in measure 7: a quarter note tied to an sixteenth note, followed by a sixteenth and an eighth note. To render the note values precise and easy to play, you need to make prosodic decisions: What notes belong together, and what roles do each note play in the group? Are these notes organized mostly as trochees or as iambs? You'll solve many technical problems by using inflection and articulation rather than muscle power.

So far, you have been playing in a sort of low-emotion mode that helps you pay attention to the metronome. Now juice it all up. If you lose contact with the metronome, backtrack to the beginning of the procedure until you become able to express yourself fully while listening to the metronome.

THE FOOT

Many musicians tap their feet irregularly. The tapping falls behind the music or speeds ahead of it, stopping and starting again for no reason. This kind of foot tapping serves no positive function and is little more than a compensatory, nervous tick.

Tensions in the feet can travel up the leg and go beyond it to reach the pelvis, the back, and the head and neck. With the help of a partner, do the following experiment. Take your shoes off. Play or sing something in your usual manner, sitting or standing. Ask your partner to crouch at your feet; place his or her hands flat on the top of the feet; and apply gentle pressure downward, toward the floor. Your partner's pressure will relax your toes and stabilize the feet. The body thrives on the principle of opposing forces. Because the feet become grounded—that is, bound downward—the legs' natural reflex is to lengthen upward, in opposition to the feet. The experience is a sensorial pleasure more intense than you may imagine. The whole body is affected by the simple change in the feet, and your singing or playing benefits as a result.

Using your foot as a metronome is potentially constructive, as long as your foot is rhythmically reliable and coordinated in the manner described above. Some jazz musicians use the entire leg to keep a steady beat and generate musical excitement. On YouTube, watch Count Basie at the piano. His back and pelvis are integrated into a solid unit, his leg moves lightly from the hip joint and not from the pelvis, and his back hardly moves. Now do the following experiment. While sitting, use your leg as a metronome, lifting the foot one or two inches off the floor and bringing it down again, many times at a fast speed. What happens to your trunk? For how long would you be able to sustain the exercise? What would happen if you played the piano at the same time?

Revisit the exercise of Coincidence in chapter 5, and train your foot to become a prosodist, able to "speak" its rhythms with a lively energy and a clear linguistic intention. In chapter 12 you'll learn how to rock sideways while seated, which connects your pelvis to your back, thereby allowing your leg to move from the hip joint without affecting the back. Put the two skills together, and you'll become able to sit and tap your foot in a manner that is rhythmically reliable and physically healthy.

RHYTHMIC SOLFÈGE, VOCALIZED SUBDIVISIONS, AND THE LATENT METRONOME

The next two metronomes are Rhythmic Solfège, which we covered in the last chapter, and the vocalized subdivisions we have just learned. The last metronome is latent. It exists inside you as a potentiality, combining all the other metronomes and their multiple dimensions: the reliable steadiness of the mechanical metronome, the vitality of your conducting arm and your tapping foot, and the vibrations of your voice as it speaks and sings varied subdivisions. The latent metronome involves no visible bodily movements or audible efforts of any type. If you stay connected with your invisible and inaudible metronome, your rubato becomes organic and well proportioned. Then you'll have achieved the paradoxical, desirable (im)precision that is the hallmark of an integrated musician.

CHAPTER 8

SUPERBAR STRUCTURES

THE JOINTS IN BETWEEN PHRASES

We first looked at superbar structures (or "measures of measures") in chapter 4. Reread the relevant section before studying this chapter.

Generally speaking, the questions you ask yourself when interpreting a piece of music concern themselves with tension and relaxation. How much tension and of what kind (melodic, harmonic, rhythmic) is there in a piece's opening chord or arpeggio? How long does the tension last? Does the second chord have more tension than the opening chord, or less? How will you translate these qualities of musical tension and relaxation into gesture and sound? How much of the tension should come from the gesture, how much from the music itself?

Superbar structures will help you answer these questions regarding the lengths of phrases and paragraphs, and the space in between them.

The end of a musical phrase is called a *cadence* (not to be confused with an improvised solo in a concerto, called a *cadenza*). Depending on its cadence, a phrase will come across as a declarative statement, a question, an answer, or as an instance of equivocation, explanation, wit, and so on. It's a mistake to consider the cadences at the end of phrases as invitations to relax. It's more constructive to consider that cadences in music allow for the renewal of tension. In some instances, the renewal comes about immediately after a lessening of tension, but "less tension" doesn't mean "relaxation."

The superbar structure can be seen as a study in joinery—in other words, the degrees of integration and separation between parts, the hierarchy of parts within the whole, and the amount of tension that must exist at the joints for the whole to hold together. In architecture, joinery is the ensemble of the wooden components of a building, such as stairs, window frames, and doors. Where do you put them in your building? How do you measure and cut them? How do you affix them to the larger framework? Wood contracts and expands according to heat and humidity. It's a more pliant, dynamic element than concrete or steel (although they, too, contract and expand). Throughout the world there have existed techniques for building entire houses without using nails or screws: the wooden parts are cut and assembled in such a way that beams fit snugly one against the other thanks to the use of sophisticated joints of many types. In *mortise and tenon* joinery, for instance, the mortise is a hole or recess cut into a piece of wood and meant to receive a corresponding projection or tenon.

It may be useful for you to think that your cadences are like wooden joints in a building. Much like wood itself, the cadences are pliant and dynamic. They contract and expand. They can be taken apart and put back together, and the fit of the parts can be tighter or looser, the tighter fit making for a more stable building. Cadences, like wood, have some "give," unlike steel parts soldered together. Too much give, however, makes for a wobbly construction.

STUDYING THE SUPERBAR STRUCTURE IN PRACTICE

When studying the superbar structure, start with feeling and sensation before bringing in your analytical capabilities. In time, you'll see that the superbar structure is a breathing, living entity rather than a theoretical construct. Here I propose practical strategies for you to sense superbar structures and shape them in performance.

1. SEE, HEAR, AND SENSE THE SUPERBAR STRUCTURE

In the music of the Classical period, superbar structures tend to be clearly articulated through silences, cadences, changes of rhythmic texture, modulations, and so on. For this reason, the works of Haydn, Mozart, Beethoven, and Schubert, among others, are useful guides in studying the superbar structure. Their compositions offer both a wealth of standard four- and eight-bar phrases and a wealth of departures from the standard. Listen to a recording of piano sonatas by Haydn while looking at their score. Take note of unequivocal cadences that mark the arrival points of four- and eight-bar phrases. Then start discerning the extensions and contractions from the four-bar norm. Here and there Haydn will use four plus four plus four: a twelve-bar phrase that extends the habitual eight-bar phrase. Elsewhere he'll use another twelve-bar phrase, though now subdivided into two halves of six bars. At yet another point he'll be a devil and introduce a five-bar phrase all by itself.

Not all phrases will be unambiguously articulated. At some point, you might be unable to tell where exactly a phrase ends and another one begins. Most likely Haydn chose to make the phrase ambiguous on purpose, to tease his audience and tug at their expectations. If a composer's ambiguity is purposeful, your performance of the passage also ought to be purposefully ambiguous!

After Haydn and Mozart, approach Beethoven and Schubert, then Schumann, Chopin, and Brahms. (We look at an example of a four-bar phrase that Brahms extends to five bars in the next chapter.) Take on the Italians: study the Baroque "Arie Antiche" that are so useful in building the voice. There, too, you'll see four-bar phrases with contractions, extensions, and a broad interplay of symmetry and asymmetry. Then approach the French and the Russians. You'll see that superbar structures are ubiquitous throughout the musical universe.

Turn on the radio at random and listen to whatever the station is playing. Hear the lyrics, and sense the pulse and the changes in harmony. Snap a metronome-like beat to it; then conduct its measure; then sense and conduct its superbar structure. Compositions that strike our ears as logically constructed usually have relatively predictable superbar structures. More often than not you "know what's coming next" even when you've never heard the piece before.

2. LEARN WORDS AND PHRASES, NOT PHYSICAL ACTIONS

The music of Haydn and Mozart is conversational and rhetorical by nature, and their musical language is easily recognized as a sort of Italianate variant of German. Other composers may write in languages we don't apprehend at once, but their compositions are texts all the same. Superbar structures are simply a composition's sentences and paragraphs. Use the superbar structures to study your paragraphs, and the simple awareness that you're working on texts rather than bunches of notes or physical gestures will change the way you practice.

Practice in linguistic units, big and small. Suppose you want to isolate a tricky moment in a single bar: a trill, a change of position, an interval that requires an awkward fingering. Even if you isolate the difficulty down to a single note, that note will represent a syllable or word; to tame its physical difficulties is to "say" the word well. Develop the habit of singing or playing a whole word, a whole sentence, or a whole paragraph, rather than disparate notes that don't form a self-contained linguistic unit. Then develop the habit of performing sequences of paragraphs, letting the superbar structure guide you in analysis and performance.

3. FROM END TO BEGINNING

Oftentimes musicians practice their pieces from beginning to end, repeating the beginning many times, the middle section fewer times, and the last section fewer times still. The risk exists that the piece's beginning will be overpracticed and overripe, while the piece's end will be neglected and insecure.

Once you figure out the superbar structure of the piece you're studying, number each phrase in sequence. Suppose that, according to your analysis, your piece has four phrases of eight bars each, which you number 1, 2, 3, and 4. Perform the piece from the end to the beginning in the following manner:

```
            4
         3  4
      2  3  4
   1  2  3  4
```

The procedure gives you a rock-solid understanding of the passage's construction, plus the comfort of knowing where you're going and how you're getting there. (We'll look at a version of the procedure in chapter 10.)

Imagine a movement lasting 700 bars that may take ten or twelve minutes to perform—the last movement of a Beethoven symphony, for example. You can think of it as a long race, with physical demands that require muscular training; or a battle of wits in which the composer tests your capacity to outlast him in a spirited debate. Seven hundred bars of accented downbeats would kill you first, then your audience. But seven hundred bars organized into a few dozen spirited statements—each one of them a superbar structure—will give life to the composition, to you, and to the audience. If you practice and memorize those few dozen statements from the end to the beginning ("4321"), you'll win the debate.

4. STRIP A MUSICAL PHRASE TO ITS BARE ELEMENTS

The core elements of a work of art have a sort of magnetic force that draws in the viewer, the reader, or the listener and won't let go of him or her until the last scene of the last act or the closing chord of the last movement. If you can sense a composition's magnetic force, you can ride it in performance. Then the work of art will guide your gestures, not the other way around.

You can isolate a contrapuntal core in tonal pieces, as proposed by Heinrich Schenker (who thought that the contrapuntal core was the most important element in all of music). You can isolate a harmonic skeleton by reducing a piece to a series of chords that give you a sense of where the piece "goes." You can isolate a bass line, which might hint at both harmonic and contrapuntal forces. Finally, you can isolate a rhythmic core that, all by itself, has the capacity to drive your performance. Rhythmic Solfège is one way of doing it. Here's another way, using the superbar structure.

Take an eight-bar phrase from your current repertoire, or exercise yourself on "Oh! Susanna" or "Happy Birthday" if you prefer. Sing or play the phrase at high speed, eliminating as many details as necessary for you to be able to speed through the phrase comfortably. You might sense the phrase as eight impulses coinciding with the downbeats of each measure. The impulses are organized in twos and fours, each impulse prodding you forward almost despite yourself:

BOUNCE, bounce, BOUNCE to *here*!
BOUNCE, bounce, BOUNCE to *there*!

The superbar structure of anything you play holds the same potentiality to propel you. You can also sense the superbar structure's power by conducting and walking it. These procedures are so rich that they deserve their own sections.

CONDUCT THE SUPERBAR STRUCTURE

You can use Rhythmic Solfège to conduct the beats, time signatures, the subdivisions, and prosodic impetus of any measure. Since superbar structures are "measures of measures," they also lend themselves to being studied and mastered through Rhythmic Solfège.

🔊 This exercise is illustrated in video clip #18, "Conducting the Superbar Structure."

We'll study the Menuet in G Major, BWV Anh. 114, from J. S. Bach's "Notebook for Anna Magdalena Bach." Its authorship is usually attributed to Christian Petzold (1677–1733). (Example 8.1)

Play the piece normally, just to insert its sounds into your brain and ears. Most likely you're familiar with the piece already, since it's one of those basic compositions that

EXAMPLE 8.1. Christian Petzold (attributed): Menuet from J. S. Bach's "Note book for Anna Magdalena Bach," BWV Anh. 114 in G Major

thousands of music students have learned over centuries. If you aren't a pianist, play a version of it on your instrument, sing it, or whistle it. Then speak the piece in Rhythmic Solfège, snapping the beat and conducting the time signature of $\frac{3}{4}$.

A four-bar phrase in $\frac{3}{4}$ can be considered a single bar with 12 beats—that is, a $\frac{12}{4}$ bar. In conducting, a $\frac{12}{4}$ bar looks something like this, with the downbeats of each original $\frac{3}{4}$ bar marked in bold:

$$\Uparrow \textbf{10}\text{-}11\text{-}12$$
$$\Leftarrow \textbf{4}\text{-}5\text{-}6 \qquad\qquad 7\text{-}8\text{-}9 \Rightarrow$$
$$\Leftarrow \textbf{1}\text{-}2\text{-}3$$

While conducting a $\frac{12}{4}$ bar, speak the Menuet in Rhythmic Solfège. Remember that the Menuet has a total of eight phrases of four bars each. To cover the whole piece, you'll need to conduct a total of eight $\frac{12}{4}$ bars.

The preceding diagram numbers all the *beats* in four measures of $\frac{3}{4}$. We can also choose to number the *measures* instead. In the following diagram the bold numbers indicate the downbeat of each measure, and the syllable "and" represents the second and third beats.

⇑ **4**-and-and

⇐ **2**-and-and   **3**-and-and ⇒

⇓ **1**-and-and

In studying superbar structures, it's more convenient to use numbers to refer to entire measures, not single beats. From now on in this chapter, every number in a schema indicates the downbeat of a three-beat measure.

The following schema organizes an eight-bar phrase in $\frac{3}{4}$ into a single, slow bar of four beats with six subdivisions each—the equivalent of a $\frac{24}{8}$ bar. The bold numbers indicate every *second* downbeat from the original bars in $\frac{3}{4}$. Superbar structures create a hierarchy of downbeats, making some stronger and others weaker. This will go a long ways in helping you organize your piece and perform it with less muscular effort, as the right hierarchy of beats gives your playing or singing a terrific amount of rhythmic forward motion.

⇑ **7**-and-and **8**-and-and

⇐ **3**-and-and **4**-and-and   **5**-and-and **6**-and-and ⇒

⇓ **1**-and-and **2**-and-and

Speak the piece in Rhythmic Solfège and conduct it in different ways:

- Snap every beat (that is, every number and every "and").
- Snap every number (which corresponds to the downbeats of every measure), but not the intermediate beats.
- Snap the numbers in bold only (which correspond to the downbeats of every second measure).

In the preceding exercise, one complete conducting cycle covered an eight-bar phrase. Now you're going to cover a sixteen-bar section in a single cycle. Study the following schema.

⇑ **13** 14 15 16

⇐ **5** 6 7 8   **9** 10 11 12 ⇒

⇓ **1** 2 3 4

Each number corresponds to a bar of three beats. Each group of four numbers (such as **1** 2 3 4) corresponds to a four-bar phrase. Your conducting can show the hierarchy of beats within a superbar structure. Beats **1**, **5**, **9**, and **13** receive the heaviest metric accents, as they mark the beginning of each four-bar phrase. Beats 3, 7, 11, and 15 receive secondary metric accents. After each four-bar phrase there is a renewal of rhythmic energy. Your hand and arm must travel in space to go from beat 4 to beat **5** (or, in terms of cardinal points, from south to west), then from 8 to **9** (from west to east), then from 12 to **13** (from east to north), then from 16 to **1** (from north to south). As you move from one cardinal point to the other, make your gestures broad and sweeping, indicating that a phrase comes to an end and another phrase starts with a momentum of its own.

You're beginning to embody a multiplicity of speeds within the piece—the beat, the measure, and the four-bar, eight-bar, and sixteen-bar phrases. Figure 8.1 will help you visualize some of this information.

1 2 3 | 1 2 3 | 1 2 3 | 1 2 3 | 1 2 3 | 1 2 3 | 1 2 3 | 1 2 3 |

1 2 3 | **1** 2 3 | **1** 2 3 | **1** 2 3 | **1** 2 3 | **1** 2 3 | **1** 2 3 | **1** 2 3 |

1 2 3 | **2** 2 3 | **3** 2 3 | **4** 2 3 | **5** 2 3 | **6** 2 3 | **7** 2 3 | **8** 2 3 |

1 | **2** | **3** | **4** | **5** | **6** | **7** | **8** |

1 | | **3** | | **5** | | **7** | |

1 | | | | **5** | | | |

FIGURE 8.1. A multiplicity of musical speeds

Other pieces use three-bar phrases, five-bar phrases, the alternation of phrases of different length, and so on. Take the procedure you studied here and reshape it in accordance with the pieces you study and perform.

After you become comfortable conducting the superbar structure, learn to walk it.

WALK THE SUPERBAR STRUCTURE

Rhythmic patterning has the capacity to grab hold of you and "make you do things." This has been recognized in every culture, for good and for evil. Little kids simply cannot resist marching bands: Their bodies *must* move once they hear the music. Some children might move in perfect coincidence to the music, stomping their feet to the beat. Others become so excited that they move in discombobulated patterns, arms and legs flying about willy-nilly. Regardless of their movements, children demonstrate that rhythmically strong music causes a rhythmically strong physical reaction.

When you walk a piece's superbar structure, a paradox takes place: Your locomotion seems to drive the piece to "go" somewhere, at the same time that the piece itself seems to drive your locomotion. The superbar structure plays you, not you it.

🔊 This exercise is illustrated in video clip #19, "Walking the Superbar Structure."

Imagine that you're standing on the center of a square map, about three feet in length and width. The map has four cardinal points: south, west, east, and north. You'll touch each cardinal point in turn, using your right and left feet in alternation. Start with feet close together. After each step with the right foot, bring the left foot quickly next to it, so that feet are side by side as in the starting position. Do the same thing after each step with the left foot.

1. Lead back with the right foot: *south*.
2. Lead leftward and forward with the left foot: *west*.
3. Lead rightward and forward with the right foot: *east*.
4. Lead forward and centerward with the left foot: *north*.

This manner of walking draws a cross on the floor—the same geometric figure that your arm waves in the air when you conduct a four-beat measure. Sing or speak the Menuet again, which you have memorized by now. Walk as described above, making each step coincide with the downbeat of a measure in the Menuet. A cycle that takes you back to your starting point corresponds to a $\frac{12}{4}$—that is, four bars of $\frac{3}{4}$.

Now you're going to walk eight bars of $\frac{3}{4}$, using each cardinal point for the downbeats of two bars in succession. In the previous exercise, you brought your feet close together quickly after each step. In this exercise, every step with each foot will correspond to a distinct downbeat, so you'll bring your feet close together more deliberately. The following instructions include the measure numbers that correspond to each step. Mark the start of each four-bar phrase within the eight-bar phrase by stepping more heavily on beats 1 and 5.

1. Lead back with the right foot (**1**), and bring the left foot next to it (2): *south*.
2. Lead leftward with the left foot (3), and bring the right next to it (4): *west*.
3. Lead rightward with the right foot (**5**), and bring the left next to it (6): *east*.
4. Lead forward with the left foot (7), and bring the right next to it (8): *north*.

While walking, conduct a $\frac{3}{4}$ bar in the basic manner, snapping your fingers for each beat and waving a triangle up in the air (down, right, up) and speak the Menuet in Rhythmic Solfège. It'll take a lot of practice, but when you get the hang of it you'll be an extremely well-coordinated prosodist!

Speak the piece's first two measures, then insert a minuscule fermata—either by sustaining the last note of the second bar for a moment, or by waiting a fraction of a second in silence. Then go on to the next two bars, at the end of which you insert another fermata, a little longer than the first one since now you have reached the end of a four-bar phrase. At the end of an eight-bar phrase this "breathing fermata" or *luftpause* can be a little longer still. Every fermata gives you time and space to organize your psychophysical energies, in perfect coincidence with the Menuet's structure.

Everything you have done so far—speaking, singing, conducting in various numerical combinations, inserting fermatas here and there—can and ultimately must become not something that you do, but something that you carry inside you as a permanent possibility or latency. Become ready to conduct, to walk, to sing, to insert fermatas ... then choose

TABLE 8.1 The Superbar Structure and the Grid

	1	2	3	4	5	6	7	8
1.	1 2 3	1 2 3	1 2 3	1 2 3	1 2 3	1 2 3	1 2 3	1 2 3
2.	1 2 3	1 2 3	1 2 3	1 2 3	1 2 3	1 2 3	1 2 3	1 2 3
3.	1 2 3	1 2 3	1 2 3	1 2 3	1 2 3	1 2 3	1 2 3	1 2 3
4.	1 2 3	1 2 3	1 2 3	1 2 3	1 2 3	1 2 3	1 2 3	1 2 3

not to conduct, not to walk, not to sing, not to take time. Instead, play the piece with a simple richness informed by your deep knowledge of prosody.

Superbars are in integral part of the metric grid on which the game of music is played. Table 8.1 lays out a grid for the Menuet we've been studying. There are four phrases (numbered on the left column) of eight measures each (numbered on the top row). I've indicated a hierarchy of stresses by using **bold** for stressed downbeats; **underlined bold** for the downbeats that start each four-bar phrase; and ***underlined bold in italics*** for the heaviest of stresses, which is on the first downbeat of an eight-bar phrase.

THE LINGUISTIC LAYOUT

The visual display of information influences how you interpret the information, digest it, remember it, and transform it into practical knowledge.

> The visual display of information
> influences how you interpret the information,
> digest it, remember it,
> and transform it into practical knowledge.

Let's call the second version a *linguistic layout*, in which the visual display follows the words' logic instead of simply fitting into the printed page's physical limits. Music scores are printed mostly to fit the page, without following the logic of music itself. If you displayed musical information differently, you'd affect the way you interpret it, digest it, remember it, and transform it into sound.

For this exercise you'll need multiple photocopies of a movement or section from a work you're studying, scissors and glue, and extra-large sheets of paper. Make a few decisions regarding the superbar structure of the movement in question. Cut up the photocopy in such a way that each cut section corresponds to a self-contained phrase or series of phrases. Then glue the phrases on to the large piece of paper, laying the phrases out more or less like a poem. As an illustration, I've used the opening of the Gigue from J. S. Bach's Suite for Solo Cello in D minor, BWV 1008. In example 8.2 it's laid out in the normal manner, and in example 8.3 it's laid out linguistically.

Many layouts of the same score are possible, depending on your analytical decisions and on what levels of hierarchy you want to consider. In the case of a thirty-two-measure piece with four phrases of eight bars you can lay out the score as eight phrases of four bars,

EXAMPLE 8.2. J. S. Bach: Second Suite for Solo Cello, BWV 1008 in D Minor, Gigue

four phrases of eight bars, or two sections of sixteen bars. If you're studying a piece that is particularly important, difficult, or fun, create multiple layouts for it.

Phrases coalesce into groups. When you glue each series of phrases onto the big sheet of paper, allow more white space in between groups than in between phrases. This allows you to visualize, at one glance, the length of each phrase and how phrases relate to one another in groups.

The linguistic layout is like all other exercises: You can do it once or twice and learn something from it; or you can do it many times over many years, fundamentally altering your way of making music. Use the linguistic layout to visualize and understand complex structures like the sonata form, applying the prosodic tools of integration, separation, and direction on a large scale. Photocopy a sonata movement in reduced format, so that the entire movement fits onto a single sheet of paper. Cut it up in phrases and groups, and glue the resulting strips of paper in sections: exposition, development, and recapitulation. Vary the amount of blank space according to the hierarchy of phrases, groups, and sections.

The linguistic layout is also like all other exercises in that it contains risks and dangers. You risk seeing compositions as skeletons made of more or less independently articulated limbs and bones. Without a fluid energy running through it, however, a skeleton is essentially lifeless. Schenker believed that tonal pieces were wholly shaped by the energies of consonance and dissonance, and he dismissed the skeletal approach altogether:

EXAMPLE 8.3. The linguistic layout

I...reject those [formal] explanations which are based upon phrases, phrase-groups, periods, double periods, themes, antecedents, and consequents. My theory replaces all of these with specific concepts of form which...are based upon the content of the whole and of the individual parts; that is, the differences in prolongations lead to differences in form.[1]

"Prolongation" was Schenker's term for a contrapuntal core of a few notes spun and elaborated into an entire movement.

You might choose to embrace Schenker and dismiss the skeletal approach, embrace the superbar structure and dismiss Schenker, or take something meaningful from each perspective, synthesizing them and internalizing them for your own purposes.

In the remaining chapters I'll make few further references to the superbar structures, but there's nothing wrong with your singing, conducting, walking, and otherwise enjoying the superbar structures of all the music examples in this book.

CHAPTER 9

OPPOSING THE GRID

We can think of most compositions as the interaction between a grid and the forces that push against it. Johannes Brahms took this oppositional principle to heights of rhythmic complexity. In this chapter we'll consider a number of his piano pieces in order to deepen our grid-opposing skills. You don't need to be a pianist to enjoy studying these materials, which are illustrated in audio clips on the dedicated website.

First let's briefly revisit the metric, agogic, tonal, and dynamic accents that we encountered in chapter 4. Metric accents are inherent in time signatures. Downbeats receive a primary metric stress, while other notes may receive secondary or tertiary metric stresses. An agogic accent is the energy carried by a note longer than its neighbors. A tonal accent is the energy carried by the highest note within a group; a reverse tonal accent is the energy carried by the lowest note. Dynamic accents are added markings such as wedges, *sfz*, and *fp*.

We'll be making constant mention of the five basic prosodic patterns and their permutations of preparation, stress, and release. Here they are again, for ease of reference.

to BE	ta-DUM	iambic
NE-ver	DUM-ta	trochaic
WASH-ing-ton	DUM-ta-ta	dactylic
come on DOWN	ta-ta-DUM	anapestic
ba-NA-na	ta-DUM-ta	amphibrachic

INTERMEZZO, OPUS 10 #3 IN B MINOR

The piece starts with an upbeat to a silence. It's very daring of Brahms, because it makes it seem as if he's ignoring the grid altogether—which, as we'll see, isn't the case (example 9.1).

In isolation, accented short notes or chords tend to be prosodic stresses. In this piece, however, they're preparations to stresses that have been amputated. A note or chord of preparation points to a destination to be reached, and has a propulsive momentum lacking in a stress. Brahms's upbeats, then, make sense only if the pianist somehow points them toward their missing destination, which is supplied by the grid.

EXAMPLE 9.1. Johannes Brahms: Intermezzo, opus 10 #3 in B Minor

Physically and musically, it's preferable for you to have a reliable, internalized aural memory of the grid. In its absence you risk either placing the upbeat willy-nilly, robbing it of its meaning and emotion; or trying to feel the amputated downbeat in your body, using your head, neck, and shoulders as substitute metronomes. The solution lies in temporarily restoring the downbeats until you feel their power to moor the grid. Then amputate them again, making the grid live inside you.

This exercise is illustrated in audio clip #1, "Intermezzo, op. 10 #3: Amputated Downbeats."

Conduct a few bars of $\frac{6}{8}$ in silence, at the tempo you have chosen for the piece. Then speak the patterns in example 9.2.

1. The first pattern uses a plain unit of upbeat/DOWNBEAT, repeated twice per bar. Had Brahms wanted to compose something musically square and technically easy, he might have chosen this version.

2. The second pattern is a little harder than the previous one, since it contains relatively long silences between spoken or sounded units. A silence can be surprisingly difficult to manage. Most musicians tend to get either nervous or bored, and to mangle the silence's length as well as its emotional content.

3. The third pattern introduces the concept of the amputated downbeat, but is easier than Brahms's actual version since you don't have to deal with an uncomfortably long silence.

4. The fourth pattern mimics Brahms's writing of an eighth-note upbeat to a long silence that lasts five eighth notes.

EXAMPLE 9.2. Placing amputated downbeats

Now you have an internalized metric grid that allows you to place the upbeats correctly. Play the passage as written.

Starting in bar 9, Brahms creates a new event in opposition to the grid (example 9.3).

We know that Brahms loved hemiolas, and at first we might want to believe he's up to his usual tricks, turning a bar of $\frac{6}{8}$ into one of $\frac{3}{4}$—that is, turning two groups of three eighth notes into three groups of two eighth notes. My theory, however, is that Brahms hasn't shifted into hemiola mode, but that he continues to tease the pianist and the listener with amputated metric stresses.

Suppose a gang of rogues steals a secret airplane from the U.S. Air Force. They dismantle it from top to bottom, starting from the outside until they reach the airplane's core. Then they put it back together again, in the process understanding exactly how the plane was designed and built. Now the rogues are ready to start manufacturing their own copies of the prized plane. This is called *reverse engineering*. In musical reverse engineering,

EXAMPLE 9.3. Metric ambiguity

you rewrite a bar, phrase, or passage by eliminating from it every layer of complexity and elaboration, leaving in place nothing but the barest, most banal version of the passage. Then you put the elaborations and complexities back in one by one, until you have understood what elements give the passage its emotion and meaning.

🔊 This exercise is illustrated in audio clip #2, "Intermezzo, op. 10 #3: Reverse Engineering."

How would this passage look in its most basic form? Dynamic and agogic accents wouldn't fight metric accents for primacy, and the bars would be composed of running eighths with no accents (example 9.4).

EXAMPLE 9.4. Reverse engineering

Given the melodic shapes that Brahms starts with and the rhythmic choices at which he eventually arrives, we might speculate that the passage's impetus is amphibrachic. We can schematize it as {3 4 5, 6 1 2}, in which 1 is a primary metric stress and 4 a secondary one that actually precedes it, organizing the amphibrachic units into a larger iambic grouping of upbeat/DOWNBEAT (example 9.5).

EXAMPLE 9.5. Amphibrachic schema

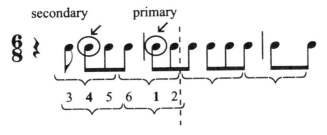

In his elaboration of the passage, Brahms slurs the 3 into the 4 in the right hand, thereby amputating the secondary metric stress and creating an agogic one instead. To the resulting quarter note he adds a dynamic accent. In the left hand, Brahms slurs 2, 3, and 4 together, making for an even longer agogic accent, to which he also adds a dynamic accent. Instead of highlighting the metrically stressed 1 and 4, Brahms highlights 2 and 3, creating a lively opposition of forces where dynamic and agogic accents push and pull asymmetrically against the metric accents. But if you perform the passage as if consisting of hemiolas—that is, bars of $\frac{3}{4}$ and not $\frac{6}{8}$—the oppositions are much diminished, and the only noteworthy event would be the offbeat dynamic accent of the left hand. I believe Brahms doesn't shift to $\frac{3}{4}$ at all until he reaches bar 13, when indeed he plays a plain hemiola for one bar, starts another hemiola on bar 14, and breaks it off by reintroducing the subversive upbeat that had started the piece.

Ideally, there ought to be a fight between the grid and Brahms's rhythmic inventions, not between the pianist and the piano. For that to happen, the pianist must sense the grid, internalize it, and allow the opposition between the grid and Brahms to be the real show on stage.

CAPRICCIO, OPUS 116 #1 IN D MINOR

Brahms opens the piece in almost immediate disregard for the metric grid—or so it might seem at first (example 9.6).

Dynamic accents on the right hand and agogic accents on the left both conspire against the metric accents, which "go missing," so to speak; the upbeats are louder and more strongly affirmed than the downbeats. But if Brahms had wanted metric accents to

EXAMPLE 9.6. Johannes Brahms: Capriccio, opus 116 #1 in D Minor

EXAMPLE 9.7. Dactylic re-barring

disappear altogether he'd have written the piece differently, re-barring it and making the dynamic accents coincide with the downbeats (example 9.7).

In fact, the piece makes sense only if the pianist and the listener both perceive the grid—the better to feel how Brahms opposes it with agogic and dynamic accents. Rewrite the piece to bring the grid to the fore. Change the left hand to a pattern of upbeat/DOWNBEAT, eighth-note/quarter note, not slurred; and eliminate the sforzandi from the right hand altogether (example 9.8).

Play the rewritten version a few times, absorbing its unambiguous metric accents. Then play the piece as written, keeping the feeling of the metric accents as a sort of pulsating energy *within* your body, not as movements of your head and neck. The opposition with the grid will become clearer both to you and to your audience.

⊙ This exercise is illustrated in audio clip #3, "Capriccio, op. 116 #1: Amphibrachic/Dactylic Opposition."

Brahms spins the phrase twice, changing the roles of the left and right hands a bit. Then, after four bars of something relatively ordinary, he launches a long series of

EXAMPLE 9.8. Amphibrachic re-barring

EXAMPLE 9.9. Long hemiolas

hemiolas. Sixteen bars of $\frac{3}{8}$ become eight bars of $\frac{3}{4}$, though without a time signature change (example 9.9).

To better to sense the passage's superbar structure, reimagine the eight bars of $\frac{3}{4}$ as two long bars of $\frac{12}{4}$ each. Conduct them in Rhythmic Solfège, saying the left hand's rhythms out loud; or conduct with the right hand while playing the left hand (example 9.10).

EXAMPLE 9.10. Long hemiolas rewritten in $\frac{12}{4}$

🔊 This exercise is illustrated in audio clip #4, "Capriccio, op. 116 #1: Hemiolas in $\frac{12}{4}$."

By design or by default, information can be unequivocal (crystal-clear and not open to differing interpretations) or ambiguous (carrying the possibility of multiple meanings and interpretations). Music notation is inevitably ambiguous, since it's impossible to notate enough aspects of a composition to render the printed page an unequivocal guide to interpretation. Phrase markings are more ambiguous than we think when we glance at a page of music. Prosodic energies of preparation, stress, and release sometimes override phrase markings. Notation apart, music itself carries its own ambiguities of prosody, meaning, and emotion. What does Brahms mean? And what does the pianist mean when he or she plays something that Brahms wrote?

The left hand's hemiolas can conceivably be played as a series of dactylic, anapestic, or amphibrachic units. For the first eight measures, nothing in the passage indicates that it *must* be played in one of these three ways, or that it *must not* be played so. In the second half of the passage, slurs group two bars together, possibly indicating that they must be played as dactylic, except that there is also a crescendo marking, which might override the dactylic impetus, where a release follows a stress. Take the first eight measures of this passage and perform it as a series of dactyls first, then a series of amphibrachs (example 9.11).

EXAMPLE 9.11. Dactylic and amphibrachic hemiolas

🔊 This exercise is illustrated in audio clip #5, "Capriccio, op. 116 #1: Dactylic and Amphibrachic Hemiolas."

Go back to the beginning of the piece and look at measure 4 and its upbeat. Three notes slurred together over a bar line make for an amphibrachic unit of preparation, stress, and release. But the sforzando on the note of preparation is ambiguous. It might be saying,

"Maybe this is a metrically displaced dactyl, not an amphibrach." Perhaps the left-hand hemiolas, too, are organized into a series of amphibrachic units, spiced by a little dactylic ambiguity. Indeed, this ambiguity may be the piece's main prosodic feature.

The entire section is an elaborate statement of the dominant of F major, the relative of the piece's main key of D minor. The second half of the section, where the left hand's slurs appear, reaffirms the F-major dominant a bit more unequivocally than the first half of the section, and using a dactylic energy for these groupings will reinforce the C (the root of the dominant chord) and clarify the section's overall structural role. Interestingly, Brahms will spend almost no time dwelling in the *tonic* of F major, but sounding its dominant with the long hemiolas does settle the piece for a moment.

The hemiolas' relative simplicity comes to an end, and a more complex passage starts (example 9.12).

The right hand's agogic accent (the long A-flat in the second bar), together with the left hand's dynamic accent (the sforzando), undermine the metric accents of the downbeats. The passage risks feeling unmoored, unless the pianist senses the grid and internalizes it. Rewrite the passage as a series of eighth notes organized anapestically. Add a sforzando on the A, right hand downbeat, and delete the sforzando on the left hand. The resulting passage favors the metric accents and brings the grid to the fore (example 9.13).

This exercise is illustrated in audio clip #6, "Capriccio, op. 116 #1: Metric, Agogic, and Dynamic Accents."

EXAMPLE 9.12. Agogic and dynamic accents

EXAMPLE 9.13. Rewritten accents

Play the passage this way until the metric grid is imprinted in your musical and muscular memory. Then add the left-hand sforzando and play the passage again. Keeping a strong downbeat on the right hand, revert the rest of the right hand to its original note values, and play the passage again. Now play the passage as written, retaining the feeling of the grid and placing the various accents and amputated downbeats against the grid.

While creating intricate structures brimming with hemiolas, displaced accents, and missing downbeats, Brahms keeps using four- and eight-bar phrases, as if he were a country musician playing simple folk tunes and dances. It'd probably overwhelm the listener if Brahms used jagged superbar structures on top of his metric oppositions. This isn't to say he writes bland superbar structures all the time; on the contrary. We'll look at an example of an interesting superbar structure later on.

In a contrasting section, Brahms writes a long sequence of amphibrachs, with the left and right hands alternating chords in a regular manner: one chord with the left, one with the right (example 9.14).

The prosodic pattern is three-pronged while the physical gesture is two-pronged. The pianist's hands have to become alert to the switching prosodic energies and adapt their gestures accordingly. To start the passage, the left hand sounds a stress and the right hand a release. Then the left hand sounds a preparation, the right a stress, the left a release. Then

EXAMPLE 9.14. Amphibrachic hands

the right hand sounds a preparation, the left a stress, and the right a release, and the cycle starts again.

🔊 This exercise is illustrated in audio clip #7, "Capriccio, op. 116 #1: Amphibrachic Hands."

Your hands must become adept prosodists, so to speak. In fact, every body part needs to become a prosodist. The arms, hands, and fingers are natural candidates, since most musicians use them as a matter of course. The legs and feet are prosodists for organists, pianists, and drummers. The lips, tongue, and jaw are prosodists for singers and brass and wind players. Whether or not you use these body parts in your musical domain, train them all to become *latent prosodists*, ready to contribute to the whole body's rhythmic energy.

INTERMEZZO, OPUS 116 #5 IN E MINOR

Here Brahms creates an ambiguity of iambic and trochaic energies, a favorite device that you'll subsequently detect in dozens of his compositions (example 9.15).

Metrically, the figures he uses throughout the first section are iambic: upbeat/ DOWNBEAT, preparation/STRESS. But the upbeats are pedaled six-note chords, making the downbeats' two-note chords seem weak in comparison. Brahms gives so much weight to the upbeats that they threaten to become downbeats themselves, rendering the two-note pattern trochaic: DOWNBEAT/offbeat, STRESS/release. Had Brahms wanted the phrase to be a sequence of straightforward trochees, however, he'd have barred it differently (example 9.16).

EXAMPLE 9.15. Johannes Brahms: Intermezzo, opus 116 #5 in E Minor

EXAMPLE 9.16. Trochaic re-barring

🔊 This exercise is illustrated in audio clip #8, "Intermezzo, op. 116 #5: Iambic and Trochaic Pulls."

Rewrite the piece to eliminate the opposition between iambic and trochaic energies. Delete four notes from each six-note chord, retaining two notes that give the right hand a melodic shape. Just to be sure, think "crescendo" from upbeat to downbeat, and give weight to the dissonances at the downbeat. In this simplified, wholly iambic version, the metric grid is explicitly displayed. Play it a few times until you internalize the iambic impetus. Then restore the notes you had deleted from the upbeats; add the pedal; and add Brahms's crescendo and diminuendo indications, recreating the opposition between the iambic impetus (which you've internalized) and the trochaic impetus (which Brahms externalizes in composition).

The opposition grabs you by the ear and plays tricks with your perception of time. "Where exactly is the downbeat? Where is Brahms taking me? Am I pulling, or am I being pulled?" This goes on for twelve bars, and then the tension dissolves into a lyrical passage in which the metric grid asserts itself more clearly. After several bars, the left hand sounds offbeats that announce Brahms's intention to pull your sense of time out of shape again. The clash of iambic and trochaic energies returns for eight bars. At the very end of the piece, the left hand is in syncopation to the bar line (example 9.17). Brahms concludes the piece as he started it, in exquisite metric ambiguity!

Unless we see, hear, sense, or otherwise capture the opposition between the grid and the forces that oppose it, we miss out on the vitality of music itself.

CAPRICCIO, OPUS 116 #7 IN D MINOR

From this capriccio, we isolate an eight-bar phrase in the middle section, in the key of A minor (example 9.18).

Its meter is ⁶⁄₈ and we can take it for granted that Brahms will use hemiolas, as indeed he does from the beginning of the passage. But the hemiolas are syncopated, creating a metrically vacillating melody.

Using the technique of musical reverse engineering, isolate the melody and rewrite it in its "square hemiola" version: unsyncopated, plainly in ³⁄₄, a steady stream of eighth notes running underneath it in ⁶⁄₈ (example 9.19).

The melody employs a series of three-note units. Are they dactylic ("WA-shing-ton") or amphibrachic ("ba-NA-na")? The second syllable of each word coincides with the

EXAMPLE 9.17. Metric uncertainty

secondary metric accent of a $\frac{6}{8}$ bar, making the word seem amphibrachic; but if the melody is in $\frac{3}{4}$, we expect its first syllable to receive a dactyl-making metric accent. Using an apparently simple melody, Brahms has created a multiplicity of oppositions: between $\frac{6}{8}$ and $\frac{3}{4}$, between amphibrachs and dactyls, and between strong beats and syncopations (example 9.20).

🔊 This exercise is illustrated in audio clip #9, "Capriccio, op. 116 #7: Eight Amphibrachs."

EXAMPLE 9.18. Johannes Brahms: Capriccio, opus 116 #7 in D Minor

EXAMPLE 9.19. Nonsyncopated hemiola melody

EXAMPLE 9.20. Syncopated hemiola in opposition to the grid

The eight-bar phrase is constructed so that every two words belong together in a larger unit, and every two groups of two words belong together in a unit larger still. Play the melody it in a conversational style, inflecting it word by word, and also in groups of two words:

word/word, word/word; word/word, word/word ...

Brahms's dynamic markings seem to indicate an iambic organization to the first two pairings, as he writes a crescendo for the second word:

word/WORD, word/WORD;

Bars 5 and 6 have no dynamic markings, then bars 7 and 8 receive a decrescendo, with perhaps a hint of a trochaic organization for the last pairing:

word/word, WORD/word ...

Visualize the words strung together like lines of verse in a poem, then organize the melody accordingly (example 9.21).

EXAMPLE 9.21. Word-like note groupings

word/WORD, word/WORD;
word/word, WORD/word ...

The passage has a breathless, agitated quality that should come from the music itself, not from the pianist's struggles to put these rhythmic elements together.

BALLADE, OPUS 118 #3 IN G MINOR

When Brahms composes intricate patterns within one- or two-bar units, he often uses conventional eight-bar phrases divided into two symmetrical halves. But he doesn't use these conventional structures all the time; far from it. Let's look at a departure from the convention (example 9.22).

This Ballade starts with a ten-bar phrase, subdivided into two halves of five bars each. Phrases of four bars can often be subdivided into two-bar sections; phrases of eight bars, into four-bar sections; and phrases of sixteen bars, into eight-bar sections. How might we subdivide a five-bar phrase? On occasion a five-bar phrase might become 1 + 4 bars or 4 + 1 bars, but most often there tends to be a logical way to break it up as 2 + 3 or 3 + 2 bars. Which of these two choices is most appropriate for the Ballade?

You could conceivably arrive at a decision through intellectual calculation alone, using your knowledge of structure to determine that the phrases are subdivided as 2 + 3 or 3 + 2. Or you could perform these two analyses several times and let your decision arise from the muscular, aural, and emotional experience of performance.

EXAMPLE 9.22. Johannes Brahms: Ballade, opus 118 #3 in G Minor

🔊 This exercise is illustrated in audio clip #10, "Ballade, op. 118 #3: 2 + 3, 3 + 2."

Any note you play or sing carries rhythmic energy inside itself. Rhythmic energy becomes renewed and varied as you pass from one note to the next. The renewal of rhythmic energy is both constant, since it involves every note, and variable, since the intensity of rhythmic energy changes from note to note and from bar to bar. The Ballade starts with a burst of energy in the form of three notes arranged anapestically: ta-ta-DUM! The figure repeats itself in the next bar. It's likely that Brahms conceived these two bars together as a trochaic unit, the first bar as a stress, the second one a release relative to the first bar. The second bar, then, is "weaker" than the first, but it has its own strength and it represents a renewal of rhythmic energy all the same:

ta-ta-**DUM**, ta-ta-DUM ...

Within the phrase that opens the Ballade, there is a hierarchy of rhythmic renewals. If you perform the five-bar phrase as 2 + 3, the upbeat to the *third* bar will be the most important renewal of rhythmic energy; if 3 + 2, it is the upbeat to the *fourth* bar that signals the most important renewal.

The composition itself offers some evidence to support both analyses. The downbeat to the third bar doesn't have a dynamic accent, unlike all the other bars in the phrase; perhaps Brahms sees it as a relatively weak bar, and not a natural candidate for a major renewal of rhythmic energy. The fourth bar has two accented half notes, which raises the bar's energy charge. Therefore 3 + 2 explains both these factors.

The third bar represents an acceleration relative to the first two, since the rhythm of the melody goes from dotted half notes to two dotted quarter notes, raising the bar's energy charge. The third bar also marks the start of an unbroken sequence of running eighth notes, all the way to the end of the phrase. Therefore 2 + 3 explains both these factors.

We need to look elsewhere for enlightenment. The contrasting section is largely in the key of B major, a marvelous and daring departure from the piece's main key of G minor. Within it, Brahms sounds the piece's opening melody in a four-bar version ... in D-sharp minor (example 9.23)!

EXAMPLE 9.23. A four-bar phrase in D-sharp Minor

This version of the phrase is organized into two halves of two bars, and it gives us a clue as to how Brahms created the five-bar phrase: He took a four-bar phrase, split it in two halves, and added a one-bar extension to the first half. What started as 2 + 2 became (2 + 1) + 2. This makes the analysis of 3 + 2 for the opening phrase more likely than the analysis of 2 + 3.

🔊 This exercise is illustrated in audio clip #11, "Ballade, op. 118 #3: 2 + 2 extended."

Unless I miscounted it, the ten-bar phrase at the opening of the Ballade contains 262 notes plus five rests, for a total of 267 bits of musical data. If you get the superbar structure clear in your mind, ear, and body, the phrase's energies become so well organized that you don't need to make 267 separate decisions to perform it.

1) Take the opening five bars of the Ballade. Assign prosodic values to their downbeats, organizing them as a dactyl plus a trochee:

STRESS-release-release; STRESS-release.

2) Organize those two units into a larger trochaic unit, in which the first downbeat is the strongest of them all:

STRESS-release-release; STRESS-release.

3) The second five-bar phrase has the same prosodic structure. Together, the two five-bar halves form an even larger trochaic unit:

STRESS-release-release; STRESS-release |
STRESS-release-release; STRESS-release.

Here's the same information, abbreviated:

S-r-r; S-r | **S**-r-r; S-r.

4) Translate the information above into a numeric sequence you can use to count the superbar structure mentally as you perform the passage:

1-2-3; 4-5 | **1**-2-3; 4-5.

🔊 This exercise is illustrated in audio clip #12, "Ballade, op. 118 #3: The Superbar Structure."

Now you have a metric and prosodic grid with a clearly defined hierarchy of energies. Hundreds of individual notes fit into the grid nicely, every note finding its right place within the hierarchy of energies, every note pushing and pulling against the grid in some way or other. The piece's propulsive energies come from the superbar structure, the prosodic qualities of preparation, stress, and release, the alternation of consonance and dissonance, and the interplay of metric, agogic, tonal, and dynamic accents. It's the piece that drives your playing, not the other way around!

🔊 The ideas in this chapter are further illustrated in three bonus video clips: #20, "Internalizing the Grid I: Missing Downbeats," #21, "Internalizing the Grid II: Hemiolas," and #22, "Internalizing the Grid III: Provocations."

CHAPTER 10

PATTERNING AND SEQUENCING

INFORMATION AND INTERPRETATION

Most compositions are made of patterns in sequence. Your task as a musician is to become able to discern these patterns analytically and to have the technical means to translate them into sound in performance. For the purposes of our study, we'll take a thorough look at the first half of the last movement from J. S. Bach's Sonata in G minor, BWV 1001, for Solo Violin (example 10.1). If you aren't a violinist, join up with a violinist friend and study the piece together. With a few adjustments, the piece can also be performed at the piano, the flute, and other instruments. Or read the score while listening to the recording posted online.

🔊 This exercise is illustrated in audio clip #13, "J. S. Bach, Presto for Solo Violin."

Musical notation is a compromise between the possible and the desirable. Few things in music can be annotated in a completely unambiguous manner. In this piece, even the time signature is ambiguous.

Example 10.2 shows a few note values notated in $\frac{3}{8}$ and $\frac{6}{16}$.

Some note values are written the same way in both time signatures. Out of context, you might be unsure if six sixteenths flagged together correspond to a bar of $\frac{3}{8}$ or of $\frac{6}{16}$. The piece's printed meter is $\frac{3}{8}$, and you might be tempted to take this information at face value. This would be a big mistake. Play two versions of the opening phrase, in $\frac{3}{8}$ (three groups of two sixteenths per bar) and in $\frac{6}{16}$ (two groups of three sixteenths per bar). Exaggerate the groupings a little, just to make sure they correspond to the chosen time signature (example 10.3).

🔊 This exercise is illustrated in audio clip #14, "$\frac{3}{8}$ versus $\frac{6}{16}$."

The test demonstrates that, indeed, the piece starts not in $\frac{3}{8}$ but in $\frac{6}{16}$. You could probably have concluded as much by simply looking at the melodic shape of the opening phrase. Whether you do it visually or aurally, however, you need to be permanently alert to implicit information that might trump explicit information. As we study the piece we'll see that its meter actually shifts between $\frac{6}{16}$, $\frac{3}{8}$, and $\frac{3}{4}$.

> Lesson #1: Musical notation is a compromise, leading to information that may be incomplete or illogical. The work of interpreting information never ends; the work of making the interpreter smarter never ends.

EXAMPLE 10.1. J. S. Bach: Sonata for Solo Violin, BWV 1001 in G Minor, Presto (first half)

EXAMPLE 10.2. A comparison between $\frac{3}{8}$ and $\frac{6}{16}$

EXAMPLE 10.3. Testing the differences between $\frac{3}{8}$ and $\frac{6}{16}$

A₃B₃C₃

Our test determined that the opening phrase was in $\frac{6}{16}$. We performed the test using exaggerated dactylic groups for the whole phrase. It's not impossible that the dactylic choice is the best one for this passage, but we must test it further before being sure. We'll use a method called $A_3B_3C_3$. It consists in choosing a number of prosodic options and testing them in several ways. In this passage our options are: dactylic, A; amphibrachic, B; and anapestic, C. In other pieces you might test fewer or more options. Then adjust your ABC accordingly.

🎧 This exercise is illustrated in audio clip #15, "ABC, 123."

Play version A under tempo, inserting silences between groupings so that the passage's dactylic construction is unambiguous. Imagine you're giving a lecture to a dozen fidgety students who have never encountered prosody before. Your performance should be clear enough for every student in the room to sense and understand, upon first hearing, the pattern you're demonstrating. This is version A_1. We annotate it with a variety of signs to help us analyze and perform it (example 10.4).

Now play the passage with less exaggeration, but still making your prosodic choice unambiguous. Don't insert silences between the groupings, and play it only slightly under tempo. You might sound like someone giving a deliberately calm yet compelling performance of the piece. This is version A_2 (example 10.5).

EXAMPLE 10.4. A₁

A₁ **Andante con moto**

EXAMPLE 10.5. A₂

A₂ **Allegro moderato**

Now play the passage as if in concert: a tempo, and with subtle inflections rendering the dactylic groupings clear to the listener. This is version A_3. Notice that in A_3 the only graphic sign we add to Bach's score is the dotted line, which indicates a little separation between groupings. The idea is for you to use signs freely when you first approach a piece, and ever more sparingly as you become comfortable with the piece. In time, aim to internalize all the information the signs provide (example 10.6).

EXAMPLE 10.6. A_3

Now play the passage in an exaggerated amphibrachic manner, B_1; in an unambiguous but unfussy manner, B_2; and in a concert version, B_3 (example 10.7).

EXAMPLE 10.7. B_{123}

Apply the procedure for the anapestic grouping, C_1, C_2, C_3 (example 10.8).
To be conscientious, play the passage twelve times in a row:

A_1, A_2, A_3;
B_1, B_2, B_3;
C_1, C_2, C_3;
A_3, B_3, C_3.

If you make a mistake anywhere along the way, backtrack to the beginning of the procedure and start over from scratch, until you can go from first to last version flawlessly. Consider it a form of meditation. It may take several hours until you execute a single

EXAMPLE 10.8. C₁₂₃

sequence without mistakes, but by then your connections between intention and gesture, analysis and performance, musicianship and technique will be rock solid.

The sequence A₃B₃C₃ at the end of the procedure is crucial. It allows you to compare each prosodic alternative in its concert version—which is the version that counts the most when it comes to making final interpretive decisions.

> Lesson #2: Know your ABCs and your 123s. In other words, know the interpretive options at your disposal and have the technical means to perform each option reliably.

Musicians often play through a passage slowly many times, hoping to conquer technical difficulties through repetition alone. But in the absence of prosodic energies, slow practice is meaningless and perhaps even harmful. Musicians also "practice in rhythms," breaking up a phrase into fragments of fixed length, overlaying fixed rhythmic patterns upon the fragmented phrase, and performing the resulting combinations a few times each. Most of the results are musically absurd and technically awkward, but musicians persist in practicing this way in the hope of acquiring good mechanical reflexes. Practicing slowly and "in rhythms" becomes useful only when the rhythms are prosodically plausible and the slow practice is musically charged.

PATTERNS AND SEQUENCES

The piece starts with a two-octave, descending G-minor arpeggio—that is, an intervallic pattern repeated several times. You'll soon see that the entire piece is made of sequences of patterns. Instead of learning the piece note by note, you can and must learn it pattern by pattern: descending arpeggios, ascending arpeggios, descending and ascending scales, scale segments, and whatever other patterns occur in the piece. The piece has nearly 140 bars and more than 800 notes, but it's built on a small number of patterns; a ballpark figure might be fifteen patterns or so. Would you rather learn 800 bits of disparate information or fifteen sets of organized information?

🔊 This exercise is illustrated in audio clip #16, "Patterns in Isolation and in Sequence."

Practice a pattern in isolation and make yourself thoroughly comfortable with it. Go on to the next pattern and repeat the procedure. Then put the sequences of patterns together. Each of these tasks is time-consuming, but becoming an expert in all of them will make you a much faster learner in the long run.

In example 10.9, the first pattern is the descending arpeggio, repeated over three bars.

EXAMPLE 10.9. The first pattern in a sequence

The next pattern is an ascending arpeggio followed by a descending scale. We hear two complete sets of this pattern and one incomplete one: the last ascending arpeggio is broken off before we hear its corresponding scale (example 10.10).

EXAMPLE 10.10. The second pattern in a sequence

Then a new pattern emerges for three bars: arpeggios descending and ascending again within the bar (example 10.11).

EXAMPLE 10.11. The third pattern in a sequence

It feels as if the music is accelerating. To be precise, more things are happening more quickly within the music. This new pattern breaks off abruptly, with a big interval that necessitates a potentially awkward string crossing. The meter suddenly changes, and we finally have a passage in $\frac{3}{8}$, not $\frac{6}{16}$ (example 10.12).

EXAMPLE 10.12. The fourth pattern in a sequence

Learning each pattern is important, but passing from one pattern to the next is the more difficult task. The joints between patterns tend to have structural weight and come with challenges of coordination and awareness. Before long we'll take a closer look at joinery.

Lesson #3: Become able to enter a pattern with ease and to benefit from the pattern's ability to organize information for you. Then become able to exit the pattern with the same ease, to avoid being boxed in by the pulls of an old pattern when you should be adapting to those of a new one.

UPBEATS IN BAROQUE MUSIC

The musicological consensus regarding Baroque music up to about 1760 is that upbeats shouldn't play a big role in performance. According to the ideology of the times— embraced by composers, performers, and listeners alike—the first beat of a bar symbolized God, the second beat the king, and the third beat the individual. Therefore, the first beat should always be strongly sounded, followed by a weaker beat, followed by a beat weaker still. Not to do so would amount to an attack on God's primacy over all humans and on the king's power over his subjects. The beats' hierarchy mirrored society's, and it had to be respected at all times.

This argument would invalidate some of the prosodic ideas I have been presenting, since feet such as the amphibrach and the anapest are based on the existence of upbeats. The pull of the upbeat, however, is so strong in human nature that even the most diligent Baroque performers never bypass upbeats entirely.

Lesson #4: Understand the rules before you break them. And know to obey the rules as well as to disobey them.

The new section, clearly in $\frac{3}{8}$, uses a pattern of intervals, articulations, and changes of string that is more elaborate than the preceding patterns. If we rewrite the passage as a series of straightforward chords, we see that Bach is using the circle of sevenths (example 10.13).

EXAMPLE 10.13. The circle of sevenths

Seventh chords in sequence have a forward motion of their own. Every seventh chord is dissonant and cries out for a resolution that never comes, since the next chord is another seventh chord also crying out for resolution! Bach breaks off the pattern after the fifth chord. Isolate the downbeats from the passage, which coincide with the roots of the seventh chords. Play them not as a physical exercise empty of musical meaning but as a marvelous message from the gods above, using the momentum implicit in the sequence of descending fifths as a driving energy (example 10.14).

EXAMPLE 10.14. A passage reduced to its downbeats

> Lesson #5: The interplay of consonance and dissonance, the expansion and contraction of motivic materials, and the acceleration and deceleration of structural pace all create musical tensions. Use their energies, rather than your muscular effort, to drive your performance.

Now isolate the downbeats of each bar together with their preceding upbeats. In performance you might decide to emphasize the downbeats and lessen the upbeats in accordance with musicological tenets, but knowing how to ride your upbeats' inherent energies can only help you play the best possible downbeats (example 10.15).

EXAMPLE 10.15. Downbeats and their upbeats

Insert silences between words in a sentence. This helps you clarify the sentence's structure while giving you time to coordinate yourself before speaking each word in the sentence. We call this procedure *delayed continuity* (example 10.16).

EXAMPLE 10.16. Delayed continuity

Now play five versions of the passage, in sequence (example 10.17):

1. Roots alone;
2. Roots and their upbeats under tempo;
3. Roots and upbeats a tempo, with silences between them;
4. Delayed continuity;
5. The passage exactly as written.

🎧 This exercise is illustrated in audio clip #17, "The Circle of Sevenths."

EXAMPLE 10.17. A five-step procedure

Lesson #6: Capture your piece's innermost musical content, and then invent intermediate steps and indirect procedures to go from musical content to physical comfort. A difficult passage is a "problem." The intermediate steps are "the solution." Work on the solution, not the problem.

JOINERY

In this section we'll look at ways of improving the most important aspect of patterning and sequencing: your joinery—or how you pass from pattern to pattern.

The sequence we've been studying breaks off after five bars. The meter shifts again, from $\frac{3}{8}$ back to $\frac{6}{16}$, and a new pattern occurs. In fact this isn't a new pattern, but the piece's first pattern, inverted: the piece opened with descending arpeggios, and here we have the same arpeggios but ascending. The pattern is two bars long and is repeated four times, for a total of eight bars (example 10.18).

There's a psychological aspect in joinery: The way you perceive your patterns will determine whether you tighten up or open up to perform them. The next pattern "feels

EXAMPLE 10.18. An inverted pattern

faster." It's only one bar long, and inside it two different musical figures vie for attention. If a pattern is "fast," it doesn't mean your own energies have to speed up, which would have negative consequences for your performance. Look for cues in the music itself to help you not rush in mind and body. In this pattern, the prosodic elements are straightforward: the three slurred notes create a dactyl, and the three detached notes another dactyl. Use the relative simplicity of the pattern's prosody to play it in such a way that the music will seem to speed up without your tightening (example 10.19).

EXAMPLE 10.19. An accelerating pattern

> Lesson #7: The way you react intellectually and emotionally to a musical challenge will determine your physical attitudes and gestures.

This piece abounds in step progressions—hidden scales and scale fragments that buttress the piece's structure. In many pieces, step progressions offer a stable element underneath an agitated surface. (We make a deeper study of step progressions in chapter 20.) Isolate the step progression that underpins this particular pattern and the pattern that follows it, perform it in isolation, and then add the arpeggios to it. If you stay in sync with the step progression's slow-moving pace, you'll find it easier to play the seemingly fast arpeggios attached to it (example 10.20).

EXAMPLE 10.20. Step progressions

🔊 This, together with the passage from bars 35 to 47, is illustrated in audio clip #18, "Step Progressions."

The sequence appears easy to perform, lulling you into a feeling of security. If you relax, however, you'll find it hard to face the provocative event that comes next. Joinery

EXAMPLE 10.21. A provocative fragment

requires you not to freak out when something looks difficult, and not to get lazy when something looks easy (example 10.21).

Bach structures the piece using different types and intensities of tension: now elaborate, now simple; now faster, now slower; now smooth, now jagged. Here the meter changes from $\frac{6}{16}$ back to $\frac{3}{8}$. For two bars the composition seems to be going up and down at the same time. The passage's jaggedness is closely related to a momentous harmonic event: Bach has taken the piece from the opening key of G minor to its relative major, B-flat, and this point signals the start of a modulation toward the dominant key of D minor.

> Lesson #8: A piece's structural arc, made of an interplay of tension and relaxation, gives you clues on how to husband your own energies as a performer. Pace yourself as the composer paces his compositions.

One way to improve your joinery is to isolate a sentence fragment that includes the joint in between patterns, and become comfortable "speaking" the musical word that corresponds to the joint. Example 10.22 can be broken up into four word-like units, which we number "1234." The fourth word is the joint between patterns. Speak each word with calm deliberation. Use the upbeats' energies to connect each word to the next. Exaggerate the pull of $\frac{6}{16}$ on bar 29 and the pull of $\frac{3}{8}$ on bar 30. This will help you feel, physically, what is happening musically.

EXAMPLE 10.22. "1 2 3 4"

Every journey is smoother if you know where you're going and how you're getting there. For this reason, joinery is made easier if you work from the end of a passage (in other words, the journey's destination) back to its beginning. In the case of our current sentence fragment, it means inverting "1234" into "4321."

🔊 This exercise is illustrated in audio clip #19, "4321."

Take the last word and repeat it a few times. Take the last word plus the one that precedes it, and repeat them a few times. Continue this way until you have reached the beginning of the passage (example 10.23).

EXAMPLE 10.23. "4 3 2 1"

4 ... 4 ... 4;
3 4 ... 3 4 ... 3 4;
2 3 4 ... 2 3 4 ... 2 3 4;
1 2 3 4 ... 1 2 3 4 ... 1 2 3 4.

Joints between patterns tend to involve interesting rhythmic and prosodic events. If you understand what's going on rhythmically, you'll become better able to navigate the joints' technical challenges. In bar 34 the meter changes again. This time it doesn't go back to $\frac{6}{16}$ as we might reasonably expect; instead it becomes $\frac{3}{4}$. More precisely, two bars in $\frac{3}{8}$ are fused into a single bar in $\frac{3}{4}$, after which the meter shifts back to $\frac{3}{8}$.

It's conventionally assumed that a bar's downbeat receives a metric stress. If you take the information on the printed page literally, you'd consider the B-flat on the downbeat of measure 34 a metrically stressed note. But the melodic shape of bars 34 and 35 seem to indicate that the metric accents ought to fall on the D, the G, and the C-sharp at the end of each group of four slurred notes. To put it simply, Bach composed a hemiola: two groups of three eighth notes (the normal construction of a $\frac{3}{8}$ bar) have become three groups of two eighth notes (the normal construction of a $\frac{3}{4}$ bar).

The way information is imparted inevitably affects how we interpret it. The design of signs in a bus station can make you confident about where to go or confused and even lost. We read CAPITALIZED words differently from **bold** or *italics*. Bach's hemiola is rendered confusing by its orthography, as it were; the bar line marking the downbeat of measure 34 shouldn't really be there. Train your eye to ignore the misleading information, or actually rewrite the passage to eliminate its distractions (example 10.24).

Whether or not you choose to rewrite the passage, play it under tempo and exaggerate its metric construction: a primary metric accent on the A (downbeat of measure 33), secondary accents on the D and G, and a new primary accent on the C-sharp (downbeat of measure 35).

🔊 This exercise is illustrated in audio clip #20, "The Hemiola in Bars 33 and 34."

Now manage all the excerpt's challenges from bars 29 to 37 in succession (example 10.25).

EXAMPLE 10.24. Hemiolas

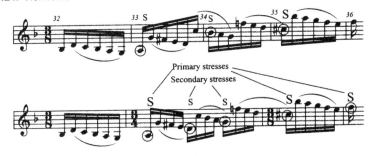

EXAMPLE 10.25. Joining fragments

This exercise is illustrated in audio clip #21, "Joinery."

You can take time at the downbeat of measure 32 since it's a cadence, and at the downbeat of measure 33 since it marks a change of meter. Travel deliberately from stress to stress, landing comfortably on a metric stress and rebounding off it to reach the next one. Use inflection and punctuation to create space inside the musical text, so that notes and measures—or your thoughts and gestures—don't run into one another.

> Lesson #9: Every problem contains the seeds of its own solution. Metric challenges cause you to lose your head, and yet a clear understanding of metric constructions can actually help you coordinate yourself.

After the $\frac{3}{4}$ bar the meter changes back to $\frac{3}{8}$. The new pattern is two bars long, repeated four times. It juxtaposes the descending scale from measure 5 and the intervallic design from measure 30. The sequence is broken off in measure 42 with a pattern of descending arpeggios. The preceding pattern lasted two bars and was repeated four times; the new one lasts one bar and is repeated three times. In effect the new pattern is a form of acceleration: the pattern is shorter, its sequence is also shorter, and the pattern itself is somewhat jagged (example 10.26).

We've dealt with similar challenges before, and we found a solution thanks to step progressions. Starting with the C-sharp on the downbeat of measure 35, the downbeat of every two bars belongs to a step progression in the form of a descending scale. At bar 43, the step progression accelerates, from one note every two bars to two notes per bar. But it's the music that should "rush," not the musician!

EXAMPLE 10.26. Patterns and step progressions

ARCHITECTURAL ELEMENTS

By manipulating building blocks, skillful builders can determine how uniform or how varied their building will be. Measure 46 contains a descending scale that has been used in several contexts. Isolate all instances of this building block, and perform them in sequence. Prove to yourself that you can play them with a uniform sound and articulation. If afterward you decide to play them in a varied manner, it'll be by choice rather than by accident (example 10.27).

🔊 This exercise is illustrated in audio clip #22, "Architectural Elements."

Our next pattern is one bar long, repeated four times (example 10.28).

The pedal-point A, sounded on the downbeat of three of these four measures, is the dominant of D minor. On the one hand the pedal point says, "Listen to me, I'm the dominant of D minor! You *must agree* that we can only be in D minor!" On the other hand, it prepares the return to the beginning of the piece, which of course is in G minor.

EXAMPLE 10.27. Architectural elements

EXAMPLE 10.28. A pedal point on the dominant

The moment the violinist takes the repeat, all that talk of D minor goes out of the window. It's a dramatic and highly meaningful procedure. For it to work, however, the section must end with a Picardy third—that is, a chord of D major rather than the expected D minor.

Many Baroque pieces (as well as sections of pieces, as in our example) in minor keys end with a major chord. One of the reasons is acoustic, having to do with the harmonic series, which we study in detail in chapters 16 and 17. Another reason is the struggle between the tonic and dominant chords, which is at the core of tonal music. The D-major chord works as a clear dominant in G minor; a D-minor chord, lacking the leading tone F-sharp, doesn't point toward G minor with the same urgency.

UNRESOLVED AMBIGUITIES

Baroque pieces in triple meters often end with a hemiola, in which two bars of $\frac{3}{8}$ become a bar of $\frac{3}{4}$ or two bars of $\frac{3}{4}$ become a bar of $\frac{3}{2}$. Here are two clear examples from other pieces by Bach for solo violin: the end of the Sarabande in B minor from the first Partita, BWV 1002, and the end of the Chaconne in D minor from the second Partita, BWV 1004 (example 10.29).

Is it possible that our piece also ends with a hemiola? Test it by performing it in two different ways: as two bars of $\frac{3}{8}$, and as one bar of $\frac{3}{4}$. The metric accents must be different in each version. In $\frac{3}{8}$, the downbeat of measure 53 (the high A) receives a metric accent; in $\frac{3}{4}$, the downbeat of 53 is unaccented but the D in measure 52 and the A in measure 53 receive secondary metric accents (example 10.30).

🔊 This exercise is illustrated in audio clip #23, "The Closing Hemiola."

EXAMPLE 10.29. Two hemiolas

EXAMPLE 10.30. Hemiola or not?

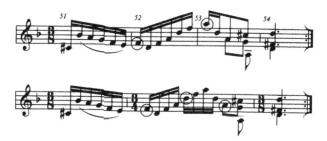

A case can be made for $\frac{3}{8}$: The high A at the downbeat of 53 is a melodic climax that begs for a stress. A case can be made for $\frac{3}{4}$: The eighth notes in bar 53 are exceptional in a piece otherwise filled exclusively with running sixteenth notes, and the first of those two eighth notes is surely worthy of receiving a metric stress.

Some performers would simply play it "as they feel it." Others would say, "If Bach wrote it in $\frac{3}{8}$, it *must* be in $\frac{3}{8}$." Some would study the question and choose one version over the other after due reflection. Some would delight in the ambiguity of the passage, performing it with a subtle mix of melodic, agogic, and metric accents. Some would play the passage in $\frac{3}{8}$ the first time around and in $\frac{3}{4}$ when it is repeated. There are many valid possibilities. There are also some "invalid" possibilities, one of which is fumbling through the passage in ignorance of its richness.

> Lesson #10: To become a master of your choices takes hard work. You need a clear head to see the choices at your disposal, multiple tools to put every choice into practice, and the courage to assume the consequences of your choices.

THE GRID, YET AGAIN

Bach uses two types of bar lines: a short one after one bar and a normal one after two bars, alternating throughout the piece with absolute regularity. Is it possible that Bach wants us to consider the entire piece as being built upon a regular series of two-bar units? Should there be two different metric accents alternating throughout the piece, one heavier, one lighter? Might the piece really be in $\frac{6}{8}$ and $\frac{12}{16}$, rather than $\frac{3}{8}$ and $\frac{6}{16}$?

The two types of bar lines may or may not be important, or they may be important some of the time but not always. All information must be interpreted in context, and we know this piece is complex and filled with metric ambiguities. It'd be surprising if the bar lines themselves carried no complexities or ambiguities.

In certain passages the two-bar construction is straightforward. The pattern of ascending arpeggios starting in measure 17 is perfectly organized in trochaic two-bar units, in which the first bar represents "STRESS" and the second "release." The section starting in measure 35 is also organized in two-bar units, but they contain much more rhythmic and melodic variety. An overly trochaic impetus of STRESS-release for these two-bar units would be unsatisfying, since the units' musical tension begs to be sustained over the bar, not released immediately after the first downbeat.

EXAMPLE 10.31. Two-bar units

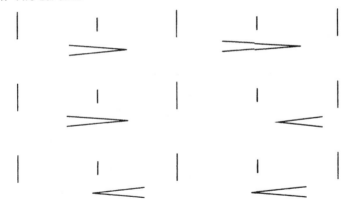

In the section from measure 17 onward, the heavier downbeats are starting points for the ascending arpeggios. In the section from measure 35 onward, the downbeats seem to play a double role, as starting points but also destinations; the tensions within the two-bar unit might resolve at the following downbeat, implying an iambic impetus of preparation-STRESS.

Go back to the beginning of the piece. Suppose we embrace the two-bar organization of the phrase and choose to give primary metric accents to the downbeats of measures 1, 3, 5, 7, and 9, and secondary accents to measures 2, 4, 5, and 8. What happens *in between* the downbeats? Look at the ascending arpeggio that culminates with the G at the downbeat of measure 5. Few violinists would fail to play a crescendo for the ascending arpeggio, which would then become a de facto upbeat to the high G.

The grid of repeated two-bar units is never-changing, but what Bach writes into the grid is ever-changing. He varies the distribution of tensions within each bar, within each two-bar unit, between units, and at the end of sequences and phrases. Suppose you removed the time signature and the bar lines and played the piece *ad libitum*—in other words, suppose you took away the grid and lessened the opposition between order and disorder. The piece would be less of a masterpiece, and much less fun to play.

With a pencil, circle the downbeat of every second bar, which all receive primary metric accents. Then study how Bach prepares them, leads to them, bounces off them, and links them in superbar sequences (example 10.31).

FURTHER STUDY OF PATTERNING AND SEQUENCING

In this chapter we have studied the first half of the piece. Now we have a pretty clear idea of its structure and how to practice and perform it. What about the second half (example 10.32)?

Bach hews to the principle of patterning and sequencing. He creates further melodic, prosodic, and harmonic complications, crowding more information into the phrases and accelerating the pace of patterns and sequences alike. I leave it to you to analyze the

EXAMPLE 10.32. J. S. Bach: Sonata for Solo Violin, BWV 1001 in G Minor, Presto (second half

section by yourself, using the chapter's lessons and exercises. If you aren't a violinist, remember that you have several choices at your disposal, only one of which is to team up with a violinist friend and study the piece together.

Patterning and sequencing aren't the exclusive domain of J. S. Bach. In a short piece by Arnold Schoenberg, melodic shapes, rhythms, meters, and dynamics change so quickly that you can't discern the repeating elements that comprise patterns and sequences of the sort we have just considered. But close examination will show that Schoenberg's pieces are as intricately and tightly patterned as anything by Bach, perhaps even more so. To learn the specific language of each composer, era, or style takes time and effort, but your task is easier if you understand that what underpins most compositions is the phenomenon of patterning and sequencing.

PART II

COORDINATION

CHAPTER 11

CONNECTION AND FLOW

First Principles

LAYERS OF CONNECTION

As you go through daily life, you tend to perceive your various body parts in relative isolation, according to what you're doing from moment to moment. You punch in a phone number, and you sense your fingertips pressing against the phone's keypad. You walk along a potholed sidewalk in the rain, and you're more or less aware of your legs and feet as you negotiate the traps along the way. You carry a heavy laptop bag while rushing through an airport, and you feel your neck and shoulders straining under the effort. But these perceptions are somewhat misleading, as they distract you from sensing that, in truth, every part of your body is interconnected.

A violinist who plays a trill using two fingers of her left hand is, in fact, using both hands, both arms, both shoulders, and her head, neck, back, and legs at the same time. If she doesn't direct her back and legs to support her upper body, she'll compensate unconsciously by stiffening her neck and shoulders, thereby affecting the fingers of her left hand. If she doesn't command her right arm to bow smoothly and steadily, her left hand will lose some of its own stability. If she sways her pelvis forward and backward, she'll hollow her lower back and shorten her spine. Directly or indirectly, all these misuses will affect her trill.

The principle is universal: Every part of your body plays at least some role in every gesture of yours, and it's impossible for you to use any body part in total isolation. In making music and in your daily life, you need to sense, activate, and nourish the connections that exist naturally between all the parts of the body.

These bodily connections can't exist without a connection between your gestures and your intentions—that is, between your body and your mind. As our violinist trills, a whole mental, emotional, and aesthetic impulse animates the lifting and dropping of every finger. It can't be otherwise, just as a child's laughter can't be anything other than an action of her whole self.

In ideal coordination there's a natural, organic connection from gesture to gesture. A cat walks around your backyard. Suddenly it smells its prey. It breaks into a fast run, jumps and catches a bird, lands on its feet again, comes to a stop, and eats its dinner. Each action is different from the ones that precede and follow it, but they all belong together in a continuous flow of energy and motion. Whether you're an instrumentalist, a singer, or a conductor, your music making can and must embody the same principle of connection. (In the next chapter we'll study the Cat's Leap, an exercise designed to improve continuity of gesture.)

Leading an electrifying interpretation of a complex work of art, a conductor shows no gaps in his or her thinking. Thoughts follow one another in an unbroken chain of imagination, perception, insight, and gesture. The orchestra responds to the wholeness of his or her approach with its own collective wholeness. In ideal coordination, thoughts are interconnected, gestures are interconnected, and thoughts and gestures are one and the same.

Sometime after murdering Hamlet's father, Claudius starts feeling pangs of regret. He prays, but he's disturbed and insincere. In a famous couplet, he acknowledges the disconnection between his sentiments and his prayer, between his thoughts and his words:

My words fly up, my thoughts remain below;
Words without thoughts never to heaven go.[1]

Only too often a musician's words fly up, yet his thoughts remain below. For all the hustle and bustle of his performance, he says nothing, and his words don't reach heaven. To be well-coordinated means to say what you think and think what you say, establishing in your discourse a connection from sentiment to thought, from thought to thought, from thought to word, and from word to word. To coordinate yourself in performance, then, you need to find a connection between the musical text and yourself. You must understand the text, speak it well, and mean every word of it—every note in every measure, however short or fast. Further, you must find within the text itself the very energies that animate your gestures.

Every sound is the manifestation of some sort of connection: between you and your instrument, for instance, or between your breath and your vocal mechanism. We study sound in detail in part III of the book. For now it's enough to note that there's no sound without connection, and a healthy sound is the result of healthy connections.

In short, connection is everything. Here's a brief summary of the connections you must develop:

- Connections between body parts (finger to hand, hand to arm, arm to shoulder to back to legs . . .).
- Connections between body and mind, between intention and gesture, between what you think and what you do.
- Connections from thought to thought and from gesture to gesture.
- Connections from note to note as you sing or play.
- Connections between you and the physical world, including a connection between you and your instrument or voice.
- Connections between you and the composer, and between you and your audience.

Connection and disconnection are visible, audible, and tangible. You can see the cat's connections as it runs and hunts. You can hear a child's connections when she laughs. You can feel the connections between your back and legs when you carry a heavy weight. Similarly, you can see the conductor's disconnections when he squirms in front of his orchestra; you can hear the disconnections in a poor singer, huffing and puffing from note to note; you can feel the disconnections in your own body when stage fright causes your legs to shake.

AN INTRODUCTION TO THE ALEXANDER TECHNIQUE

Many of the principles and procedures in *Integrated Practice* are inspired by the Alexander Technique, a method of self-awareness developed by Frederick Matthias Alexander (1869–1955). My companion volume *Indirect Procedures: A Musician's Guide to the Alexander Technique* covers it in detail. Here I introduce its basic principles briefly.

1. END-GAINING

If ideal coordination springs from connection, why do we disconnect? Many answers have been suggested, including education, imitation, the stress of modern life, lack of time, and so on. But if misuse is what we *do*, its origin lies in what we *wish* to do, since an intention animates every gesture. And, by and large, we wish to attain quick, easy, measurable, direct results in all that we do. Alexander called the universal tendency for us to set wrong goals or to pursue a goal in the wrong manner *end-gaining*.

End-gaining is so prevalent that we take it for granted. Economic policy and political discourse, for instance, are often affected by the end-gaining of officials who try to produce short-term results despite the long-term costs to the nation. A tennis player who, overly keen on the win, smashes the ball into the net, has committed a small act of end-gaining. A young artist decides to paint splashy canvases like Jackson Pollock or geometrical ones like Piet Mondrian. But Pollock and Mondrian arrived at their mature styles after long, organic processes; to imitate the results of their processes is to end-gain.

End-gaining is present in every aspect of music making. There exists an end-gaining rubato, an end-gaining vibrato, an end-gaining way to turn a page or bow to the audience. The philosopher Roland Barthes didn't use the term "end-gaining," but he talked about the same thing when he described the baritone Gérard Souzay singing Gabriel Fauré:

> [H]aving to sing, for instance, the words *tristesse affreuse* ["terrible sadness"], he is not content with the simple semantic content of these words, nor with the musical line which supports them: he must further dramatize the phonetics of the *affreux*, must suspend and then explode the double fricative, releasing misery in the very density of the letters; no one can ignore the fact that it is a question of particularly terrible pangs. Unfortunately, this pleonasm of intentions muffles both word and music, and chiefly their junction, which is the very object of the vocal art.[2]

Barthes went on to note the literal-mindedness of such a performance, the surfeit of exaggerated details, and above all the performer's lack of confidence in the work of art to make its own case. Ideally, the listeners ought to be given a chance to find out for themselves what mysteries the work of art holds and to respond with their own emotions. Instead they're force-fed the emotions of the end-gaining performer.

The simple act of moving from a standing to a sitting position illustrates end-gaining to perfection. You sit down as if looking for the chair with your buttocks; the chair itself is your desired end, which you pursue unthinkingly and inattentively. In the process you contract the head into the neck, lift and round the shoulders, and hollow the lower back. To stop end-gaining, you need to give up your immediate goal altogether and go through a number of intermediate steps and indirect procedures. In the case of sitting and standing, these may include suspending the action for some time; becoming aware of the assumptions you make about where the chair may be and how to reach it; executing gestures seemingly unrelated to sitting and standing; and approaching the chair in a spirit of open-minded curiosity, until you "forget" how to end-gain when sitting and find yourself moving in a totally new way. In time, these procedures—many of which I describe throughout the book—help you sense, understand, and eliminate your end-gaining not only when sitting and standing, but in everything that you do.

2. FAULTY SENSORY AWARENESS AND HABIT

Two interrelated obstacles make it difficult to conquer end-gaining. First, most people are unaware of how they use and misuse themselves. You may have had the experience of watching yourself on video and exclaiming, "That isn't me! I can't possibly look and sound like that!" Alexander called this *faulty sensory awareness*, a universal phenomenon that plays a fundamental role in his pedagogy.

Muscles, joints, and tendons have sense organs called *proprioceptors*, which send feedback to the nervous system about the position of a body part relative to the rest of the body, and the effort being made to achieve, maintain, or change that position. Let's call *proprioception* your body's sense of itself, which determines your sense of your whole self. The neck muscles are particularly well supplied with proprioceptors. If you misuse your head and neck, your proprioception ceases to be reliable, thereby affecting your sensations of position, movement, balance, effort, and fatigue. The more you misuse yourself, the less reliable your sensory awareness becomes. And as your sense impressions grow ever more inaccurate, your use deteriorates accordingly.

The second obstacle to change is habit. We get so used to our gestures, our voices, and our smells that we end up ignoring them. We don't pay attention to the habitual in the misguided hope of being better able to process and understand the unfamiliar. Habit, sensory awareness, and the way we use and misuse ourselves are intimately related. We misunderstand information and react wrongly to it, which causes us to misunderstand the next batch of information and react wrongly again. How to break this vicious circle? Alexander had a good idea, which he called *non-doing* or *inhibition*.

3. NON-DOING AND INHIBITION

The child at play, the wild animal evading its hunter, and the athlete preparing to pole-vault all have a degree of choice in what they do. They can wait, sense, process information, and decide (however quickly or slowly) what to do; or they can rush or stumble into reaction before sensing and processing the information at hand. Alexander named the process of refusing to react in a habitual and automatic manner *inhibition*.

Most people think of inhibition as the unhealthy suppression of emotion: "He's a very inhibited little boy." But physiology uses the same word to mean simply the contrary of "excitation." In movement, for instance, a body part can be excited or inhibited; you excite your arm into movement, you inhibit your shoulder from stiffening at the same time. The dictionary defines inhibition as "any of a variety of processes that are associated with the gradual attenuation, masking, and extinction of a previously conditioned response." Wouldn't it be wonderful to attenuate and extinguish a nasty habit you have spent years suffering from?

The cheetah that stalks its prey and waits for the right moment to pounce demonstrates an innate capacity to inhibit. We too are born with this instinctive attribute, which we use as a matter of course. Every time you go on stage, for instance, you "inhibit in action," making hundreds of decisions "to do" or "not to do" while performing. As with all of your innate capabilities, you can develop and refine your inhibition, learning how to keep the channels of energy and direction continuously open.

Since your reactions are animated (consciously or not) by your intentions and desires, you can't change your reactions if you don't change the intentions and desires behind them. What makes your neck stiff and your shoulders tight? The culprit may be your desire to produce an effect in the audience and to "express your emotions." If you'd like to free your neck and your shoulders, you may have no choice but to change your aesthetic goals. Truth be told, passing from habit to freedom is very difficult, since your habitual "doing" feels familiar and safe while the "non-doing" of inhibition feels strange and threatening. It takes time, thought, and dedication to master this fundamental principle.

4. DIRECTION AND FLOW

When you shake someone's hand, you receive enough information to draw a partial portrait of the person's temperament and character. The handshake contains qualities such as temperature, humidity, and skin texture. It also contains muscular energies that you perceive as being floppy, hard, pointy, supple, and so on. Similar energies are present throughout the body, in ever-changing combinations of contraction and expansion that are unique to each individual; the handshake is only one example of how the energies manifest themselves. Alexander called these energies *directions*.

Directions are independent of bodily positions. Two people standing next to each other in similar postures may be directing their energies differently, one heavy and sluggish, the other nimble and ready for action. Directions prepare and guide movement. Well-directed movement flows with good energy, while misdirected movement disperses energy or blocks it.

Healthy direction depends on the opposition between different forces. If not harmonized, these antagonistic pulls put the body out of whack. If harmonized, however, they give you tremendous power. For instance, you can direct your head toward the ceiling and your coccyx toward the floor, causing your spine to lengthen; and direct your left shoulder leftward and your right shoulder rightward, causing your back to widen. We'll study opposition throughout the next chapters.

Like inhibiting, directing is an innate capacity that you can develop to a higher level of efficiency. Inhibition and direction are closely intertwined. To inhibit is to say, "I will not do *this one thing*," and to direct is to say, "Let me make *all these things* possible." This double decision-making process determines the outcome of all your actions.

5. THE PRIMARY CONTROL

Watch a baby attempting to stand on her legs and walk. Unless the baby finds out how to "wear" her head and neck, she won't be able to maintain her balance. The head and neck, then, act as a *primary control* in the coordination of the whole body.

Given the right conditions, all positions of the head and neck can be healthy. Visiting the Sistine Chapel and admiring the frescoes on its ceiling, you tilt your head backward in order to look at the artwork. If you let the weight of the head bear down on the neck, you'll shorten your neck and disconnect it from the spine. But if you direct your head up toward the ceiling even as you tilt it back in space, you'll protect your neck and lengthen your spine. In itself, then, tilting the head back is by no means harmful.

The primary control is the first step in creating a circuit of connections between all body parts. The circuit works very much like a grid, organizing your flow of energy, breath, movement, and sound. As with all grids, there exist an opposition between the relatively rigid grid and the fluid and unpredictable energies that push against it. If you wish to maximize your flow, work on your connections. And if you wish to maximize your connections, work on your oppositions. Figures 11.1 and 11.2 show two well-connected individuals flowing to the brim with the energy of opposing forces.

THE PROSODY OF GESTURE

Make a partial list of the actions you performed in the past few hours: reading a few pages in a book; sitting, standing, and sitting again; making a phone call. Every action contains multiple rhythmic elements such as duration, speed, upbeats, and downbeats. Wherever there is rhythm, there's a prosody that clarifies its organization. If the prosody of a language is the study of its rhythms and the way they relate to all other elements of style, the prosody of the self is the study of your rhythms and interaction with all other elements in your style.

FIGURE 11.1. Marianne at play.

FIGURE 11.2. Arthur at play.

Prosody concerns itself with integration, separation, and direction. What parts of speech or music belong together in units of varying sizes, organized hierarchically? How are those units articulated? Where do those units point to? The same questions can be asked of your coordination. What parts of your body belong together, in integrated units that are organized hierarchically? Your neck and spine form one such unit; so do your back and shoulders, and your back and pelvis. What parts of your body are articulated? There are dozens of joints throughout your body, and although they all ought to be bendable, not all of them should bend at all times. To find out where your joints are and how best to use them is to find out points of integration and separation throughout the body. How will you direct each part of your body, and all parts together in a complex ensemble? The head goes forward and up, the back opposes it; the shoulders go outward, one in opposition to the other; the spine lengthens upward, the lower back opposes it downward. Integration, separation, and direction—the main tools of linguistic and musical prosody—are also the main tools of the prosody of gesture.

Your life is a multiplicity of rhythms. Some are fast, others slow; some are habitually recurrent, others dependent on context. At the same time that you live your own rhythms, you must deal with the rhythms of the people you interact with, the rhythms of daily obligations, the rhythms of the seasons, and so on. To be in good health is to navigate all these rhythms in the best possible way, in sync with their ever-changing flow. Good health means knowing to listen to all rhythms; knowing when to follow, when to lead, when to allow, when to impede; knowing when to ride a rhythmic pull, when to counter it, when to evade it. Finding the proper rhythm for your actions means letting rhythm itself do most of the work for you. Throughout the next chapters we'll study the prosody of gesture and the road to its mastery.

CHAPTER 12

THE JUGGLER

A Cello Lesson

In this chapter you'll draw inspiration from the art of juggling and learn how to take care of many musical and technical challenges at the same time. You'll learn how to sit comfortably and how to develop latent mobility and latent resistance. You'll start your study of pronation and supination in the use of the arms. The question of sound will come up briefly—we'll study it in detail in later chapters. You'll learn or relearn seven simple but effective practice strategies. You'll learn the Cat's Leap, an exercise that provides a showcase for the basic principles of all exercises you'll ever practice. You'll study bilateral and quadrilateral transfer, which is the essential dialogue between your arms and your legs. Finally, you'll learn how to integrate technical exercises, improvisation, and repertoire in practice.

MUSIC IS JUGGLING

A juggler spins a plate on top of a long stick until the plate achieves dynamic equilibrium. She then inserts the stick, together with the plate, in a hole on a wooden horse. She spins a second plate on top of another stick until the plate is balanced, then inserts the stick in a second hole on the wooden horse. She spins a third, fourth, and fifth plate, by which time the first is beginning to wobble. She runs back to it and spins it afresh. Then she spins a sixth plate and a seventh one. By now the second and third plates are wobbling, so she runs back and revives their momentum. The act goes on, ever more excitingly and dangerously, until she has balanced fifteen plates on top of fifteen sticks, inserted in three wooden horses. It takes dexterity, alertness, and sangfroid to accomplish this exploit. Although the juggler rushes from plate to plate as if desperate not to break anything, she does so only to entertain the public, since she's in absolute control of her act. The plates spin, but her head doesn't!

In many ways, musicians are like jugglers, attending to a large number of challenges in alternation and in combination. Like jugglers, musicians need dexterity, alertness, and

FIGURE 12.1. Roberta.

FIGURE 12.2. Antonio Janigro.

sangfroid. And, also like jugglers, musicians need to become so comfortable with their skills that making music doesn't feel like a desperate attempt not to break anything.

Some aspects of music are universal to all musicians. Others are specific to each player or singer. Universal aspects include the following:

1. The unselfconscious awareness of the whole body.
2. The orientation of the head, neck, and spine.
3. Sitting and standing positions.
4. The body's latent resistance and latent mobility.
5. The coordination of all limbs and their collaboration with one another.
6. The details of music itself: notes, rhythmic patterns, nuances, and so on.

Now I'll make a partial list of the specific plates a cellist needs to juggle. For yourself, make a list covering your own needs as an instrumentalist, singer, or conductor. Your list doesn't need to be exhaustive. The important thing is to appreciate the juggling metaphor and use it constructively.

7. The comfortable placement of the cello in its playing position.
8. Left-hand techniques such as articulation, changes of position, finger extensions, intonation, vibrato, and so on.
9. Right-hand techniques such as drawing the bow along a precise path, crossing strings, legato and staccato, and so on.

Examine the images of an emblematic plate breaker whom we'll call Roberta, depicted by the painter Robert Berény in 1928; and the Italian concert artist Antonio Janigro (1918–1989), who juggles all his plates with great ease (figures 12.1 and 12.2).

It's possible that Roberta is just a painter's model holding the cello for the first time in her life, and yet her posture is typical of many working cellists. I'll take the liberty of retaining Roberta as an imaginary but plausible cellist to whom I give lessons in the art of plate spinning.

RESISTANCE AND MOBILITY

Let's compare our two models from head to toe. Janigro wears his head high, atop an elongated spine. His neck and spine form a single unit, and his head appears mobile and unconfined. Roberta's head and neck look as if fused together, and they hang forward and down, breaking the line between the neck and spine. Janigro's head leads his body into expansion, Roberta's into contraction.

Janigro integrates his shoulders into a unit with his back, and he doesn't lift them when he uses his arms. Roberta lifts and contracts her shoulders, and whenever she moves her arms she moves the shoulders with them. Janigro's elbows and wrists are harmoniously organized, and his lengthened fingers are active only to the degree needed to do their work. Roberta raises her elbows and twists her wrists, and hers hands grip the bow and fingerboard with excessive force.

Janigro's cello rests lightly on his legs, leaving them unimpeded. His feet are in firm yet light contact with the floor, allowing him to stand up at once if he wanted. Roberta splays her legs, impeding the mobility of her whole body. She chokes the cello with her knees, reducing its resonance. Her ankles are twisted in a mirror image of her wrists, and her heels and toes are positioned so that the feet seem to be hindering the body rather than helping it. It'd be an effort to stand up from this position.

Roberta needs to coordinate herself before she can handle the cello, so she and I start our work with the sitting position, minus the cello. With the help of a partner, you can reproduce and practice these exercises.

Many musicians practice and perform sitting with their backs leaning against the back of the chair. It seems paradoxical at first, but to release wrong tensions in the neck, shoulders, and arms you need to *increase* the right tensions in your back and legs—right in quantity, quality, placing, and timing. To awaken your back, sit fairly far forward on the chair, resting the weight of your trunk more on your sitting bones than on your thighs and allowing the back to remain erect on its own, rather than propped by the chair.

After Roberta arranges herself in this position, I stand behind her and apply gentle pressure to her body, asking her to resist me. I push her down with both my hands on her shoulders, then I push her forward with a fist in between her shoulder blades. By resisting my pressure, Roberta connects her back to her shoulders, her spine to her pelvis, and her pelvis to her legs and feet, distributing and projecting her energies throughout her body. If I stop applying pressure to her body, Roberta retains *latent resistance*, or the capacity to resist again immediately if so needed.

While resisting my pressure, Roberta is free to turn her head in every direction, stand and sit again, rock from side to side, lean her trunk forward and backward from the hip joints, or turn her trunk in circles, half-circles, or ellipses clock- and counterclockwise. If she chooses not to move, she retains *latent mobility*, or the capacity to move in any way she wishes at any time. Latent resistance and latent mobility become basic plates that Roberta must spin at all times.

A chain of events with a clear cause-and-effect relationship takes place when I apply pressure to Roberta's back. By resisting my pressure, she creates connections between many body parts. Her connections allow for the release of energy: the spine lengthens, knotty spots on the back and shoulders soften, breath flows more easily. Roberta's sound gains in strength and richness, her rhythm becomes stable, and her phrasing becomes more coherent. Let's call the chain of events *pressure, resistance, connection,* and *release.* To facilitate the release of sound, energy, movement, emotion, or thought, you must work on resistance and connection, not on the release—which does itself!

SITTING AND ROCKING

I ask Roberta to perform one of the most useful of all exercises: to rock from side to side while seated.

🅰 The exercise is illustrated in four video clips: #23, "Sitting & Rocking I: The Basics," #24, "Sitting & Rocking II: At the Cello," and, at the piano, #25, "Sitting & Rocking III: From the Side," and #26, "Sitting & Rocking IV: From the Back."

Suppose I offer you a glass of water. By accepting it, you run a few risks. The glass or the water might be unclean. The glass might slip out of your hands and shatter on the floor. You might dribble water on your blouse. These risks may be small, but they're present every time you drink a glass of water. Once you start thinking about it, you'll realize there are risks and dangers in every situation, without exception. It's impossible to do, say, or think anything that's completely free from all risk. Nevertheless, it's possible to learn how to detect and navigate the risks inherent in each situation. When practicing any exercise, make a mental list of its risks and dangers and determine how best to navigate them. Then the exercise will become constructive.

While rocking sideways, you risk moving your head too far to the side, thereby disconnecting the neck from the spine. How to navigate this danger? Imagine that your head is a piece of metal, and the ceiling a powerful magnet. At the same time, imagine that your coccyx is another piece of metal, and the floor another powerful magnet. Your head and coccyx are magnetized in opposite directions, and your spine becomes elongated and yet supple, since the magnetic forces don't actually lock your head in a fixed position. Now you can move without losing the all-important connections between the neck and the spine. We'll call the magnetic pulls of the head and neck the *primary directions*, since they affect the coordination of the whole body.

Keeping the buttocks glued to the chair when you rock sideways prevents the pelvis from following the back in movement, thereby breaking up their connection—which is as important as the connection between the neck and the spine. How to navigate this danger?

Lifting the right buttock when you lean leftward and the left when you lean rightward will help the pelvis and back stay connected.

While rocking you risk stiffening your legs and feet in an attempt not to lose your balance. How to navigate this danger? Actively engage your legs and feet on purpose. When rocking rightward, gently push your left foot down and point your left knee out; when rocking leftward, use your right foot and knee in the same way.

Correctly performed, rocking allows sitting to become a comfortable position. You don't need to actually rock, but just to know how to do it and to be ready to do so at a moment's notice. *Latent rocking* infuses your body with latent mobility and resistance. Add it as an important plate in your juggling act, and remember that your primary directions make or break the exercise.

THE INSTRUMENT AND THE ARMS

I ask Roberta to place the cello in its playing position. She senses the instrument as a sort of invasive presence, and she twists her head, neck, and back as a result. Roberta thinks she needs to "work on the cello," but in fact she needs to "work on herself at the cello." When she manages to make herself the priority and the cello a secondary concern, she begins to handle the instrument as a friendly presence against her body. Her back meets the cello's gentle pressure with gentle resistance, and the cello's pressure becomes another plate for her to spin permanently.

In ideally coordinated people, the arms support the back as much as the back supports the arms; good dancers and athletes demonstrate the point whenever they perform. Roberta will use her back better and rock sideways more easily if she puts her arms to action. I ask her to place her left fingers on the fingerboard and her bow on the string, but she starts worrying about the arms and neglects her head and neck—with predictable results. The only solution is to backtrack to the beginning of the sequence and spin all plates in order. It goes like this:

1. Head, neck, and back;
2. Head, neck, and back, plus latent resistance and mobility;
3. Head, neck, and back, plus latent resistance and mobility, plus latent rocking sideways;
4. Head, neck, and back, plus latent resistance and mobility, plus latent rocking sideways, plus the cello against the body;
5. Head, neck, and back, plus latent resistance and mobility, plus rocking sideways, plus the cello against the body, plus the arms and hands.

The arms can rotate in two directions, called *pronation* and *supination*. Stand with your arms hanging. To pronate the arms, rotate them so that your palms face back. To supinate the arms, rotate them so that the palms face forward. Now lift your arms in front of you. To pronate the arms, turn your palms toward the floor. To supinate the arms, turn your palms toward the ceiling. The words apply to other body parts such as the legs and feet, and to overall bodily positions. You're supine if you lie on your back, and prone if you lie on your stomach.

Pronate your arms in front of your body as if preparing to bounce a basketball, with elbows slightly bent and your palms facing downward. Within this position you can point your wrists out, bringing the little fingers in; or bring your wrists in, pointing your little fingers out. Janigro directs his arms with "elbows out, wrists in," while Roberta holds her arms with "elbows up, wrists out," creating plenty of tensions and distortions. Pronation and elbow-to-wrist opposition are two more plates for her to spin at all times.

🌀 Pronation and supination are the subject of a multipart video study. The following are the relevant clips:

#27, "Pronation & Supination I: Shoulders & Arms"
#28, "Pronation & Supination II: Arms & Hands"
#29, "Pronation & Supination III: Convex/Concave"#30, "Pronation & Supination IV: Resistance"
#31, "Pronation & Supination V: Direction"
#32, "Pronation & Supination VI: Movement"
#33, "Pronation & Supination VII: At the Viola"

In chapter 15 you'll find another section on pronation, with an exercise illustrated in video clips #56, "The Song of Pronation I: An Introduction," and #57, "The Song of Pronation II: An Application."

MAKING SOUNDS

Is it possible to make music without making any sounds? John Cage once composed a piece consisting of nothing but four minutes and thirty-three seconds of silence. Metaphysical notions apart, however, sound vies with rhythm as the most important element of music, as well as of a musician's individuality. Anatomy, coordination, habit, taste, instrument quality, hall acoustics, and dozens of other physical and psychological variables ensure that no two musicians could ever produce exactly the same sound.

The traditional approach to sound says, "First imagine a sound, then find the physical means to produce it." The problem is that the search for sound is often predetermined by taste and habit. You like or dislike that which you know already, and the unknown is often unimaginable. Each gesture you make produces its own sound. By simply exploring gesture, you may well be surprised by new, unplanned, and unimagined sounds.

The physical instrument itself has something to offer other than what you expect. I once knew an accomplished cellist who bought an expensive instrument. He tried to impose his imagined sounds on the new cello, but the instrument refused to produce them. In the ensuing struggle, the cellist developed serious tendonitis. When he let go of the preconceived, habitual sounds of his imagination, he was able to take the lead from the instrument itself and produce wholly new, free, and health-restoring sounds. Needless to say, there are many aspects to sound production other than the workings of one's imagination, and every musician needs many technical tools in order to produce healthy sounds. My point is that every gesture is animated by an intention, and if your intentions are rigid, so will be your gestures.

I ask Roberta to play an open string, sustaining a long note over a single bow stroke, drawing it slowly and as close to the bridge as possible, and making the note swell and diminish. It's at the same time the simplest and the most difficult of all exercises. Every millimeter along the way, Roberta risks scrunching her sound or letting the bow skid on the surface of the string. Producing a simple yet perfect tone becomes even harder once Roberta adds the left hand, intonation, vibrato, rhythm, changes of bow stroke, and so on. Meeting this challenge is so important that it merits several chapters. In chapters 16 and 17 we study the acoustic phenomenon of the *harmonic series*, which underpins the entire edifice of sound. In chapters 18 and 19 we study the *messa di voce*, the art of swelling and diminishing a tone.

A musician's preoccupation with sound is rightly all-consuming. Roberta, too, will pay permanent attention to her sound—a plate she'll spin ceaselessly whenever she plays the cello.

PRACTICE ROUTINES

Roberta would find it easier to spin all her plates at the same time if it felt to her as if they spun in slow motion. This is different from playing the cello slowly, of course; it's the psychological time that needs to slow down, not the actual physical actions. There exist several practice strategies to get there. They're illustrated on separate video clips using the Bourée from J. S. Bach's Third Suite for Solo Cello, BWV 1009 (example 12.1).

EXAMPLE 12.1. J. S. Bach: Third Suite for Solo Cello, BWV 1009 in C Major, Bourée

The first strategy consists in giving priority to the coordination of the whole body. Take time to sense your body, direct your head, neck, and back, and find your latent resistance and mobility—then play a few notes.

🔊 This exercise is illustrated in video clip #34, "Practice Routines I: Coordination."

Now give priority to sound. Take a few aspects from the piece—the key of C major, the piece's tempo and time signature—and play a simplified version of it. As you become attuned to the instrument's natural resonance, transform the simplified version into the actual piece.

🔊 This exercise is illustrated in video clip #35, "Practice Routines II: Sound."

We studied the exercise called Coincidence in chapter 5. It links your intentions with your gestures, and it trains your arms, hands, and fingers to become good speakers. Practice Coincidence with the left hand alone, for instance, thereby eliminating many of the coordinative challenges of playing the cello. This allows you to play up to tempo without breaking plates.

🔊 This exercise is illustrated in video clip #36, "Practice Routines III: Coincidence."

When you find a certain rhythm for your actions, the rhythm itself carries the actions forward. Rhythmic Solfège allows you to perform a cello-less version of the Bourée that captures the piece's rhythmic drive, which you can then ride in performance.

🔊 This exercise is illustrated in video clip #37, "Practice Routines IV: Solfège and Superbar."

Suppose you have to speak a text full of tongue twisters and complicated sounds. If you insert silences between words, you can say the words themselves at their normal speed while having time in between words to gather your wits.

🔊 This exercise is illustrated in video clip #38, "Practice Routines V: Delayed Continuity."

The feeling of a slow psychological time inside a fast-moving physical reality arises when you stay in the moment, not letting your mind rush forward or drag backward. In some disciplines you pay attention to your breathing in order to bring the mind to a state of calm focus. The focus comes not from breathing itself, but from the attention you pay to it. Breathing is one trigger of attentiveness; for this exercise we select listening. Establish a basic quality of sound that becomes the standard you'll uphold throughout your piece. Then match every note in the piece to the chosen standard. The attention to sound will focus the mind and bring you to the moment.

🔊 This exercise is illustrated in video clip #39, "Practice Routines VI: Norms."

Alternate and combine all these procedures. Then your performance will arise not from a determined effort of the conscious mind but from a playful, improvisatory attitude.

🔊 This exercise is illustrated in video clip #40, "Practice Routines VII: Improvisation."

THE CAT'S LEAP

In the previous chapter we watched an imaginary cat walking, running, and jumping in your backyard, and we marveled at the natural continuity of its gestures. Vocal and instrumental technique is much like the cat's actions: healthy when the gestures are connected and continuous, unhealthy when disconnected and jagged. I show Roberta an exercise that renders her left hand catlike. Keep in mind that Roberta's lessons are applicable to playing every instrument, to singing, and to conducting. Your effort to understand the universal behind the particular will pay great dividends! Go to the end of this section and read the list of seven universal principles illustrated by this exercise. If the principles seem useful to you, then you'll enjoy reading about the Cat's Leap whether or not you're a cellist.

🔊 This exercise is illustrated in video clip #41, "The Cat's Leap."

I ask Roberta to play the following sequence of notes, using the left hand alone (example 12.2).

EXAMPLE 12.2. The Cat's Leap

The exclamation mark means a gentle but audible percussive effect when the finger drops on the string. The cross means a left-hand pizzicato, in which the finger plucks the string. The numbers indicate fingers, string-player style: 1 (index), 2 (middle), 3 (ring), 4 (little), 0 (open string). The line between the first and second notes indicates that the index fingers stays down on the string as the hand changes position, causing a sliding sound or *glissando*. The Roman numeral indicates the string (in this case the A, the topmost cello string).

The cellist's left hand plays multiple roles. Alternately lifting and dropping, the fingers articulate specific notes—one at a time, or in double, triple, and quadruple stops. Fingers, wrist, hand, and arm collaborate on various kinds of vibrato, using oscillatory motions involving each joint along the arm. The fingers can pluck the string and produce a pizzicato. The hand and arm move up and down the fingerboard, changing positions and sounding higher or lower pitches. This list isn't exhaustive, but it covers everything we need for the exercise. Recapitulating, we can say that the left-hand actions include articulation, vibrato, pizzicato, and changes of position with or without glissando. The Cat's Leap engages these four capabilities.

It starts with a note articulated by the index finger as it drops on the string. Immediately after articulating the note, the arm oscillates, thereby creating a vibrato. There follows a change of position: the arm and hand travel along the fingerboard, going toward the bridge and away from the scroll. Once the hand arrives at the new position, it articulates a short grace note with the little finger. Immediately afterward, the little finger plucks the string, thereby sounding a new note, held by the index finger. Again the arm oscillates and creates a vibrato. Then the index finger plucks the string, sounding the open string. And the whole cycle starts anew.

A note ideally articulated contains a latent vibrato. One action is borne of the other, or, more precisely, the energies needed for one action encompass the energies needed for the other. The principle applies throughout the entire exercise: The ideal articulation also contains the energies needed for changing positions and for plucking the string with a pizzicato; the ideal change of position contains the energies needed for articulating new notes; the ideal pizzicato contains the energies needed for a vibrato. All left-hand functions spring from the same source, each function containing, latent within itself, all other functions. The operative word is "latent." Roberta doesn't need to vibrate every note that she ever articulates, but she needs to become *able* to do so at will.

The fingers' evident importance in instrumental technique distracts many musicians from sensing how much the whole body participates in each and every gesture. However strong an individual finger is and must be, it never acts separately from the arm and shoulder (and, less perceptible at first, the head, neck, back, and legs). Indeed, its very strength comes in part from its connection to the rest of the body. At first Roberta is tempted to "concentrate" on her fingers—or more radically still, on her fingertips. In time she learns to deploy the entire arm, which actually enhances her fingertips' sensitivity to the feel of the string and fingerboard.

Timing is crucial. The elbow moves with a reflex rebound almost immediately after the finger hits the string to articulate a note. Most important, it moves *because* the finger has hit the string, in reaction to it, in tandem with it. If your elbow hasn't moved by reflex after a few microseconds, you'll need to *make* it move; the source of movement won't be a rebound against gravity but a conscious pulling back, disconnected from the gesture that precedes it.

The grace note, played by the little finger, is very short, in itself and in comparison with the notes that precede and follow it. Its shortness, its placement within the sequence, and the fact that it's articulated by the little finger all conspire to make it potentially weak. Every instrumentalist is tempted to deal with this little note with brute force or willpower. Roberta plays the exercise once. The grace note doesn't sound fully. The second time around she focuses on the little finger, bangs it down hard on the string, and finds no success. The third time around she misuses her head and neck, trying to do with them what the little finger refuses to do. Soon she's caught in a vicious circle, misusing herself ever harder, sounding ever worse.

Stop playing for a moment. Renew your primary directions. Sense your head, neck, back, and legs anew. Enjoy the mobility of the back and its capacity for resistance. And, before playing the exercise, listen in your mind's ear to the pattern's rhythms, its lilt and swing. The pattern says,

Tam...chee-KOM-pah | Tam...chee-KOM-pah ...
Mac...a-RO-ni | Mac...a-RO-ni ...
Damn...the-YAN-kees | Damn...the YAN-kees ...

It doesn't matter what the pattern says exactly; it *says* something, and it does so rhythmically and compellingly. The key to playing the grace note as freely as possible is a clear prosodic intention, the desire to communicate and be understood. If you perform the exercise correctly, you'll have the longest, strongest little finger in the history of anatomy. Why, the little finger goes all the way to your elbow! No, to your back! No, no, to your *foot*!

We're ready to draw some of the universal principles that lie behind this particular exercise.

1. Good technique is a web of latencies, built on qualities of strength, stability, and elasticity.
2. Most gestures combine conscious, willed actions, with reflex, automatic ones. It's as important to know how to "allow" the reflex aspects of your coordination to

take care of themselves as it is to "do" those aspects of your coordination that require the active participation of your conscious will.

3. Gestures exist in context; they're preceded and followed by other gestures. When practicing a gesture, take its context into account.

4. Muscle power and the local initiative of specific body parts are often unneeded, if not downright harmful. Weight, gravity, elasticity, the opposition of forces, and the inherent recoil and rebound of the body in movement all do the job better than muscle power.

5. Timing is essential. Though you have some leeway for each and every gesture, you must become alert to the window of opportunity within which the gesture's combination of willed and reflex qualities is best balanced.

6. Riding the rhythmic release of energy inherent in movement requires a lot less physical effort than "doing" and "controlling." The resulting musical effects are more satisfying too.

7. All good techniques contain linguistic and prosodic dimensions. Healthy gestures "speak" with elegance and meaning.

BILATERAL TRANSFER: A FIRST APPROACH

I ask Roberta to play the Cat's Leap yet again, but this time her right arm comes into action, drawing an open string. The left hand travels along the A string; I ask her to draw a G string with a slow bow stroke (example 12.3).

EXAMPLE 12.3. The Cat's Leap with added bow

This exercise is illustrated in video clip #42, "Bilateral Transfer."

Roberta's bowing arm moves in spurts, imitating the left hand. The pianist Alfred Cortot (1877–1962) once said—and I paraphrase—that it's dumb to imitate a model, but smart to draw inspiration from it. It's dumb of the right hand to imitate the left, since their gestures are rather disparate. I ask Roberta to play the open string alone, with a steady and easy contact. Now her left hand can find inspiration in the right, and become steady and easy too. In this way, Roberta transforms the communication between her left and right arms from a dumb, imitative dialogue into an intelligent, inspirational one.

I ask Roberta to play a pattern of string crossings over the three lower strings, while the left hand travels along the upper string (example 12.4).

EXAMPLE 12.4. The Cat's Leap with added string crossings

The bowing arm falls into the trap I set for it and moves in jerks and starts. We devise a series of intermediate steps and indirect procedures to encourage the two sides of her body to collaborate. This involves giving up the immediate goal, letting go of frustration, renewing her primary directions, sensing anew the prosody of the left hand, working on her string crossings separately from the left hand, and so on.

The unceasing dialogue between the two sides of the body is called *bilateral transfer*; the dialogue involving all four limbs, *quadrilateral transfer*. Bilateral and quadrilateral transfer are two more plates for Roberta to spin. We study both in greater detail in chapter 15.

FROM EXERCISE TO IMPROVISATION AND COMPOSITION

A man who bikes to work, plays team sports every week, and practices ballroom dancing with his wife doesn't need to do push-ups and jumping jacks—his life *is* his exercise. A sedentary slob who sits at the computer all day and in front of the TV all evening might benefit from going to the gym and exercising, though he'd risk becoming a version of Dr. Jekyll and Mr. Hyde: slob at the computer, hunk at the gym. Unless Roberta applies the insights she obtained from the Cat's Leap to all musical endeavors, she'll be Dr. Jekyll when exercising and Mrs. Hyde when performing. To avoid this trap, she needs to internalize the exercise's principles and apply them to everything she does.

◐ This exercise is illustrated in video clip #43, "Discarding the Framework." A related exercise, called "Improvising Fauré's Sicilienne," is discussed in chapter 20 and illustrated in video clips #69, 70, and 71.

The starting exercise offers an organized framework for a series of principles. In the Cat's Leap, the framework is a left-hand exercise in $\frac{3}{4}$, using the index and little fingers in a combination of actions that include articulation, vibrato, changes of position, and pizzicato. The principles include the continuity of gesture, the release of rhythmic energy, the web of latencies, and the prosodist's art.

Roberta's first step is to master the framework. This means performing the original exercise perfectly in all its details. Her second step is to alter the framework. She can do so by playing the exercise on a different string, starting on different positions, or using other

FIGURE 12.3. Work principles. Calvin and Hobbes å 1991 Watterson. Dist. by Universal Uclick. Reprinted with permission. All rights reserved.

finger combinations and intervals. Her third step is to discard the framework. With all the combinations and variations at her disposal, it becomes easy for Roberta to bring her bowing arm into play and to improvise a melody inspired by all the lessons learned but not bound by them.

Now Roberta can take anything from the repertoire and play it with the same freedom. Practicing becomes playing, playing becomes practicing, and she can grow simply by improvising and performing her repertoire every day.

Figure 12.3 encapsulates the main principles Roberta learned from our work over the years.

CHAPTER 13

OBJECT WISDOM

An Oboe Lesson

In this chapter you'll practice the standing position, using a simple procedure called the Lunge, from which you'll draw strength, stability, and mobility. Then you'll study the relationship between the arms and the back, using a procedure called the Plunge. You'll study an Anti-Nodding Strategy that helps you prevent the misuse of the head and neck. You'll develop Object Wisdom, or the art of improving your coordination thanks to the playful manipulation of everyday objects. You'll study seven exercises to help you coordinate your fingers. And you'll learn how to remain free of crippling habits while approaching a composition from the inside out.

THE LUNGE: RESISTANCE AND MOBILITY REVISITED

Melanie is an accomplished professional oboist who suffers from recurring backache and incipient tendonitis on both arms. She's convinced she's "too tense" when she plays, so she comes to me for lessons on "how to relax."

I ask her to play something. For our purposes, her choice of music is immaterial; she'd reveal her habits of thought and gesture by playing a scale, a passage from the repertoire, an improvisation, or anything else. As it happens, she chooses the opening of J. S. Bach's Sonata in B minor, BWV 1030, originally for flute and obbligato harpsichord (example 13.1).

Melanie accompanies her playing with a strange dance. She shakes her head and neck for most of her attacks and accents, sways her arms up and down, and bends and straightens her knees every few seconds.

To move while playing isn't necessarily problematic; it depends on why, how, and when you move. We might distinguish between four types of movement:

1) Needed, such as the motions of your lips, tongue, and jaw when you speak
2) Not needed but harmless, such as gesticulating gently when you speak

EXAMPLE 13.1. J. S. Bach: Sonata for Flute and Harpsichord, BWV 1030 in B Minor, first movement

3) Not needed but potentially harmful, such as scrunching your neck when you speak
4) Not needed but potentially helpful, such as pacing the room while you speak to a group of students

Melanie's movements are a disorganized mixture of the above. To help her become aware of her potentially harmful movements, I teach her an exercise called the Lunge. With a partner, reproduce the following sequence of steps, taking up the roles that Melanie and I play in the exercise.

🔊 This exercise is illustrated in video clip #44, "The Lunge."

1. Melanie and I stand facing each other. I tell her that, in a moment, I'll fall forward, and I'd like her to catch me by placing her hands on my shoulders. When I fall forward, however, Melanie is surprised by how heavy I seem. Straining her neck, shoulders, and arms, she nearly drops me. In truth, my apparent heaviness is only a reflection of Melanie's relative weakness, which has two causes. First, she tries to catch me primarily by using her arms and hands, but they're insufficient for the task. She needs to bring her back and legs into play. Second, she tries to remain loose and relaxed, when in fact she needs to be grounded and stable.

A spring resists when squeezed and twisted, always seeking to return to its normal shape. We may liken the body to a system of interconnected springs. The spine is one such spring, as are the legs, the shoulders, the arms, hands, and fingers. Their innate tendency is to resist any pressure applied to them. Given the right conditions, each spring within the body calls forth the resilience of all the other springs in a collaboration of astounding power.

I ask Melanie to take a small step forward and sideways; to flex her front knee a little and keep her heels in contact with the floor; to firm up her trunk, instead of softening it; and to lift her arms in front of her with slightly bent elbows, like a choral conductor preparing to start a slow piece in *mezzo forte*. Then I apply gentle pressure to her body, pushing into her open palms, her spine, or her hips, asking her to resist my pressure. I increase and decrease the pressure, so that Melanie learns how to gauge resistance and how to distribute it throughout her body. I return to my original standing position in front of her; I ask her to resist me; and again I fall forward into her arms.

This time around she catches me by using her entire body, coordinated from head to toe. If earlier she was surprised by how heavy I seemed, now she's surprised by how light I have become. Needless to say, my weight hasn't changed; it's Melanie who has gained a great deal of strength.

The bodily position in which one foot is planted forward from the other, with the front knee bent, is called the *lunge*. I recommend it as the default position for standing up and singing, playing, or conducting. Within the position, the feet can be far apart or close together. For most needs, it may be enough for you to place one foot just a few inches away from the other, the front knee very slightly bent. The position may be so discreet that a concert audience might not even notice that you're "lunging" on stage.

To diminish the effort needed to accomplish a physical task—moving a heavy load, for instance—you might use, among others, a lever, an inclined plane, or a system of pulleys. In physics and engineering, a tool's force-amplifying effectiveness is called *mechanical advantage*. The more effective the tool, the greater mechanical advantage it offers. "Give me a lever long enough and I will move the Earth," Archimedes once said. Two children of different weights can balance themselves on a seesaw by moving nearer or closer to the seesaw's pivot point; in this way, the lighter kid uses mechanical advantage, rather than muscle power, to achieve equipoise with the heavier one.

Alexander borrowed the term from engineering and used it to speak not of tools, but of positions. A *position of mechanical advantage* allows you to achieve greater results with lesser efforts. The lunge's mechanical advantage helps Melanie use the power of her back and legs to support her shoulders and arms, lessening the burden of holding the oboe that she habitually places on the neck, wrists, hands and fingers.

2. Having discovered how stable the lunge is, we set out to examine how much mobility it allows. Within the lunge, you can lean forward and backward from the hips, turn the trunk leftward and rightward, bend the legs each in turn or both together, turn the head in whatever direction, use the arms freely, and combine all these possible movements. You can use the hip, knee, and ankle joints without bending, slackening, or shortening the spine. If while walking you suddenly stop, with one foot ahead of the other and both heels down, you'll find yourself in a basic lunge. To some degree, walking is nothing but shifting from one discreet lunge to another.

3. Again I ask Melanie to place herself in a lunge. I stand four feet away from her—that is, farther than before. I let her know that on the count of "three" she must take a step forward, bring her arms and hands up, and catch me as I fall. I count and start falling, and Melanie steps forward to catch me. Somehow I seem to have become terribly heavy again, and she nearly drops me. When she moves, Melanie forgets to direct her spine. Instead, she lets the power of her back and legs disperse, and as a result she stiffens her neck and arms. This is why her habitual way of moving at the oboe is harmful.

4. Melanie assumes the lunge position again. I stand close to her and apply pressure here and there on her body—on the shoulders, on the spine, on the hips. While resisting the pressure, she leans forward and backward, turns the trunk from side to side, and raises and lowers her arms. Mobility and resistance begin to coexist and collaborate. Now Melanie can catch me easily even if she has to move quickly and suddenly to do so.

5. Melanie has a number of choices when playing the oboe. She can stop all extraneous movements and limit herself only to needed ones; she can learn to move without losing her connections; or she can carry on moving in her habitual manner, if that is what she wants to do.

There's a lot of merit to moving little beyond the strict minimum, which is the way many master musicians choose to perform. On YouTube, look up the pianists Arthur Rubinstein and Mieczysław Horszowski, the jazzmen John Coltrane and Charlie Parker, and the conductor Yuri Temirkanov. Whole orchestras and choruses perform with minimal movement; look up the Vienna Philharmonic or the Sardinian folk group Coro de Iddanoa Monteleone.

The historical record indicates that J. S. Bach himself barely moved when he played.

> At the clavichord Bach is virtually still. He plays effortlessly, the movements of his fingers "hardly perceptible." Those fingers not in action remain motionless, "quietly in position." The rest of his body takes even "[less] part in his playing." His hands do not contort or register any strain even in the most difficult passages. . . . Bach plays expressively but his body expresses nothing.[1]

To move and dance to your own playing isn't necessarily bad. Niccolò Paganini and Franz Liszt, the archetypical Romantic superstars, apparently pranced onstage in extravagant fashion. But the record indicates that both were supremely integrated musicians, past masters of every aspect of music making. In all likelihood they didn't lose their connections when they moved. To emulate their stagecraft and succeed, you need to establish solid connections throughout your body and to become an expert on rhythm, sound, and all other aspects of the musicianly art. Then, and only then, dancing and prancing will do you no harm.

Some musicians are so invested in their disconnected movements that they choose to carry on, regardless of the pain and handicap. It's a trade-off like any other: "I like this too much to give it up, and I agree to pay the price for it (although I'll also complain a lot about it!)." As it happens, there are many audiences who love watching a disconnected musician struggling on stage, possibly amalgamating the musician's struggle with the emotional meaning of the musical text itself. Melanie might conceivably decide to embrace her habit in all its consequences, including the pain that bothers her so much.

THE PLUNGE

Thanks to the lunge, Melanie has improved the use of her back and legs. But whenever she lifts her arms, she hollows her back and stiffens her shoulders. I lead her through a new exercise. Ostensibly it addresses the coordination of the arms, shoulders, and back. In reality, it's a multidimensional meditation that heightens the awareness of the whole body. I call the exercise the Plunge. As usual, practice it with a partner.

⬥ This exercise is illustrated in video clips #45, "The Plunge I: From Above, the Basics," #46, "The Plunge II: From Above, Variations," and #47, "The Plunge III: From the Side."

1. Stand facing a wall or door at arms' length, touching it with the outstretched fingers of both hands at shoulder height and width, elbows slightly bent. You're likely to hollow your back and stiffen your shoulders when you lift your arms. Your first task in this exercise is to make your back primary, your arms secondary, and the wall tertiary, the better to lift your arms without misusing your back.

2. Keep your arms up in front of you, elbows gently bent. Flex your wrists and point your fingers upward, creating some distance between your palms and the wall. Hinging from the ankle joints and keeping the rest of the body straight, lean forward until your hands touch the wall. It's as if you're poising yourself to do a push-up while nearly vertical, the wall playing the role of the floor in an ordinary push-up.

Many things can go wrong when you perform the plunge. You risk dropping your head and neck forward; contracting your shoulders; shifting your pelvis forward; lifting your heels off the ground; and stopping your breath. If your pelvis and legs are too relaxed to support you, your neck and shoulders will stiffen in compensation. Logically, you need to firm up the pelvis in order to release the excessive tension in the neck and shoulders.

3. Stay in the plunge position, and ask your partner to apply pressure to your back— for instance, by pushing a fist onto the spine between your shoulder blades. Ask your partner to start gently and increase the pressure gradually. Use your whole back—as well as your hands, arms, and shoulders—to resist the pressure, and keep in mind that pianissimo pressure requires only pianissimo resistance from you.

By resisting with the whole body, you create a web of well-distributed tensions. Your resulting strength comes not so much from muscle power but the connections and oppositions within the body: the hands connected to the arms, the arms to the shoulders, the shoulders to the back and pelvis, the pelvis to the legs and feet.

4. Perform the exercise with one arm only; hands closed, open, arched, with pointed fingers; the body close to the wall or far away from it; the feet next to each other, far apart, or in lunge-like asymmetry. The important thing is not the form of the exercise but its substance. The plunge is a meditation on the ability to lose your balance without losing your directions, on mobility and resistance, on the circuit of connections throughout the whole body, and above all on the mental attitudes that allow you to become self-aware but not self-conscious.

5. Stay in position with both palms against the wall, and ask your partner to apply pressure to your back again. Bend your elbows slightly, as if doing a push-up, and then unbend them. Stay attentive to the spine and pelvis and don't overrelax them when using other joints such as the elbows or wrists. We can broaden the principle and state that all joints need permanent latent mobility, but joints that don't need to bend or flex for a particular movement need permanent latent resistance.

6. Walk away from the wall and take up your instrument, sensing how your arms have become natural extensions of the back and the instrument a natural extension of your arms. Now play, and note how it feels compared with the old habits.

MOVEMENT, RHYTHM, AND PERSONALITY

I started this chapter by noting that Melanie danced to her own playing, and conjectured that her dancing sabotaged her music making. There are at least three reasons why she moves this way. The first, as we saw already, was physical. The second is related to prosody, and the third to psychological and aesthetic issues.

To better understand the prosodic causes of misuse, we focus for a moment on the head and neck, without forgetting that other body parts have as much potential for misbehavior. Many musicians make quick movements of head and neck, often in tandem with the movements of their hands. Picture a pianist playing an agitato passage in $\frac{4}{4}$, with running eighth notes and offbeat sforzandi. The pianist flings his head and neck down for each note in the measure, and more strongly still for each sforzando:

nod-nod-NOD-nod-NOD-nod-nod-NOD

You'll remember from chapter 4 that there exist four types of accent or energy in music: metric, agogic, tonal, and dynamic. The pianist in our example uses his head and neck as a metronome, marking time and indicating primary and secondary metric accents of beats and subdivisions. He also uses his head to produce and choreograph his dynamic accents, as if head and neck could physically produce his sforzandi. He uses his head and neck for tonal accents (when a melody goes up, the head goes up; when a melody goes down, the head goes down) and even for agogic ones (a longer note merits a greater sway of the head and neck).

Ideally, all types of accents would exist first and foremost in the music itself; secondly, in the pianist's imagination; thirdly, in the work of fingers, hands, and arms pushing down piano keys more softly or more heavily. Counterintuitive as it may be, the accents sound stronger and more compelling when the head and neck do their proper job—which is not to choreograph accents but to orient the body in space.

At the oboe, Melanie nods much like the pianist of our example, and for similar reasons. In fact, the tendency to nod is universal, and it merits treatment.

This exercise is illustrated in video clip #48, "Anti-Nodding Strategy."

Sit at a piano. Make loose fists of both hands and use the piano as a percussion instrument and your fists as mallets. Bang in $\frac{2}{4}$, $\frac{3}{4}$, $\frac{2}{4}$, $\frac{6}{8}$ and so on; bang in iambs, trochees, amphibrachs, and every imaginable pattern. Add sforzandi, sometimes on the downbeat, sometimes on an offbeat. Keep your spine erect and firm. Let your arms and fists—not your head and neck—be the agents of prosody, the speakers of your dynamic and agogic accents. Now carry on banging your fists and rock sideways on your buttocks, just as Roberta did in the previous chapter, slowly taking your whole torso far to the left, then far to the right again.

In principle, you should be able to move your trunk slowly, your hands quickly, and your head and neck not at all. So should Melanie when she plays the oboe, and in a moment we'll go through a series of procedures to make it easier for her not to mimic the comings and goings of the musical phrase.

Melanie misuses herself in movement, then, for physical and rhythmic reasons. But she also does so for a third reason. One of the greatest challenges for all musicians is to trust themselves to succeed on the stage, trust their audiences to be receptive, and above all trust music itself to touch the audience. Trust and confidence allow you to present your work in a sober, straightforward manner: "Let me shine some light on what Bach wrote. I hope you and I will manage to focus on Bach, not on how I engineer the lighting!" If a musician is unsure of her technique, her interpretation, or the ability of her public to seize her musical message, sometimes she moves to compensate for her lack of clarity. Her movements convey the following message: "If you can't *hear* what I mean, perhaps you can at least *see* it. And if I can't *play* what I mean, perhaps I could at least fool your ears by distracting your eyes."

Through music, a musician connects to the creative source; through music, a musician connects with the audience. Indirectly, then, the audience can feel its own connection with the creative source. It takes courage for a musician to trust music itself—and not the mechanics of performance—to do the job of taking the audience closer to the creative source.

OBJECT WISDOM

Melanie has now developed some fundamental connections between the head, neck, shoulders, back, pelvis, legs, and arms. She keeps these connections when walking, sitting, standing, losing her balance, performing a vertical push-up against the wall, and so on. But when it comes to the oboe, she has so many accumulated habits that simply picking up the instrument causes her to revert to her long-standing misuse. When she plays, for instance, Melanie's hands look awkward, as if they were being required to do something outside their natural range of motion—fingers crooked and pained, veins and bony stuff visible.

We turn our attention to a series of objects—*non-oboes*, we might call them—to help Melanie free up her arms and hands. The choice of objects is limited only by what we find in my teaching room: an eyeglass case, a cell phone, a paintbrush, a basketball, or anything else. Objects invite you to discover the hands' capacity to hold, squeeze, pinch, poke, caress, slap, throw, catch, and so on. Each object teaches you different lessons. You can hold an eyeglass case, open it and shut it, and throw it from one hand to the other. With a cell phone, you can do all that plus punch in numbers, thereby involving fingers and thumbs in a way the eyeglass case does not.

Objects are multilayered and multidimensional. Take a tennis ball, for instance. It's round and bouncy. Its outer surface is fuzzy, its core rubbery. If you squeeze it, the ball seems to yield to your pressure and resist it at the same time. Hold the ball between your palms and roll it about, massaging the ball with your palms and your palms with the ball. The ball "teaches" the hands how to absorb its qualities of elasticity and bounce. The ball's shape, texture, and weight all contribute to making the experience delightful, although the delight comes not from the ball itself, but from your hands as they play with the ball.

Every object in your life has lots of wisdom to impart. All you need is to approach each object with a playful child's frame of mind: "What can I do with this? In how many ways can I amuse myself? What nearly dangerous thing can I do? How can I use this object to annoy my mother?"

The following exercises will help you develop Object Wisdom in its many dimensions.

1. THE BROOM: ALLOW THE OBJECT TO GUIDE YOU

Get hold of a normal kitchen broom, with a long handle and short bristles. It's best if the broom's handle has a flat top on which you can rest your palms without being uncomfortably poked.

🔊 This exercise is illustrated in video clip #49, "Object Wisdom I: The Broom."

1. You know you can use the broom to sweep the floor or to prop a window open, but your mind risks becoming limited by this knowledge. Spend time handling the broom without preconceived ideas. Run your hands over the broom's surfaces, noticing the different shapes and textures. Turn the broom upside down and feel the bristles' texture with your palm. Take the broom in one hand and use it to tap the palm of the other hand. These actions inform you about the broom's anatomical qualities, so to speak: size, shape, weight, texture, and component materials. After you become thoroughly familiar with the broom's construction, start exploring its functional capabilities.

2. Stand with your feet spread at about hip width. Hold the broom upright in front of you by pushing it down with your palms on the flat end of the stick, one palm on top of the other. Keep all body parts neither tense nor relaxed: elbows poised, hands open, fingers spread out. Push the broom gently down, sensing both the stick's firmness and the bristles' elasticity. Partially release the pressure of your hands, and the broom will rise up a little bit as the bristles straighten up. If you really become attentive to the broom's resistance and elasticity, you'll also become aware of the resistance and elasticity in your hands and arms. The feeling will travel beyond them to go to shoulders, back, pelvis, legs and feet. The broom becomes a fifth member, collaborating with your arms and legs to make your whole body stable.

3. Take the broom by the handle, near the broom's balance point close to the bristles. Keeping the broomstick upright, throw the broom from hand to hand. At first, the broomstick will wobble and lose its uprightness. It may also escape your grip and fall on the floor. This is all to the good, as you can then learn not to panic and not to fear the loss of control. Once you throw it in the air, and before you catch it with your other hand, the broom becomes independent and autonomous. If you throw it in a certain way, you can determine the broom's flight path and behavior. Use your whole arms to make the throw, not just the hands and wrists, and use your back and legs to support the arms.

Do you throw the broom immediately after catching it, or do you wait a moment? Do you let your receiving arm move a little with the broom, or do you resist it? How far apart do you keep your hands? How forcefully do you throw the broom? All these elements influence the game. Your throws must have a rhythmic component if they are to succeed (and by success, I mean a throw safely and easily caught, and a throw-and-catch cycle that awakens your body's intelligence). Hold the broom for a moment. Just before you throw it, your throwing arm moves in the opposite direction of the throw; then it rushes into the throw, letting go of the broom; then it relaxes, though only a little. It's an amphibrachic cycle of preparation, stress, and release.

4. While standing, hold the broom's handle at about its center of gravity with one hand, the arm stretched to about three-quarters of its full length, the broom vertical. Turn your arm in pronation. The arm leads, the broom follows; then the broom gains momentum and takes over the leadership role, twisting the arm a little—a twist that you can accept or resist as you wish. Use your hand to change the direction of the broom's movement. You need only a little effort, and then the broom itself will acquire momentum and start turning the other way, taking the arm with it. This is a good way for you to learn how to "do" something while "allowing" something else to take place. Now find a way to pass the broom from hand to hand in mid-twirl. Keep your elbows relatively fixed while the broom twirls, and you'll have the feeling that the broom is giving you a sort of massage, stimulating the arms, shoulders, and neck.

5. From the broom, you've learned elasticity and resistance, the interconnection of body parts, the mastery of timing and rhythm, and the capacity to let objects do some of the physical work for you. If you aren't literal-minded, you'll see that drawing a bow across a string, striking a chord at the piano, or indicating a crescendo to an orchestra all have similarities with the gestures the broom has taught you.

2. THE PAINTBRUSH: DEGREES
OF FIXITY

Take a normal-sized paintbrush and use it to mock-paint a surface: a table, a door, or a wall-length mirror in which you can observe yourself in action. It's the brush that paints the surface, not you; you half-guide the brush, half-follow it. The joints of the whole arm (fingers, wrist, elbow, shoulder) come into play, constantly varying their degrees of activity and passivity. Your arm moves in circles, figure eights, and ellipses of every shape and dimension, clock- and counterclockwise. Indeed, every single one of your motions is circular; for you to draw a straight line with the brush, your arm, hand, wrist, and fingers must each pivot or rotate or otherwise move along a curved path, and their combined curves produce the straight line.

Some of your painterly movements may be more elegant, powerful, and agreeable when certain areas of the body remain relatively fixed. A point of fixity within a mechanism doesn't necessarily render the whole mechanism fixed. Instead, it regulates its movements, encouraging some motions, allowing others, and preventing others still.

You "dance and paint" rather differently when your spine is floppy and when it's directed. Stand in a lunge in front of the mirror, and use the brush to draw figures on the mirror. Test varying levels of bodily mobility:

1. Let your whole body accompany the movements of arm and hand, every joint in the body free to do as it pleases.
2. Prevent the spine from bending, but allow all arm and leg joints to move if needed.
3. Hold your body still, and move only the painting arm and hand.

For every gesture (for instance, drawing a bow across the string), study its points of possible fixity. Isolate these points, each in turn, two or more in combination. Then test how they feel at your instrument, and see what combinations of fixity and mobility allow for the greatest freedom in each technical and musical situation.

3. THE BALL: RHYTHMIC ASPECTS OF OBJECT WISDOM

This exercise is illustrated in video clip #50, "Object Wisdom II: The Basketball."

1. Take a soccer ball, volleyball, or inflated rubber balloon. While standing, wrap your palms around the ball and hold it in front of you. Rotate the ball by turning the hands and wrists; raise and lower the ball or take it to the left or to the right; invent variations and combinations of all these actions. Sense the articulations of shoulders, elbows, wrists, and fingers and use them as needed.

When first rotating the ball, some people raise and contract their shoulders. Others tend to keep their elbows nearly stuck to the side of their trunks without engaging the upper arms, therefore losing the connections from the back to the arms and fingers. Underinvested elbows are as problematic as overinvested shoulders. Your arms and hands work better if your elbows aren't fixed or inert but in a state of lively readiness.

2. Take the ball in your hands, and turn it at moderate speed. Now start walking in a circle around the room. While walking, change the speed in which you turn the ball; go from very slow to very fast; stop turning the ball all of a sudden; restart it just as suddenly. Notice how your arms' movements affect your gait. If your legs can move at their own speed, unbothered by the arms, they'll be better able to make a positive contribution to your overall coordination. (We study the collaboration between arms and legs in chapter 15.)
3. Throw the ball from hand to hand, using the same qualities of resistance and elasticity you developed when handling the broom. While throwing the ball continuously, improvise a scatting song with a steady rhythm, making your catches coincide with the song's metric accents:

Ta-DUM, ta-DUM, ta-TA-ta ta-DUM!

Paraphrasing what William Christie said back in chapter 2, all dances contain a hidden text. Throwing the ball from hand to hand is a kind of dance. If you discover its hidden text—perhaps by making it audible—you'll dance with much greater ease.

🅐 Bonus video clip: #51, "Object Wisdom III: The Piano."

4. FROM OBJECT TO OBOE: HELPING THE NEW PREVAIL OVER THE OLD

Melanie might love the oboe, but that doesn't change the fact that her instrument is a trigger of misuse. She's likely to misuse herself by picking the oboe, by playing two notes on it, or just by thinking about it. She needs to find a "new oboe" in her hands, because the old one keeps leading her astray.

In my room, I have a wooden stick half the size of a broom handle. Its greatest merit is that it can become a pretend-oboe, which Melanie may touch and hold without any of her old psychophysical or musical habits. I ask her to handle it while remembering what it felt like to have her arms be connected with her back, the way she did in the plunge. The stick becomes an extension of her arms, and therefore an extension of her back. She moves the stick first with one hand only, then with both hands, and finally with both hands as if she were holding an oboe. The stick is our ultimate *non-oboe*, an object that allows Melanie to adopt her oboist's attitude without any of her oboist's misuses.

I ask her to retain her stance. I remove the stick from her hands and place the actual oboe in its place. Before she plays even a note, I ask her to trade her oboe back for the stick. We do this a few times in succession: stick, oboe, stick, oboe. Then we have our breakthrough: Melanie "forgets" her old habits and finally holds the oboe in a completely new manner. The oboe has become the *non-non-oboe*: a new instrument that doesn't trigger Melanie's misuses anymore. Before making music, however, Melanie needs to work on those awkward, painful fingers of hers.

THE PARADOX OF FINGERS

Fingers perform such complex feats of dexterity in instrumental technique that players obsess about how to control their behavior. Exercising your fingers in isolation from the whole circuit of body-mind connections, however, is counterproductive and potentially harmful. Further, fingers receive an enormous emotional charge from musicians: joy and pleasure, of course, but also frustration, anger, and fear. When the fingers begin to hurt and disobey the musician's commands, the emotions become obsessive and self-defeating. "I worry about my fingers because they're hurting. And the more I worry, the more they hurt."

The paradox in instrumental technique, then, is that you *must think* about the fingers and you *must stop thinking* about them. Like the problem, the solution is also paradoxical. In this section I propose several exercises for you to work on your fingers without working on them.

1. THE LOOPING CIRCUIT

With your elbow slightly bent, stand at arm's length in front of a wall and touch it with your index finger. The objective is to sense a circuit called "wall, finger, hand, wrist, arm, shoulder, back, pelvis, legs, feet, floor." Visualize a grid with a thousand little lights shining all along your body from wall to floor. After a moment sensing the circuit and charging it up, reverse your perception of it, going from floor to wall instead: "floor, feet, legs, pelvis, back, shoulder, arm, wrist, hand, finger, wall." You won't know anymore if the circuit begins with the finger or ends with the finger. Your finger is a small link in the circuit and wholly dependent of it, and yet you might feel that your finger is such a powerful entity that it alone can connect the floor to the wall. This is the "looping circuit" that you must nourish for the benefit of your fingers.

Keep your fingertip on the wall and take small steps forward, backward, and sideways: The looping circuit remains charged with energy. Tap the wall rhythmically with your finger: The circuit remains charged. Do the same exercise with different fingers, with several fingers in combination and alternation, sitting or standing, at the piano or at your habitual instrument: The circuit remains charged.

2. POWER FROM THE HAND, POWER FROM THE BACK

Stand next to a partner, put a hand on his or her shoulder, and command your hand to push the partner. Now start anew. Put your hand on the same spot and take a little time to firm up your hand, arm, shoulder, back, and legs. Then command your back to push the partner slowly and surely. Pushing with the hand is an act of aggression; pushing with the back, an act of connection.

Do the same exercise and, while pushing with your back, tap your partner's shoulder gently with your index finger. The finger's movement ought to be secondary, the push from the back primary. Then sit at a piano and put your hands in playing position; push with your back ever so gently; and tap a few notes. The playing finger becomes a collaborator to the supporting back and legs. Subsequently, apply the same principle to playing your habitual instrument.

3. FINGER RESISTANCE AND MOBILITY

The defining characteristic of good coordination isn't relaxation but a balance of opposing forces, or a "harmony of tensions." Intertwine your fingers softly. Take them apart, and then intertwine them again. While intertwined, your fingers are ready to let go and separate; while separated, your fingers are ready to intertwine. In short, they combine latent resistance and latent mobility. Now keep them intertwined, with your hands vaulted like the roof of a chapel. Use the left fingers to gently squeeze the right fingers, and command your right fingers to gently resist. Let the two hands alternate the roles of squeezing and resisting, and then bring them to a balance: they both squeeze and resist at the same time. Tap one index finger into the top of the chapel, making a soft percussive sound. Now tap different fingers in alternation and combination.

The intertwined fingers are ready to move, ready to stay put, ready to squeeze, ready to resist, and ready to lift and drop rhythmically. Perform this "intertwining dance" for a while, and then play a few notes on your instrument, retaining the fingers' combination of latent resistance and latent mobility.

4. PREHENSION AND OPPOSITION

With your fingers and wrists loose, rotate your arms at high speed. How do your arms and hands behave? Now firm up your wrists as if to hold a paperweight, and gently press the tips of your thumbs against the tips of your middle fingers, shaping them into little circles. Again, rotate your arms at high speed. How do your arms and hands behave?

Floppy body parts are an impediment to coordinated movement. The opposition between thumb and the other fingers is a stabilizing factor. When the thumbs are called to act (in holding an oboe, for instance), their prehensile and oppositional capabilities are potential sources of power and comfort—as long as the thumbs are fully connected to the whole-body circuit. When the thumbs aren't called to act (in certain passages at the piano, for instance, or when you're singing), they should still be charged with energy and intention. Remember the rule: Relaxation is a hindrance to healthy movement.

5. CROSSED FINGERS, DIVINE CONNECTIONS

Cross the middle finger over the index finger, as if to illustrate the saying "My buddy and I are as close as *this*." Do it with both hands. Keeping the fingers crossed with the least needed tension, move your arms and hands slowly in front of you, as if conducting a choir. Keeping your fingers gently crossed, bunch up the tips of thumbs, ring fingers, and little fingers, and then move your arms slowly about. How do your fingers feel? How do your head, neck, and back feel? Indeed, how do you feel from head to toe, back and front, inside and out? Now you know why combinations of finger positions and movements attain mystical status in certain cultures, for instance, in the classical dance styles of Southeast Asia: They create life-affirming circuits of connection, allowing energy to flow smoothly through the whole body.

Cross your fingers gently, move your arms about; uncross your fingers, pick up your instrument and play a few notes. The circuit now remains lively when you use your fingers normally.

6. FINGERS AS PROSODISTS

Your hands and fingers behave differently depending on the type of command you give them. "Lift, drop, squeeze, pinch" are commands of a certain type—let's call them *physical*. "Wake up, here, now, SPEAK!" are commands of a different type—let's call them *linguistic*. All linguistic commands have a physical charge, but it's possible for a physical command to lack a linguistic charge, in which case the command is at best incomplete and at worst harmful.

At the end of chapter 1, I suggested an exercise where you tap prosodic patterns with your fingers on a tabletop or at the piano ("ba-NA-na"). Refresh your memory by rereading the passage and performing the exercise in question. Chapter 5 shows you how to make your fingers "speak." And the exercise described in the section above, "Power from the Hand, Power from the Back," teaches your fingers to become good prosodists while remaining connected to a whole-body circuit.

The tendency for most instrumentalists is to give great importance to the dropping of fingers. Lifting the fingers, however, is just as important—and, like dropping, it can become charged with linguistic energy. Put your right hand on a tabletop, palm cupped and fingers poised as if to play the piano. Tap rhythmically with one or more fingers: tap, tap, tap, drop, drop, drop! Now place your left hand palm down above the right hand, and use the knuckles of your right fingers to tap your left palm: tap, tap, tap, lift, lift, lift! This exaggerates the active dimension of lifting your fingers. In music making, you don't need to lift your fingers so actively; you need only the latent capability to do so.

7. HANDS AS HEALING ANIMALS

With a partner, do the following exercise. Hold one of your partner's hands with both your hands. Skin, flesh, and bones create layers with different textures. The hand is hot or cold, tender or harsh, chunky or slim. Each hand has a personality and an animality of its own. ("Animal, animate, animated" come from the Latin word "animalis," meaning "living.") Holding your partner's hand quietly, you may feel the hand shifting, expanding, or shrinking as it adjusts itself to your touch. Sweet and calming energies pass back and forth between you and your partner—from hand to hand, from body to body, from person to person.

Healing lies outside the grasp of intellectual understanding, and it's difficult (if not impossible) to verbalize how healing happens and how it feels when it happens. For our purposes, we might just say that hands are "animals who can heal." Having some awareness of this capability will help you use your hands differently at the instrument, and it'll also help you heal your hands when they're hurting you after years of misuse.

8. A WORKING METHOD

Worrying about your fingers is never useful, however much they may be hurting or bothering you. Look for triggers of good mood and positive psychic energy, and then retain the mood as you ponder your fingers in the context of your entire psychophysical, intellectual, musical, and creative endeavors. Remember the juggling metaphor of the previous chapter: The fingers are one of many plates for you to spin, and certainly not the most important plate.

Revise the Lunge (which helps you direct your back and legs), the Plunge (which helps you direct the back, shoulders, and arms), and Object Wisdom (which helps you use your arms and hands in a free and playful manner). Practice them in alternation with the finger exercises and meditations in this section, until you *always* direct your whole body every time you work on your fingers. Work a bit on the whole body, a bit on the fingers; a bit on sound production, a bit on the fingers; a bit on Rhythmic Solfège, a bit on the fingers. Let's call this the *principle of alternation*. Trial and error will teach you how to practice it over the months and years.

J. S. BACH, REBORN

Melanie needed to learn how to play the "new oboe," since the old one was a long-standing trigger of misuse. Now she needs to learn how to play the "new Bach," because in fact the old one is also a trigger of misuse.

Look at the excerpt from the sonata again (example 13.2). Play it, sing it, whistle it, or bring it to life in any way you can.

EXAMPLE 13.2. J. S. Bach: Sonata for Flute and Harpsichord, BWV 1030 in B Minor, first movement

It's often possible to reduce a long phrase to a handful of notes that form the phrase's core. Bach builds his opening phrase on a descending scale of six steps, in which an F-sharp is the most prominent pitch. Within the sonata's tonality of B minor, an F-sharp can take on many roles, the most important of them being the root of the dominant and the fifth of the tonic chord. The pitch establishes the piece's tonality and gives it stability and dynamism at the same time (example 13.3).

EXAMPLE 13.3. The F-sharp as both tonic and dominant

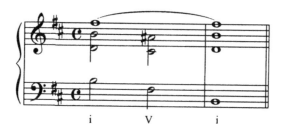

In the Baroque era, a crescendo and diminuendo on a long note was a prized ornament called the *messa di voce*. Its importance in sound production, coordination, and interpretation—in all of music, not only in Baroque repertoire—is such that we devote chapters 18 and 19 to it. I ask Melanie to play a single, sustained F-sharp and make it grow and diminish. Her task is to produce an ideal sound in ideal coordination, unencumbered by the task of performing an elaborate phrase that normally provokes her into a dance of disconnection (example 13.4).

EXAMPLE 13.4. A messa di voce on an F-sharp

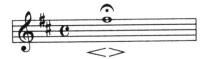

Once Melanie finds her connections while playing that all-important single pitch, I ask her to play a scale fragment without disconnecting herself. The fragment links the dominant to the tonic and serves as a sketch for the more intricate phrase Bach will eventually use (example 13.5).

EXAMPLE 13.5. A melodic descent

Melanie continues to nourish her bodily connections, her connections to the instrument, and her connections to sound and breath, and she adds an upbeat to the F-sharp that starts the scale fragment (example 13.6).

EXAMPLE 13.6. Upbeat, messa di voce, melodic descent

Bach's phrase starts with a melodic and rhythmic provocation to Melanie's coordination: an ascending fifth constructed as upbeat/DOWNBEAT. Her habit is to choreograph the interval and its rhythm with movements of head, neck, trunk, arms, and legs. We rewrite the passage and eliminate the provocation altogether. The simplified version starts with a lesser rhythmic provocation (two notes of equal length) and with nearly no melodic provocation (the same note repeated, rather than a rising fifth). Melanie plays it a few times, using the passage's simplicity to affirm her connections. After her connections become habitual, she can face the original version without being provoked by it (example 13.7).

You may remember that this procedure is called *delayed continuity*. (It's illustrated at the cello in video clip #38, "Practice Routines V: Delayed Continuity.") The short silences

EXAMPLE 13.7. Delayed continuity

clarify the piece's prosodic construction while allowing Melanie to focus on herself for a brief moment in between sounding notes. It's as if Melanie said, "Two eighth notes for Bach, two eighth rests for me; two for Bach, two for me." Eventually the two activities converge, and in her playing she permanently affirms, "I am Bach."

I ask Melanie to play a sort of improvisation or composition using primarily the amphibrachic foot. She "speaks" Bach, as it were, riffing on his discourse, in delighted imitation of him. We annotate her improvisation for further study. It's useful to include a few graphic signs to indicate integration, separation, and direction, as well as qualities of preparation, stress, and release. On purpose, we make the annotations sparse and variable from bar to bar. In time, Melanie will internalize her prosodic decisions and won't need to mark the score altogether (example 13.8).

EXAMPLE 13.8. Improvising Bach

FIGURE 13.1. J. S. Bach.

FIGURE 13.2. Melanie.

FIGURE 13.3. Melanie playing J. S. Bach.

Melanie practiced the messa di voce until she found a stable, healthy sound on a single pitch. She learned to ascend and descend along a melodic line with a varied rhythm without losing the connections between her different body parts. She alternated between playing shorts bursts of Bach and focusing on herself for equally short bursts, until she could do both at the same time. Finally she half-composed, half-improvised the very phrase that Bach wrote, and she played it in a healthy and compelling manner.

Realistically, such a learning process takes years and years to master, but there is no better way of working! The process increases your likelihood of healing old hurts. It leads you into a state of deep creativity, and it opens up a new way of making music and of living. In brief, it's a process of integration, and exploring it over the long term will transform you.

CHAPTER 14

BODY, BREATH, VIBRATION, TEXT

A Voice Lesson

In this chapter you'll learn the Möbius Strip, an exercise for the coordination of the whole body with an emphasis on the connection between the back and pelvis. You'll learn three nonbreathing exercises that will help you understand the proper role of breathing in coordination. You'll study the art of using a text (be it verbal or musical) to coordinate yourself until you "become the text." You'll play with a party balloon and discover that you can touch and hold sound in your hands. You'll develop vocal strength and suppleness through an exercise called the Father and the Daughter. Finally, you'll study the art of harmonizing your instinctual energies and your conscious goal-setting through the Inner Animal and the Opportunist.

THE MÖBIUS STRIP

Take an ordinary sheet of paper and cut a lengthwise strip about an inch wide. Make a ring with the strip of paper by joining the ends of the strip together. The resulting object has clearly defined outside and inside faces: You can run a finger along the inside circumference of the ring or outside it, or draw a line along one or the other face. If you take the same strip of paper and twist one of its ends through 180 degrees before you join it to the other end, you create not a ring but a Möbius strip, a twisty little object that resembles a pretzel or three-dimensional figure eight. (The strip is named after Albert F. Möbius, a German mathematician who studied its topological properties in depth.) Draw a line along the strip, starting at any one point; make the line continuous, and stop drawing it only when you get back to the starting point. The line will run along both sides of the strip of paper, proving that "outside" and "inside," "back" and "front" have disappeared! The Möbius strip is a paradox that you can hold in your hand. Having no beginning and no end, no outside and no inside, no back and no front, it's a complete and self-contained circuit of connections, a symbol of infinity. I call the following exercise the

Möbius Strip because it turns your body into a similarly self-contained circuit of infinite connections.

⏺ This exercise is illustrated in video clip #52, "The Möbius Strip."

1) While standing, place one hand on your stomach, palm facing in, wrist bent, fingers pointing down, with the fingertips one or two inches away from your crotch; and place the other hand on your lower back, palm facing out, wrist bent, fingers pointing down, with the middle finger resting more or less between your buttocks (give or take an inch). Without raising your shoulders, point your elbows slightly away from your body. It doesn't matter whether you put your left hand on the stomach and the right on the back or vice versa.

You risk contracting your arms and shoulders as you place yours hands in this position. To lessen the risk, tap your body lightly with your hands and fingers, as if using the body as a delicate percussion instrument. Let your hands travel up and down the body: Tap your thighs, your stomach, your head, your sternum, and every other body part. While playfully exploring your body with this agile touch, direct your hands to land on the assigned spot, one hand on the stomach, the other on the lower back. The arms will "remember" their own mobility and lightness once they stop moving, thus avoiding becoming stiff or rigid.

2) Your hands both monitor the body and encourage certain events within it. When it comes to the connection between the back and the pelvis, your hands become "actors, receptors, and witnesses," partly causing the connection, partly sensing it, and partly understanding it. (We study the roles of the actor, receptor, and witness in chapter 19.)

Your center of gravity lies right in between your two hands, at a point roughly two inches below your navel. The two hands squeeze the body gently, as if trying to meet each other in the center of your body. The central point resists their pressure and becomes more present as a result, freeing the flow of energy throughout the body.

Touching your belly, your back, and your pelvis, the hands create an elastic envelope or cocoon for your breath. The breath enjoys the cocoon and enters it gladly, expanding against its benign pressure. The concept of the elastic envelope is useful in many situations. It has a physical component, as demonstrated by the Möbius Strip, but also a metaphorical and metaphysical one. Creating a mental, psychic elastic envelope for your creative energies helps you organize them without stifling them. The best improvisers, for instance, aren't those who put no limits on their expression but those who push against elastic limits set up by grids that may include metrical, melodic, harmonic, and other elements.

3) While maintaining the posture, take a few steps forward and backward, sideways, and in every direction. Play-act a little, and move in space as if you were a tango dancer or a fencing master. Stop for a moment with one foot slightly ahead of the other, and now bend and unbend your knees, each in turn or both together. Pivot on your feet, turning your whole body and changing the direction in which you are facing.

In an attempt to move the legs freely, you risk undoing the connection between the back and the pelvis; in an attempt to keep the back and pelvis solidly together, you risk stiffening your legs. Do the following exercise: Walk toward a chair; stand near it; then lift one foot and place it flat on the chair's seat. What happens to your back and pelvis? Most likely you'll either hollow the lower back by sticking your bottom out; or shift your pelvis forward, as if the pelvis were part of the leg and not the back. Do the same exercise again, now keeping one hand on your lower back and pelvis (as you do in the Möbius Strip). Once you put a foot up on the chair, place your other hand at the hip joint, with your fingertips inserted right where the joint bends. The hand on your back says, "Back and pelvis stay together." The hand on the hip says, "The leg bends at the hip joint, without disturbing the back and pelvis."

Retain the double feeling of connection and mobility as you walk, then also as you sit down, as you use your legs and feet to play the pedals in a piano or an organ, and so on.

4) Lungs, diaphragm, ribs, viscera, and air itself all move when you breathe. Apart from the ribcage, however, no other parts of your skeleton need to move. In the Möbius Strip your hands can feel the movement of breath while encouraging the pelvis not to move, the better to keep its connection with the back.

Stand still, breathing quietly into the elastic envelope. Now say a few words. I suggest counting metronomically, one word per beat, three words followed by a breath: "One, two, three; four, five, six; seven, eight, nine; ten, eleven, twelve." Breathe after every third beat, and have the breath last a beat: "one, two, three—breathe; four, five, six—breathe; seven, eight, nine—breathe; ten, eleven, twelve—breathe." This creates a four-bar phrase, each bar with four beats, the fourth of which is a breath that does itself.

Say something simple and brief: a description of your breakfast, a silly joke, or your siblings' names. Is your voice coming from the depths of your body? Does your voice work in tandem with your breath? Is your pelvis staying stable as you speak and breathe? Can you sense all that without working hard?

Now speak more freely, improvising a couple of sentences. If you invest yourself exclusively in the things you say you'll lose your connections, scrunch your neck, gasp for air, and generally misuse yourself. But by staying aware of your connections, you take care of yourself and your discourse at the same time, enhancing the power and authority of what you have to say.

5) Let go of your hands. You're now wearing a "latent Möbius Strip" that helps you keep your connections in daily life and in music making.

THREE NONBREATHING EXERCISES

Breathing straddles the line between voluntary and involuntary bodily functions. Cornelius L. Reid posited that "if but one member of a complex muscular system is involuntary, all members of the system must be treated as though they, too, were involuntary."[1] In other words, the involuntary aspects of breathing dictate that voluntary aspects are best left alone, otherwise you risk misusing the entire breathing system.

Navigating the bridge between conscious, controllable behaviors and unconscious, automatic ones requires a delicate mixture of "doing," "undoing," and "non-doing." There are risks and dangers in every situation, without exception. If you don't breathe, you'll die. If you breathe badly, you might die too, maybe from an attack of asthma. If you think about your breathing, you're likely to start "taking breaths," and before long you'll be self-conscious about your breathing and you'll hyperventilate and pass out.

In short, not to breathe, to breathe badly, and to work consciously on your breathing are all risky. What can you do about it?

Early on in his teaching career, F. M. Alexander was known as "the breathing man," since he helped his students overcome all sorts of breathing handicaps. And yet he paid little attention to breathing itself and discouraged his students from doing so as well. According to Alexander, "the act of breathing is not a primary, or even a secondary, part of the process. . . . As a matter of fact, given the perfect co-ordination of parts as required by my system, breathing is a subordinate operation which will perform itself."[2]

Cross your arms tightly in front of the chest, raise your shoulders, and scrunch your head and neck. What happens to your breathing? If you stay too long in this posture, you might suffocate. Now straighten up and assume your everyday posture. What happens to your breathing? It changes radically for the better.

Breathing, in sum, is a function of coordination. The posture I invited you to assume is "abnormal" and leads to an abnormal breathing pattern. Your postures in daily life are "normal" and lead to normal breathing patterns. Logically enough, ideal postures would lead to ideal breathing patterns. All the exercises in this book that deal with coordination (such as the Möbius Strip) affect your breath indirectly and positively, and working on them alone may well lead to ideal breathing patterns.

Suppose, however, that you do wish to work on your breathing. How can you access it constructively? I propose three nonbreathing exercises that don't involve controlling the breath directly. The first revisits a concept you're now familiar with: the opposition of many forces within the body. The second invites you to reconsider the breathing cycle. The third introduces the notion of the linguistic breath.

1. MOVEMENT PLUS RESISTANCE EQUALS POWER

Brace your body gently, perhaps by sitting upright at a table and holding on to the table. Back, arms, hands, legs, and feet become engaged and connected, without moving and without being stiff, in a state of "energy-charged stillness." Retain this posture and spend some time breathing and sensing your breath. The inhalation pushes against the firm skeleton, and the elastic parts of the breathing apparatus actually stretch more amply than they would if they met no resistance from the skeleton.

This desirable mixture of mobility and immobility applies to all situations: speaking, singing, playing the flute, and so on. Go for a walk. Lungs, ribs, and diaphragm move as they always do in breathing. Legs and arms are now moving too. But the central point of your body, where the back meets the pelvis, remains absolutely still (as you learned in the Möbius Strip). Your moving breath, then, can always find points of resistance to oppose it within the body, even when the body itself moves.

Brace yourself gently, as before. Sing a long note in forte dynamics, noticing how the breath behaves. Now unbrace yourself, move extravagantly (for instance, shaking your limbs and rolling your head), then sing again. What happens to the breath and the voice? Most likely you'll run out of breath much sooner. The moving breath lives longer when it meets the opposition of a relatively unmoving body.

2. THE BREATHING CYCLE

Inspiration, F. M. Alexander wrote, "is not a sucking of air into the lungs but an inevitable instantaneous rush of air into the partial vacuum caused by the automatic expansion of the thorax."[3] When your ribs open, the space inside your body becomes bigger, and air rushes in if you simply allow it. You don't need to sniff through the nose, gasp through the mouth, or do anything whatsoever: Breath does itself. According to Alexander, "It is not necessary...even to think of taking a breath; as a matter of fact, it is more or less harmful to do so."[4]

Every exhalation plays a role in determining how your inhalation takes place. Breathe out, and collapse your spine at the same time. What happens to the inhalation that follows? Whistle, sing, speak, or shout. Again, how does each activity affect the inhalation? You don't need to establish the precise relationships between specific ways of "letting air out" and their subsequent "letting air in." All you need is to notice that, in some way or another, the exhalation always influences the inhalation. In time you'll see that the exhalation not only influences the inhalation but determines it outright. Find out how to exhale, and everything else follows.

The breathing cycle, then, doesn't consist in breathing in, and then breathing out—but first breathing out, and then breathing in.

Start easy and build from there: Let air out, silently or otherwise, and then let air in, silently. Let air out...let it in, silently. Out...in...now speak or sing. One day you'll get out of breath's way and the breath will do itself. Then the difficulty will be for you to believe it and accept it.

3. THE LINGUISTIC BREATH

We breathe for two main reasons. The first is biological: Without oxygen, we die. The second is linguistic: We breathe to punctuate our discourse, to organize our thoughts and to give them meaning and emotion, and to impregnate everything we say with the energy of breath itself.

Read the preceding paragraph out loud. Where do you take your breaths, and why? The paragraph is composed of three sentences, the first quite short, the second a little longer and subdivided by a colon, and the third much longer, also subdivided by a colon and followed by a list of three elements. You might be able to say the first two sentences without taking a breath in between them. Biologically, you can certainly do so without running out of air. Linguistically, however, it may be preferable for you to take a breath in between the two sentences.

If you speak the third sentence in a single breath, you risk rushing it and mangling its meaning. Conceivably, you could take a breath with every single punctuation mark: colon, comma, and comma. Suppose you find this excessive, and you prefer to breathe only once in the middle of the sentence. Where would you take your breath? It depends on what kind of emphasis you want to give to the statement. Test a few permutations, varying the speed and volume of your speech. Remember, inspiration happens by itself if only you let it!

Linguistic breaths can play the role of biological breaths, giving you all the oxygen you need to survive and thrive. If you become an alert speaker, you won't need ever to take a purely biological breath. The next exercise will help you get there.

BECOME YOUR TEXT

This exercise is a version of *delayed continuity*, which we learned as a practice routine in chapters 10, 12, and 13. For our purposes, we define "text" as a series of words or notes grouped together. Anything you say, sing, play, or conduct, be it composed or improvised, is a text.

The text is a sort of guide, offering clues on how you can coordinate yourself. The clues are contained in the text's rhythms; its challenges of articulation and enunciation; its hierarchy of syllables, words, sentences, and paragraphs; its cadences, rhetoric, and meaning; its prosodic accents and its punctuation; and other elements still.

A comma exists for two reasons: to make the text more intelligible, and to make you more comfortable while speaking. You can conceive of all elements in the text as having this double existence. Vowels, for instance, are absolutely essential to the text, but also to your own well-being, since they give you the opportunity to vibrate, to project yourself into the discourse, and to share of yourself with the audience. If you're in harmony with the text, then the text itself energizes you. If you're at odds with the text, you harm yourself as much as you harm the text.

To learn how to use a text as a coordinative map, organize its words together in logical units. Take more time, here and there, than you normally would in performance or in ordinary speech; then use every little bit of time to coordinate yourself. If the written text is insufficiently punctuated, insert your own punctuation. Lengthen your vowels so that you have enough time to inhabit every syllable. Linger on a vowel just long enough to do a minuscule crescendo and diminuendo on it. Use your crescendi and diminuendi to connect each vowel to the next vowel or consonant. Bend a vowel for expressive reasons, but also to delight in your voice, your breath, and your whole self.

Say the following statement out loud.

Take more time, here and there, than you normally would in performance or in ordinary speech.

Here's the statement laid out like in a poem. Insert silences of varying lengths at the end of each line.

Take more time, here and there,
than you normally would
in performance or in ordinary speech.

Break the text down into smaller units, retaining its grammatical logic.

Take more time,
here and there,
than you normally would
in performance
or in ordinary speech.

Now lengthen some of its vowels, respecting and enhancing the text's grammatical, syntactical, and prosodic construction.

Take mooooore tiiiiiime...
here and theeeere...
than you noooooormally would...
in perfooooormance...
or in ordinary speeeeeech.

Now speak the phrase normally, with "latent time and space" in reserve.

Take more time, here and there, than you normally would in performance or in ordinary speech.

It's relatively easy to learn how to integrate yourself when reading out simple texts. It's another matter to do it in everything that you say in all circumstances, at the dinner table with your in-laws, talking on the phone with the tax authorities, or improvising a song on stage. Use every opportunity to practice this exercise, and over time you'll become able to coordinate yourself simply by thinking and speaking.

THE BALLOON: SOUND AS VIBRATION

We're used to perceiving sound primarily through our ears and calling it "noise" or "music," but in truth sound is tangible as well as audible. You can hold sound in your hands and call it "vibration."

🕑 This exercise is illustrated in video clip #53, "The Balloon."

Blow up a normal party balloon, and tie its spout into a knot. Holding it lightly in your hands, bring it close to your mouth and speak a few words at it—softly, loudly, low or high.

Your voice's vibrations disturb the air inside the balloon, which concentrates and magnifies the vibrations until they become a tangible reality. Ask different partners to speak to the balloon as you hold it, and your hands will perceive each voice as a completely different set of vibrations—shallow or deep, pointy or round, choked or fluid, agreeable or disagreeable. Hold the balloon near your stereo speakers. Play different music—vocal, instrumental, orchestral—and marvel at their infinite variety of vibrations.

Speak to the balloon again, using a variety of vocal effects. Let your hands help you decide when a sound is healthy (free, powerful, and resonant) and when it is not. Then use your discernment to make healthy vocal choices in speaking and singing.

Vibrations are present at all times whenever you speak, sing, or play. You don't need the balloon to feel them. Do the following three-part exercise. (1) Talk or sing to the balloon, as before. (2) Drop the balloon while keeping your hands in front of you, and talk to the space in between your hands. They'll capture some vibrations, though more faintly than with the balloon. (3) Carry on talking or singing, and slowly drop your hands. You might still capture some of the vibrations of your own voice, though more faintly still. The exercise works best if you carry on talking legato as you pass from holding the balloon to holding the space to not holding anything.

Place one of your palms flat on your sternum and the other on the back of your skull near the neck. Speak or sing, and feel your voice's vibrations under your palms. Cross your arms in front of your chest and place your hands open and flat on the sides of your body, your fingers more or less coinciding with some of the ribs on your ribcage. The posture has an interesting effect on your voice: It amplifies the vibrations of your voice inside your trunk. You may feel as if you've become your own balloon. Now let go of your arms and speak or sing normally, retaining your newly found appreciation for your voice's vibrations.

THE FATHER AND THE DAUGHTER: TWO VOCAL MECHANISMS

Take a rubber band in your hands. Hold one end of the rubber band and pull the other away from it; pull both ends at the same time; pull one and twist the other. Each action creates a different effect upon the rubber band, stretching it, making it now taut, now loose. The voice works in a similar manner. Two sets of muscles (the *cricothyroids* and the *arytenoids*) pull on each other, creating an opposition of forces. You can alter the balance of their pulls in an infinite number of arrangements, each with a particular effect on the voice.

The two sets of muscles can be recognized as separate mechanisms capable of making distinct types of sounds. In vocal pedagogy, each of these mechanisms is called a *register*. Singers and singing teachers often disagree when talking about registers. For want of better words, and despite the risk of upsetting singers who use these words to mean other things, we'll name the two registers the *chest voice* and the *falsetto*.

A little girl talking to her doll uses her falsetto, as do most people when they baby-talk. Watch a trailer for a Hollywood thriller, and most likely you'll hear an announcer with a forced chest voice, low and threatening. The French style for a movie trailer's voiceover is the opposite: the breathy falsetto of a woman pretending to be three decades younger than she is. The peculiar sounds of yodeling come from a sudden crossing between the chest voice and the falsetto.

The musical literature is full of passages in which the composer invites the singer to make one register preponderant here, and another more robust just one or two notes later. A dramatic example is Franz Schubert's Lied "Der Erlkönig" (a malevolent sprite in German and Scandinavian folklore, the king of all spirits). A father rides a horse through a stormy night, clutching his sick child in his hands. The child is afraid; the father asks him what troubles him; the child tells him that the Erlkönig has come to take him away; the father tells him it's just the wind blowing; the Erlkönig whispers in the child's ear. Things end badly. The singer has to bring four characters to life: the child, the father, the Erlkönig, and the Lied's narrator. By writing the lines of each character in different ranges of pitch and dynamics, Schubert prods the singer to alter the register balance in order to create dramatic tension. The child is a natural candidate for the falsetto, but so is the Erlkönig, who'll sound particularly threatening when sung in a wispy and ethereal falsetto.

Sing and sustain a single note, low in your vocal range, in forte dynamics, on the vowel "ah" (as in the word "car"). Now sing and sustain a single note, high in your vocal range, in pianissimo dynamics, on the vowel "oo" (as in "boot"). You'll use your chest voice preponderantly when singing the loud low "ah," and the falsetto when singing the soft high "oo." There are dozens of ways of accessing the registers; these two vocal gestures simply illustrate the principle and provide you with a practical starting point to explore your registers.

In this exercise you'll strengthen each register separately before getting them to work together. Create a dialogue between a father and a daughter. The American father, who has a booming low voice, is severe and insistent: "No," he says, lingering on the "N," lingering on the "oh." The daughter's mother is Parisian, and the little girl likes using French when picking fights with her dad. "Oui," she says. She too is insistent, but her voice is high and light.

"Noooo" (low voice, and loud). "Ooeeeeee" (high and light.) "Noooo." "Ooooooooee." "Nooooo!"

Put fermatas on some vowels and make them swell and diminish:

"NoooOOOOoooOOO…" "OoeeeeEEEEeee…"

From the low "No," fly up to the high "Oui," without taking a breath. Linger on the "Oui" for a brief moment, perform a little crescendo, then swoop down to the vowel "oh" and bounce back up again:

"NoooOOOOoooOOOeeeeEEEEeeenOOOOooooEEEE…"

The father is strongest when he meets permanent opposition from the daughter, and vice versa. Their connection—that is, the connection between your two vocal mechanisms—depends on both voices' remaining energized whether or not they're being sounded. When you use your chest voice, have a latent falsetto at your disposal; when you go into your falsetto, keep a latent chest voice at the ready.

Perform the exercise with one hand on your sternum and the other touching the back of your neck, where the spine and the skull join. You'll feel interesting vibrations traveling up and down your body. Generally speaking, the father makes the chest and back vibrate strongly while the daughter makes the skull vibrate, although the father has his own skull vibrations and the daughter, her chest vibrations. Use your imagination and intuition to make their vibrations crisscross along the entire vocal range. Then, whenever you speak or sing, vibrations will spread out, up, down, front, and back from a central point between the father's sternum and the daughter's skull.

The interplay of the vocal registers is fundamental for your voice, whether or not you're a singer. We study the registers further in chapters 17, 18, and 19.

THE INNER ANIMAL AND THE OPPORTUNIST

Imagine that you enter a darkened building for the first time. How does your "inner animal" feel about it? The inner animal is that part of you that reacts instantaneously to the world, using nothing other than sensory perception and intuition. With no input from the intellect, the animal finds the building hostile or welcoming and adjusts its behavior accordingly.

Although the function of the inner animal is essential, we can't live on it alone. The intellect is just as essential, and we become our healthiest and happiest when the two functions oppose each other in a creative and dynamic way.

By barking, growling, or howling, an animal claims dominion over a large territory. The animal also uses its voice to mate and reproduce. The animal lets it be known that it's available to start a family, and in a rush to do so. Its voice indicates that the animal is healthy and powerful, a good candidate to protect a family from predators and other dangers.

Children in a playground during recess, at a birthday party, and in dozens of other settings use their voices powerfully without being consciously aware of doing so. Like animals, they use their voice to claim territory, to make their presence known, to fight rivals, and to connect with friends. Street vendors in an open-air market and sports fans at an arena shout much like animals in the jungle, as do men at a bachelor party and women at a bachelorette party.

Your task is to act from your animal core, but under the intellect's benevolent supervision. What you do freely and unthinkingly at the sports arena, you now must do just as freely, but out of a conscious choice. The process has one great built-in difficulty: The intellect that has the potential to shape the animal power is the same intellect that tends to suppress the inner animal, because of cultural and social reasons.

For this exercise, play-acting is unavoidable. An extraverted personality will embrace the exercise more easily than an introverted one. Extraverts, however, are "doers" *par excellence* and sometimes find it hard to pay attention to what they're actually doing; they do, do, do, and never stop to think, sense, and feel. Introverts, then, may hold their own advantage in the longer run.

Imagine yourself in one of the settings I described above: at a sports arena, a big party, or an open-air street market. Your team scores a goal, but the referee disallows it. "NOOOO!" Your reaction is immediate, and you don't even think before you shout. The game is fast, and your reaction is only valid for a few seconds; soon the game resumes and the other team runs away with the ball. In this situation, then, your shout is immediate, loud, spontaneous, unthinking, and natural. Mentally put yourself in the situation and improvise a number of cries, interjections, and outbursts. Shout with all vowels at your disposal, high or low in pitch, short or long in duration. Let out multiple shouts in a row: "No, no, no, no, NO!"

You have another innate capacity, called the "inner opportunist." It manifests itself hundreds of times every day. In a restaurant you sense that the waiter is available to take your order, and you summon him with a nod of your head. If the opportunity isn't there, however, you may be better off waiting than struggling. You can seize opportunities as they present themselves or manufacture them yourself. Driving around the neighborhood, you notice a parking spot and you grab it quickly, before the opportunity is lost. Suppose that you while driving you notice another driver vying for a spot. You block him on purpose to better increase your chances and opportunities.

Train the inner opportunist to collaborate with the inner animal. In the middle of a sequence of shouts coming from the inner animal, some part of your awareness—your body, ears, or throat—tells you, "This is a good one." The opportunist adds a fermata to the shout and dwells in it with the full power of the conscious mind, reshaping it with a crescendo, a diminuendo, a change of pitch, or anything else you want to do with it. The shout comes from a source that escapes full conscious control, but the opportunist feels, sees, hears, and otherwise discerns the moments when conscious control won't destroy the spontaneity of the animal-like sound.

A good work session might involve moments of total silence, sudden single shouts, sudden repeated shouts, the occasional fermata...then a shout unlike anything you've ever produced in your life.

Suppose you become an adept animal, shouting freely in various pitches, vowels, and dynamics. Suppose your opportunist starts collaborating with the animal. Then you can shape your shouts more elaborately. Put a fermata on a shout and use it as the first note in a descending scale in mezzo forte, andante molto moderato. Let out a shout and improvise a melisma upon it. (A melisma is a group of notes sang legato to the same vowel.) Shape a shout into the first few notes of a song you've been studying, and carry on singing without losing your connection with the inner animal. Then start requesting specific shouts from your animal: a shout to start an aria, a shout to become a character in a musical comedy.

Your ultimate aim as an integrated musician is to hold these capabilities permanently inside you: the inner animal and the opportunist, the father and the daughter, the balloon, the Möbius Strip, and all the others. The more latencies you have at your disposal, the healthier you'll be. And you'll have tremendous fun when the latencies start collaborating with one another, in music and in life.

CHAPTER 15

THE QUADRUPEDAL PROSODIST

A Piano Lesson

In this chapter you'll study bilateral and quadrilateral transfer—the all-important collaboration of arms and legs. You'll learn about four types of information that flow permanently among your limbs. You'll study an exercise called Talk the World that brings together quadrilateral transfer, discourse, and communication. Then you'll learn the Song of Pronation, an exercise at the piano (simple enough for all nonpianists to learn) that coordinates the arms and charges them with musical energy. The chapter closes with an advanced application of bilateral transfer to musical and prosodic challenges at the piano, using strategies you can adapt to other musical situations.

BILATERAL AND QUADRILATERAL TRANSFER

Tap your head with your left hand and rub your stomach with your right, and—like all little kids since the beginning of time—you'll find it difficult to keep the two hands independent. The hands both imitate each other and interfere with each other. This is a demonstration of *bilateral transfer*, a never-ceasing dialogue between the two sides of the body on matters of position, movement, tension, and relaxation.

Bilateral transfer can be a collaboration or a fight. To get a fight going, hold a heavy paperweight in one hand and a light bulb in the other. One hand "wants" to relax, the other "wants" to firm up. Their contradictory intentions get crossed, and body and brain go haywire. You risk dropping the paperweight or crushing the light bulb.

To get a possible collaboration going, try the following experiment. Write a short sentence by hand on a piece of paper. Now write it again, but while writing tug at your hair with the free hand with a gentle, rhythmic motion. Your handwriting is likely to become bolder and more legible. The dominant hand has some deep-seated habits of misuse; the free hand, not invested in the same habits, sends a constructive message to the dominant hand, "transferring" its energies and capabilities to the dominant hand.

The two sides of the body often do different things, and yet they can still collaborate. Sit at a table with a smooth surface. Place one of your hands—for instance, the left—on the surface top, fingers curved, palm facing down pianist-style. Slide the hand on the table at high speed, going back and forth over distances large and small. Note how controlled or uncontrolled the gesture feels, and how the hand's motions affect your head and neck. Now hold on to the table with your right hand and repeat the gesture of the left hand. Most likely the gesture will be better controlled and more agreeable, since the right hand is helping the whole body become stable and centered.

The legs also affect the arms, and vice versa. Play a fast, loud passage at the piano while holding your feet off the floor. If the active support of the feet and legs is missing, the arms must work much harder. This is *quadrilateral transfer*, the interplay of energies among all limbs. (For the record, the dialogue between two limbs on the same side of the body—for instance, left arm and left leg—is called *ipsilateral transfer*; between an arm and its opposite leg, *diagonal transfer*.)

The following exercise, performed with a partner, will give you a feeling for quadrilateral transfer.

⊙ This exercise is illustrated in video clip #54, "Quadrilateral Transfer I: An Introduction."

1) Stand still in front of each other. Cup your right hand and hook your fingertips onto the right-hand fingertips of your partner's hand, which is equally cupped. Now pull gently on your partner's hand, asking your partner to pull back on yours. Move your arm here and there, passing from pronation to supination and back again. Thanks to the pull of opposing forces, you'll feel a rich circuit of connections between your arm and your back, your arm and your partner's, your back and your partner's.

2) Now add the left hand and arm, which will necessarily cross above or below the right one. As before, pull and oppose your partner's pull, then move your arms up and down. You'll feel a new layer of connection, this time between both arms plus the back. This is bilateral transfer in action.

3) Bring your legs into the dance. Step backward or sideways, bend and unbend your knees, stand on one leg and move the other one about. If you keep your back engaged in the dance, all limbs will communicate with one another, in a complex network of connections that crisscross the back and pelvis and give you a lot of power with little muscular effort. This is quadrilateral transfer in action.

4) Let go of your partner's hands, without abandoning the connections between your arms, your legs, and your back. The dance with the partner awakens your limbs and sets them into a circuit of connections, but in fact you don't need to move and dance in order to establish or keep the connections. Their ultimate source isn't movement but the energy of your own awareness.

5) Now employ this energy to sing, play, or conduct. Depending on your specific activity, you may need to lean on a foot here, bend a knee there, pronate or supinate an arm, rock sideways on the chair, and so on. Quadrilateral transfer is born of energy and awareness, but that doesn't mean that actual movement is forbidden!

⊙ This exercise is illustrated in video clip #55, "Quadrilateral Transfer II: An Application."

FOUR TYPES OF INFORMATION

In bilateral and quadrilateral transfer, four kinds of information pass among the limbs: permanent qualities that accompany all gestures; position in space and movement; specific techniques; and emotional charge. The flow of information is complex and highly variable, changing from second to second.

1. PERMANENT QUALITIES

If we were to catalog everything that our hands and fingers can do the array of capabilities would be in the thousands, and the combinations of what the right and left hands can do separately and together would be in the millions. The left and right limbs usually perform divergent tasks, which would seem to greatly complicate bilateral and quadrilateral transfer. Yet their divergence masks a fundamental unity that is ever-present in coordination.

Regardless of their specific activity, all limbs must be permanently strong without being rigid, and supple without being floppy. All limbs must work in opposition with the back—that is, their movements must be countered by the back's strength and stability. Limbs, like all body parts, are channels of energy. Regardless of what specific gesture you perform, your limbs can be heavy or light, extended or contracted, fluid or angular. Energy informs and animates gesture, and is independent of it. This means that the left and right hands might be doing totally separate things and yet share the same energy.

All limbs need to be in a state of permanent readiness. The violinist's left hand, for instance, contains a latent vibrato (whether it vibrates or not), latent trills (whether it trills or not), latent pizzicati (whether it plucks the string or not), and so on. The bowing arm is the same: while performing any one task, it remains permanently ready to perform any other task.

Elasticity, resistance, strength, suppleness, direction, energy, readiness, and latency are all universal qualities for all limbs, which must be present in every gesture without exception. If you use them as the backdrop for bilateral and quadrilateral transfer, you'll turn every fight among your limbs into a collaboration.

2. POSITION AND MOVEMENT IN SPACE

Imagine a violinist at play. Her bowing arm moves freely back and forth on the string, while the left arm is comparatively immobile. Suppose her left elbow is cramped and her right shoulder is raised too high. The left arm tells the right hand its story: "turned in supination, comparatively immobile, the elbow cramped." The right arm tells the left its story: "turned in pronation, lots of movement, shoulder overly raised." Because of bilateral transfer, the right arm might try to imitate the left arm's cramped position, and the left shoulder might try to imitate the right shoulder's excessive tension.

To help the two sides of your body dialogue constructively, make energy, direction, and latency primary, and movement and position, secondary. This will make it much easier to negotiate the issues of movement and position, partly because you'll be able to coordinate each limb better, and partly because each limb will interfere less with the opposite limb.

3. SPECIFIC TECHNIQUES

All musicians must sit or stand; they must pronate or supinate their arms; and they must flex their joints in order to move. There are plenty of actions, however, that occur only in specific contexts. A guitarist plucks the strings with the right fingers; a timpanist strikes the drum with a mallet. The guitarist has no use for a mallet, and the timpanist never plucks at the drum. Some of the information exchanged in bilateral and quadrilateral transfer, then, is of a particular, instrument-specific nature.

These specific techniques create their own bilateral havoc. The guitarist plucks the strings with the right fingers while sliding the left hand up and down the fretboard. The sensations of "plucking" and "sliding" contradict each other, leading to technical and musical accidents. The guitarist can deal with the contradiction by paying attention to the two other types of information we listed. Energy, opposition, and latency are primary, movement and position in space are secondary, and specific techniques are tertiary. The plucking and sliding become "smarter" when they "understand" that they fit into a larger system of coordinative elements.

4. EMOTIONAL CHARGE

We tend to think that a hand or finger that misbehaves at the instrument is "physically disobedient" and in need of "physical therapy," and we don't dwell much on the frustration, anger, or shame that the awkward hand triggers. One hand's emotions, however, will always travel to the other. If you don't factor in the emotion, doing finger calisthenics is unlikely to solve the bilateral-transfer issues that arise from a disobedient finger. Instead, put the able, joyful hand at the service of the awkward, frustrated one.

Table 15.1 lists the types of information that are exchanged between limbs. The table isn't comprehensive, but it encapsulates the complexity of bilateral and quadrilateral transfer and invites you to embrace its importance in coordination and music making.

TABLE 15.1 The Information in Quadrilateral Transfer

Permanent Qualities	Movement and Position	Specific Techniques	Emotional Charge
Elasticity	Position in space	Articulation	Identity
Suppleness	Movement in space	Dexterity	Personal history
Connection	Tension	Legato	Adequacy
Contact	Relaxation	Staccato	Inadequacy
Opposition	Effort	Sostenuto	Frustration
Strength	Fatigue	Vibrato	Fear
Flow of energy	Pain	Bowing	Joy
Latency		Fingering	Pleasure
		Embouchure	Confidence
		Tonguing	Insecurity
		Plucking	
		Sliding	

BILATERAL AND QUADRILATERAL TRANSFER IN PRACTICE

Generally speaking, bilateral and quadrilateral transfer work positively when you focus not on the limb or limbs that are moving at a particular time but on the limb or limbs that contribute the most to your body's stability. Here are three illustrations using the cello, the piano, and the trombone.

1. AT THE CELLO

Suppose a cellist is struggling with a left-hand challenge: a trill followed by a large shift up the fingerboard. The left hand articulates the trill with fingers lifting and dropping at high speed. More or less suddenly, the trill stops and the hand flies up the fingerboard to play the new note.

The left hand is busy doing different things in quick succession. Meanwhile, the bowing arm does something simple, steady, and unvarying. The average cellist focuses on the busy left hand and charges it with eagerness and worry. At the same time, the cellist neglects the right hand, assuming its role is minor and its gesture trouble-free. Needless to say, the passage remains frustratingly difficult, and the cellist puts ever more wasted energy and emotion into the left hand.

But if the cellist decides to make the bowing arm the primary motor of the passage and the left hand secondary, the bowing arm leads by example. It says, "I am strong and stable. I have a nice contact with the string and a lovely connection to the back, the pelvis, the legs, the feet, and the floor." The left hand receives the message and absorbs the right hand's strength, even though their technical tasks are so different.

Our cellist starts by bowing some open strings, giving the right arm her full attention and making the gesture free and comfortable. Then she adds a sustained note with the left hand: no trills, no shifts, so that both hands do something simple and steady. Then she adds the trill—but not yet the shift—without losing the feeling of steadiness. If perchance the trill makes her neglect the bowing arm, she must go back to the sustained until she becomes totally committed to the right arm, her source of stability and intelligence. Then she can finally trill and shift without fear.

2. AT THE PIANO

The modern piano is built so that the lower octaves are more powerful than the higher ones. The lower strings are thick and long, and on the piano frame they cross over and above some of the higher strings. Therefore the lower strings interfere with the higher ones, so to speak. For decades and centuries, every piano student has learned to underplay the left hand, in order to compensate for the inbuilt imbalance of the instrument itself. Another argument to downplay the left hand comes from the harmonic series, which we'll study in chapters 16 and 17: The low notes usually played by the left hand on the piano have a wealth of overtones, some of which coincide with the pitches being played by the right hand. If a pianist plays the low notes too strongly—so the argument goes—their overtones will crowd out the higher pitches, while a softer left hand allows for the higher pitches of the left hand to shine on their own. As a result, a conflicting bilateral transfer takes place: the left hand tends to be insufficiently present, and the right hand ends up overrelaxing (to imitate the left hand's undercharged attitude) or overtensing (to compensate for the left hand's laziness).

Instead of working ever harder with the right hand, the pianist ought to bring the left hand to the fore by playing with the left hand more loudly than strictly necessary, by rewriting the passage in question to give the left hand something extra to do, or even by using the left hand to hold on to the piano while the right hand plays solo. In time, simply being aware of the left hand's latent power may be sufficient to help the right hand, and the pianist can then go back to the usual balance of voices in performance.

3. AT THE TROMBONE

The trombonist's arms perform two very different roles: The left arm and hand hold the trombone in place, the right hand and arm move the slide in and out. Since it's the moving slide that allows the trombonist to produce the needed changes of pitch, it's easy for him or her to concentrate on the right arm and neglect the left. And yet, for the right hand to move freely, the left hand must have a secure hold on the instrument. In fact, the left hand's role in trombone playing is primary, the right hand secondary. A useful procedure is for the trombonist to assume a playing position; give mental orders for the left hand and arm to be stable; play a sustained note without moving the slide; mentally recharge the left hand and arm's energies; and then change pitches with a small movement of the slide, all the while staying fully connected to the left side of the body. To habituate the left side to "take charge" may require hundreds of performances of this exercise, with ever-increasing challenges of movement for the right hand.

TALK THE WORLD

You need a partner for this exercise. Perform it anywhere: at home, out in the street, visiting a church or a museum. For the purpose of describing the exercise, we'll imagine that you and your partner are inside a church or chapel.

Hold your partner by the arm, elbow, shoulder, or waist, as if she were your favorite sister, and walk her through the whole church. While walking, describe your environment in detail: the church's architecture, the stained-glass windows, the paintings and sculptures. From time to time, point at something that merits particular attention, using your free arm to gesticulate. Use your voice in a quiet and emphatic manner, as if you were the church's priest, enthusiastic about the building but respectful of people's privacy inside the church. This will bring together discourse, locomotion, the use of arms and legs in quadrilateral transfer, touch, breath, meaning, and emotion.

It's a wonderful exercise that merits repeated performance. Do it with different partners in different environments. Then perform a special variation of it. Have your instrument at the ready, or your singing voice if you are a singer. Again, walk and talk with your partner. Then bring your discourse to a logical end; let go of your partner; sit at your instrument; and play a piece of music in the same spirit. While playing or singing, you metaphorically "walk your listener and talk to her," taking hold of her and bringing her attention to the joys of each composition.

Gesticulation, touch, and locomotion are forms of energy. Once your body becomes infused with these energies, you don't have to actively use them; instead you can hold them as a source of latent, compressed power at the service of music making.

THE SONG OF PRONATION

When it comes to coordination, it's easy to buy into the idea of "the right position," be it sitting at the piano or standing in front of an audience. This can lead you to hold yourself upright stiffly, resulting in tremendous aches and pains. In fact, the question to ask yourself isn't "How should I sit at the piano?" but "How can I find connection and flow as I sit at the piano?"

Energy is the link between position and connection. The best coordination of the arms comes when a certain arrangement of parts is infused with a particular energy. Then the position and the energy will collaborate to give you connection and flow.

Hold your arm in front of you, the elbow slightly bent, the fingers outstretched but not stiff, the palm turned downward as if ready to bounce a basketball. When your palm faces downward, your arm is in pronation; when the palm faces upward, the arm is in supination. Pronation and supination, then, are orientations in space. But they can also become paths for your energies. Hold your arm in pronation, your palm facing down. Now picture water washing over your arm. If this imagined flow is clear in your mind, it'll infuse your arm with perceptible energy. If the water comes from outside your body and falls into the center of your body, we'll call it *pronating energy*; if water comes from the center of your body and flows over your arm and away from your body, we'll call it *supinating energy*. It becomes possible to physically pronate your arm in space while directing its energies in supination, and vice versa.

This information will become useful while we study an exercise I call the Song of Pronation.

🔊 This exercise is illustrated in video clip #56, "The Song of Pronation I: An Introduction."

Sit at a table and place your hands down as if readying to play the piano, with the arms gently pronated. Curve your wrists so that your two little fingers point inward, toward each other. Tap the table percussively with your little fingers. Now curve your wrists the other way around, so that your little fingers are pointing outward, away from each other. Again, tap the table with your fingers. Which of these two arrangements is more comfortable?

The arms and hands are better connected when the hands appear to move in opposition to the elbows—in other words, if you direct your elbows out and the wrists in, with the little fingers pointing out away from each other and the overall energies of the forearms and hands tending toward pronation. We'll explore this arrangement at the piano, playing a simple melody that all nonpianists can learn. "Elbows out, wrists in" is universally useful. After you learn it at the piano, adapt it to your specific instrumental needs.

EXAMPLE 15.1. The Song of Pronation

🔊 This exercise is illustrated in video clip #57, "The Song of Pronation II: An Application."

Example 15.1 shows both the major and minor versions of the melody. Memorizing it takes only a few repetitions. Throughout the melody, keep the elbows out and the wrists in. The fingering is nonnegotiable: You must use the thumbs to play the opening interval and all its iterations. The anchoring thumbs infuse the arms and hands with pronating energy. Other fingers as they play their notes will tend to infuse the arms and hands with supinating energy. Invest your thumbs with enough intention and weight for their pronating energy to prevail over the other fingers' supinating tendencies.

Play the opening interval, C–E, and hold it. Sense a circuit of bodily connections that go from the left to the right side of your body, and vice versa:

Fingers, hand, arm, shoulder, back, shoulder, arm, hand, fingers.

The physical gesture is charged with a particular musical energy: the consonant interval of the major third, which heralds the tonic chord of C major. Pass from the major third to the next interval, the dissonant triton B–F, and hold it. The new interval is saturated with different vibrations and emotions, and it fairly begs for resolution. Throughout the melody, the alternation of consonance and dissonance will charge you with energy and propel your hands and fingers from interval to interval. You'll be tempted to choreograph the changes of energy by moving your head and neck, shifting your trunk, or lifting your shoulders. But if you keep your body relatively still, it'll oppose the energies that pass through it, condensing and enhancing them.

Vary the melody rhythmically, playing it in ⅜, for instance. Take any two consecutive intervals in the melody and go back and forth between them repeatedly. Play an interval and add a fermata to it; then pass suddenly to the next interval. Do all of this without losing the thumbs' pronating energy or your body's stillness.

Transpose the melody to all twenty-four major and minor keys. In every key start the melody with the two thumbs. The task of transposing the melody is useful in itself. You may be tempted to calculate the number of sharps or flats, the tones and semitones in each interval, the correct fingerings, and so on. But if you sense the interplay of consonance and dissonance and the irresistible pull of physical and musical forces, then you can transpose the melody by feeling alone, not analytical calculation.

The hands' proximity makes it comparatively easy to establish and nourish circuits of bodily connection. Play the melody with your hands one or more octaves apart and the challenge grows a little. Pass from the melody to an improvisation in which intervals and rhythms vary more widely, and the challenge grows further. In all situations, maintain the relationship between the arms and hands that we've called "elbows out, wrists in." Remember that it's not a fixed position in space but a dynamic pull of energies wholly independent of whichever position the hands assume.

Play the melody in any one key. Retain the feelings of connection that the melody offers, then transform it into an improvisation, or into a piece from the repertoire. For example, play the melody in C major, improvise a little tune in C major, and then play the fugue in C major from the first volume of the Well-Tempered Clavier.

BILATERAL TRANSFER AND PROSODY

You can use bilateral transfer to deal with prosodic challenges in music. We'll take a tricky passage from Beethoven's 33 Variations on a Theme by Anton Diabelli, opus 120, for piano. If you aren't a pianist, take the working principles behind these procedures and apply them to your own needs. The basic idea is simple: Rewrite difficult passages in order to make yourself comfortable in them. Once you find your comfort, you'll be better able to navigate the difficulties in the original passages.

🎧 This exercise is illustrated in audio clips #24, "Diabelli, First Half," and #25, "Diabelli, Second Half."

The theme's impetus is predominantly amphibrachic. The second variation—which is the object of our study—uses an amphibrachic foot from beginning to end. Throughout the entire first half, the left hand always plays the basic amphibrachic foot while the right hand plays an unbroken sequence of offbeats (example 15.2).

It's only too easy to tie yourself in knots trying to play the correct notes. Rewrite the passage, eliminating the constantly changing notes and their offbeats. Instead, play a simple series of amphibrachs, first with the left hand, and then with the right. The amphibrachic impetus becomes the single most important thing, and the hands can practice the art of using the amphibrachic impetus as a source of energy (example 15.3).

Using simple chords, practice the art of playing offbeats to an amphibrachic foot. Train both hands to become good at it (example 15.4).

Now your hands are adept at riding the amphibrachic impetus and at playing offbeats. Playing the actual chord changes will become much easier.

To begin with, the variation's second half continues the pattern, but at some point Beethoven breaks the pattern in a tricky way. Instead of having the same hand constantly play the beats and another play the offbeats, the hands alternate their roles (example 15.5).

Your hands, already good at playing amphibrachic patterns and offbeats, now must become good at passing quickly between playing beats and offbeats. Write silences between the amphibrachic units, and use the silences to clarify the passage's construction and to coordinate yourself. This is the technique of *delayed continuity*, with which you're

EXAMPLE 15.2. Ludwig van Beethoven: A "Diabelli" variation, first half

EXAMPLE 15.3. Amphibrachs

EXAMPLE 15.4. Amphibrachs plus offbeats

EXAMPLE 15.5. Ludwig van Beethoven: A "Diabelli" variation, second half

EXAMPLE 15.6. Delayed continuity

EXAMPLE 15.7. Alternating left- and right-hand amphibrachs

now familiar. If you hear the silences as amphibrachic feet themselves, the articulation of the sounded notes will be easier still (example 15.6).

Rewrite the passage again so that you don't have to worry about changing notes and chords. Then your hands can come to terms with the single difficulty of going from sounding the beats to sounding the offbeats (example 15.7).

Now play the passage as written. The combination of bilateral transfer and prosodic insight virtually guarantees technical and musical mastery. And if it doesn't, at a minimum you'll have had a really good time exploring their interaction.

PART III

SOUND

CHAPTER 16

THE HARMONIC SERIES

OSCILLATION AND RESONANCE

It's summertime, and you're sitting on a swinging porch bench, moving back and forth with the smallest effort of your legs. A breeze blows across your face, and you feel contented and fulfilled, in sync with the rhythms of life itself. How nice it'd be if producing big, beautiful sounds when you sing or play were just as sweet!

In fact, a force of nature exists that allows you this ease at the instrument or the voice. It's the phenomenon of *resonance*, behind which lies the *harmonic series*.

Webster's calls *resonance* "a vibration of large amplitude in a mechanical or electrical system caused by a relatively small periodic stimulus of the same or nearly the same period as the natural vibration period of the system." A swing is a system with a "natural vibration period," or the tendency to oscillate optimally at a certain speed and amplitude combined. If you gauge and time your pushes to coincide with the swing's natural tendencies, a small input of energy will cause the swing to travel far. In short, because of resonance the swing "swings itself" if only you help it a little.

Acoustic resonance works in the exact same way: The right investment of energy at the right time will maximize your sounds' oscillations while minimizing your efforts. Sound oscillations vary in strength and amplitude depending on many factors, including instrument, voice, and room acoustics. Another factor is the presence or absence of sympathetic vibrations. If you pluck the low E string on a guitar, for instance, the high E string two octaves above it will automatically resonate. The two E strings on a guitar vibrate sympathetically because they are part of the same *harmonic series*.

Almost every note ever sung, played, or struck is a combination of several sounds. In other words, most single sounds are chords in disguise. Take the cello's open C string. The C itself—called the *fundamental* or *first partial*—is the prevailing sound, and it's so potent that listeners aren't able to perceive any other sounds at first. Yet, inseparable from it as one's skin is from one's body, a number of other partials resonate over and above the C every time a cellist plays it. Together, a fundamental and its *overtones* constitute the *harmonic series*. (The fundamental is a partial of the harmonic series, but not an overtone, which by definition lies above the fundamental.) Example 16.1 illustrates the low C's first sixteen partials. The intervals of the harmonic series are invariable; to find the harmonics for another fundamental, simply transpose the entire series.

EXAMPLE 16.1. The first sixteen harmonics

The first partial is the fundamental itself; the second, an octave above the fundamental; the third, the fifth beyond it. There follow a perfect fourth, a major third, a minor third, a very flat minor third, a very sharp major second, and a series of ever smaller seconds. Harmonics have precise mathematical relationships with one another. The octave, for instance, vibrates twice as fast as the fundamental; their relationship is 2:1. The fifth above vibrates at a 3:2 rate to the octave. Other harmonics have rates of 4:3, 5:4, 6:5, and so on. In theory, the series is infinite; in practice, it becomes aurally insignificant after a certain point.

If your fundamental is a C, the seventh partial is a pitch between an A and a B-flat that you'll perceive as being a "flat B-flat," out of tune within the equal temperament you've grown accustomed to. (We look at intonation later in the chapter.) As you go farther up the series, other partials will also be out of tune according to equal temperament. In example 16.1 these partials are marked with arrows pointing up or down according to how the partial diverges from equal temperament.

Resonance is the art of maximizing sounds while minimizing effort. Since the harmonic series is the foundation of resonance, it follows that a deep and practical knowledge of the harmonic series opens the door to easy and healthy music making.

To begin with, your ear must discover the phenomenon and attune itself to it.

DISCOVERING THE HARMONIC SERIES

For this exercise you need a piano, preferably a well-tuned grand with its lid fully open, although the average acoustic upright also provides most of the information you're about to learn. Throughout the exercise the pedal isn't needed.

This exercise is illustrated in video clip #58, "Harmonic Series I: An Introduction."

1) Press the C below middle C and hold it down, without sounding it. Now play the C below it (the equivalent of the cello's open string) with the left index, with a short, loud, accented articulation. As the note dies down, you'll hear the C above it ring out like an echo, lasting several seconds depending on the quality of the instrument and the room's acoustics. Go on to other partials, each in turn, then several partials together. They'll sound like an eerie, soft choir heard in the distance (example 16.2).

Be inventive in how you combine these partials and their fundamental. Use repetition, alternation, and combination; vary the speed, length, and volume of the notes you play.

EXAMPLE 16.2. Hold down partials, sound their fundamental

2) You can play a fundamental and directly make its partials resonate; or you can play one or more partials and indirectly reveal the fundamentals beneath them. Press down a cluster of notes with the right arm laid across the keyboard, and use the left hand to strike notes below the cluster, singly and in chords. You'll hear a variety of consonances and dissonances as the heavenly choir of overtones grows in complexity and subtlety. Then invert the procedure: Hold a cluster of notes with your left arm and play notes and chords with the right hand. The heavenly choir will sing a different hymn.

A fundamental is like a parent, and the partials are its offspring. Notes in a composition may have ascending, descending, direct, or indirect familial relationships. The more you discern these relationships, the better you control your sound. Becoming an able musical genealogist will pay enormous dividends.

3) Now play the low C alone, striking it with any number of articulations—soft or hard, sustained or short, with or without the pedal. Thanks to the preceding steps, you're likely to perceive the vibrations of quite a few of the low note's partials. These vibrations have always been there, but since you're perceiving them for the first time, you may be startled and even disbelieving!

The harmonic series is as vital to your ears as smell is to your nose, and a full awareness of the phenomenon can completely transform your musical life. For this to happen, you need to open up your ears.

DEVELOPING YOUR EARS' SENSITIVITY

We think of sound as a form of noise captured by the ear, but vibration as a type of kinesthetic or muscular experience—a shake, a rattle, a tremor. In truth, all sound is vibration. Once you open up your ears, your body, and your mind, vibrations will transform your experiences of making music and listening to it.

Strike a note at the piano and hold it own, without using the pedal. Do nothing else until the sound has died down. Do not strike another note, do not talk or hum or cough, and do not judge the experience; be *in* it for the duration. You might feel the piano keys vibrate under your fingertips, the piano bench vibrate under your butt, and the floor vibrate under your feet.

Strike a dissonant chord chosen at random and hold it down until the sounds vanish. Because of the harmonic series, a single note struck at the piano is already a chord of sorts. When you play several notes at the same time, you create a "chord of chords" with complex vibrations. As the chord of chords die down, the harmonics of all the notes keep interacting. Some notes die down quickly, others linger. The entire mass of sound moves with a will of its own, bending and contorting itself like a thin sheet of metal subject to heat, wind, and pressure.

Go to a practice room with a drum set that includes a cymbal. Hit the cymbal with a finger, or bring your mouth close to it and shout or sing a note. Depending on the room acoustics and the sound you make, the cymbal might reverberate for a minute or longer.

The harmonic series is present in the sounds emitted by machines such as elevators, fans, washing machines, fridges, helicopters, and cars. Become able to discern, in these machines, their fundamentals and the accompanying overtones. Choose one machine to start with: your electric shaver, for instance. Turn it on and spend some time just listening to the sounds it makes. Sing or hum the pitches that your ears detect. The fundamental, the third harmonic, and the fifth harmonic are clearly audible in most machines. Those are the notes that compose a tonic chord, with the fundamental at the root, although the chord is spread out over more than two octaves. The seventh partial, which forms a flat minor seventh with the fundamental, is usually detectable without too much effort. Those partials that coincide with the fundamental—one, two, three, or more octaves above it— are usually harder to detect, since they seem to fold themselves into the fundamental.

Singing and humming in tune to a machine's harmonic series can have interesting effects. You may feel that your voice's vibrations are somehow fuller and easier than when you produce them a cappella. Test this by humming alone; humming with a machine turned on; and humming out of tune with the machine—for instance, humming a fundamental a quartertone higher than the machine's.

Without knowing anything about music theory or mathematics, we all react intuitively to consonance and dissonance, to regularity and irregularity. Our inner animal listens to a sound without intellectual discernment; the animal likes or dislikes the sound, and responds with pleasure, displeasure, joy, perhaps even terror. The sounds of the harmonic series and the emotions they trigger are so powerful that in some cultures the harmonic series takes on a religious dimension, which we'll look at in the next chapter.

LEARNING AND MEMORIZING THE HARMONIC SERIES

Memorizing the names and faces of sixteen people you meet briefly at a party is quite difficult, but remembering three groups with shared characteristics is much easier: six men, six women, four children. Similarly, you can learn and memorize the first sixteen partials of the harmonic series by regrouping them according to an aural logic.

Sitting at the piano, study example 16.3. Those harmonics that don't correspond to exact pitches on an equal-tempered piano are now annotated as semitones, indicating a form of compromise: The actual harmonic is to be found somewhere inside the semitone.

1) The first group includes partials 1 through 6. Play them together as the C-major chord outlined in example 16.4.

EXAMPLE 16.3. The harmonic series as a pianistic compromise

EXAMPLE 16.4. The first six harmonics

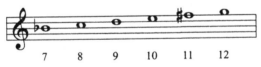

Comfortably spread between your two hands, it sounds the tonic chord of a familiar key. It has an open vibrancy that appeals to the senses and satisfies a basic aesthetic impulse that is both innate and, for people in Western cultures, developed from birth onward: the preference for consonance over dissonance. Your hands, ears, eyes, and memory all accept these six notes as an organic entity.

2) The second group includes partials 7 through 12. The sequence's intervals are ever smaller seconds. Two of its notes aren't in equal temperament: The seventh partial is somewhere between an A and a B-flat; the eleventh partial is somewhere between an F natural and an F sharp. I propose that you play the group as a scale, in two versions that I'll call an *approximation* and a *compromise*. The approximation is an ascending melodic G-minor scale. Your ear recognizes the scale and delights in its comeliness. Your mind analyzes the scale and finds it similar to dozens of passages in your repertoire. Then your ear and your mind collaborate to help you retain the information easily (example 16.5).

The compromise involves playing partials 7 and 11 as two-headed little beasts, hinting at their true pitch. At first you might feel that this makes the G-minor scale harder to recognize, but the funky partials are in fact memorable. You can remember a group of people as "six blondes, of which two have flat noses." Similarly with these partials: All six share a characteristic (being part of a G-minor melodic scale), two of them are a little different (flatter than "normal") (example 16.6).

EXAMPLE 16.5. The second six harmonics as an approximation

EXAMPLE 16.6. The second six harmonics as a pianistic compromise

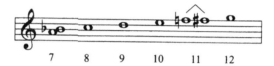

EXAMPLE 16.7. The last four harmonics

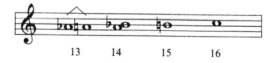

EXAMPLE 16.8. A mnemonic ditty for the last four harmonics

3) The third group includes partials 13 through 16. Partials 13 and 14 don't exist on a keyboard tuned to equal temperament. Play them as you did partials 7 and 11, as two-headed compromises (example 16.7).

The distance between partials 15 and 16 is a proper leading tone that hints at a dominant-tonic relationship and brings this sequence to closure. You may memorize partials 13 through 16 if you consider them as a variation of a famous little ditty (example 16.8).

4) Play each group as a tiny composition, complete with varied note lengths, accents, rubato, and so on. Then play the three groups in sequence: a rolling chord, a scale excerpt, and a ditty. Play them with an iambic impetus, with the fundamental as an upbeat to the second partial. Hold down the fundamental and the second partial with your left hand, and sound all other notes with the right one, without using the pedal. Insert a fermata to mark the end of each group (example 16.9).

5) You've seen, heard, felt, understood, memorized, and internalized the first sixteen partials of C. Do the same for all pitches of the chromatic scale: C-sharp, D, E-flat, E, F, and so on until you reach C again. Start your daily practice by sitting at the piano and playing the first sixteen partials for every note in the chromatic scale, going up or down the

EXAMPLE 16.9. The harmonic series organized at the piano

EXAMPLE 16.10. The undertone series

scale as you wish. It's a marvelous way of filling your house and your ears with the vibrations of the cosmos itself.

6) Now you understand the basic relationships between a fundamental and the partials above it. Your next assignment is to understand the relationship between a note and all the fundamentals underneath it (example 16.10).

The G is the fundamental of its own harmonic series, going upward in pitch. It's also the second harmonic of the G an octave below it; the third harmonic of the C a twelfth below it; the fourth harmonic of the G two octaves below it; the fifth harmonic of the E-flat two octaves and a third below it; and so on. Sit at the piano and press the key for the G, without sounding it. Then strike the octave below it, and you'll hear how it triggers sympathetic vibrations in the original pitch. Continue striking the notes in succession, moving leftward along the keyboard and striking ever lower fundamentals: G, C below it, G below it, E-flat below it, C below it, and so on.

These fundamentals form a sequence with the same intervals as the harmonic series itself: octave, fifth, fourth, major third, minor third, and so on. Theorists call this the *undertone series*. Suppose you play the violin in a string quartet, sounding pitches that almost without exception lie above the cello's pitches. Often enough the cello plays a fundamental of which the note you play is a partial. Your knowledge of the undertone series will help you figure out how the cello's fundamentals support or fight the pitches that you play yourself. Then you and the cellist can engage in a sonic conversation, making some pitches a little louder, others softer, the better to create a balanced interplay of fundamentals and upper partials.

THE HARMONIC SERIES AS THE UNDERPINNING FOR INSTRUMENTS

The construction of most instruments revolves around the harmonic series. Trombones, for instance, have only seven fundamentals, each corresponding to a position of the slide; all other notes are partials to these fundamentals. Each pitch is produced by the combination of a slide position and a degree of embouchure tension that sounds a particular partial.

The organ derives its particular sonority from a manipulation of the harmonic series. Each organ stop boosts one or more partials at the expense of the others, and the

EXAMPLE 16.11. A piano imitating an organ

combination of partials—some enhanced, others suppressed—gives the stop its individual timbre. An organ stop will sound similar to a clarinet, for instance, if it reproduces the clarinet's preponderant partials, which happen to be quite different from the flute's or the oboe's. Just as an organ can imitate another instrument, a piano can imitate the sounds of an organ, by combining pitches that exaggerate certain partials. Sit at the piano and play the tune in example 16.11. It'll create a plausible imitation of an organ stop.

On a bowed instrument, one can sound *natural harmonics* by pressing lightly on precise spots (called *nodes*) along the string and bowing or plucking the note in question. One can also sound *artificial harmonics* by stopping any note down normally and, with another finger of the left hand, pressing lightly a fourth or a fifth above that note, in each case creating a different harmonic. One can play the same pitch on different strings, using natural or artificial harmonics as appropriate, giving the instrument a tremendous range of colors and shades.

Much like a trombonist, a flutist produces his or her notes by a combination of fingerings (which create fundamentals) and overblowing (which creates partials). With the same fingering a flutist can blow the fundamental C, the C an octave above it, the G a twelfth above it, and so on. The same pitch can be sounded by different combinations of fingerings and overblowing. For instance, a high A can be sounded as second harmonic to the A an octave below it or as a third harmonic to the D a twelfth below it.

This exercise is illustrated in video clips #59, "Harmonic Series II: At the Flute," and #60, "Harmonic Series III: At the Piccolo."

By default, every musician knows at least a tiny little bit about the harmonic series, since it's impossible to make any sort of music with at least a minimal intuitive understanding of it. The problem is that our knowledge includes information felt but not understood, information felt but misunderstood, information understood but not felt, and "mis-felt" information where your ear thinks it's getting something when in fact it's getting something else altogether. If you play a brass instrument, for instance, you know that you have only a few fundamentals at your disposal, and all the notes you produce are in fact harmonics of these few fundamentals. Most likely you don't know the precise number of harmonics, their pitches, and their relationship one to the other. In fact, you learned it all by trial and error, by imitation, sometimes in dread of a mean teacher, sometimes half-asleep because you went to a party the night before your lesson. The mixture of all these experiences constitutes the average learning for all of us and leaves us with potentially handicapping gaps.

An excellent meditation for a brass player is to explain the harmonic series to a nonbrass player, or, better still, to a nonmusician. Trying to explain something to someone is a reliable way of finding out how much you know and how much you don't know about the thing in question. Present the entire phenomenon from the bottom up, from the simplest concepts of pitch to the most complex permutations, and without saying anything that might confuse your listener. If you really organize your information, your explanations could be a series of sounds, not a series of abstract explanations.

Another useful procedure is for a group of musicians—a string player, a woodwind player, a brass player, a singer, and a pianist, for instance—to get together and create a "harmonic series study group," where every member must explain and demonstrate the phenomenon to the others.

THE HARMONIC SERIES AS THE UNDERPINNING OF MUSIC

The development of Western music, from plainsong to organum (two voices singing in parallel octaves, fifths, and fourths) to modal and tonal counterpoint and beyond, largely corresponds to a climb up the harmonic series, each evolution demonstrating the willingness of composers and audiences to accept intervals of greater dissonance—that is, greater mathematical complexity—as aesthetically valid.

Medieval plainsong consisted of a single line of music. When a second, concurrent line was added to it composers, performers, and audiences wanted the concurrent lines to sound the intervals of the octave (the second harmonic) and the fifth (the third harmonic) exclusively, as "perfect consonances."

In the passage from plainsong to polyphony, it took a long time before the interval of the major third (formed by the fundamental and the fifth harmonic) was considered acceptable too—as an "imperfect consonance." The major triad consists of the first, the third, and the fifth harmonic (the second and the fourth are doublings of the octave). The seventh harmonic creates a seventh chord with the major triad, and the ninth harmonic creates a ninth chord with the seventh chord (the sixth and eighth harmonics are also doublings, respectively, of the intervals of the fifth and the octave). It took *centuries* until sevenths and ninths were widely tolerated.

Early on, the interval of the fourth was considered consonant too, until it was discarded. A case could be made that people "misunderstood" the interval of the fourth at first. If you travel up the harmonic series, the intervals *between* partials are the octave, the fifth, the fourth, the major third, and so on, and on this path the interval of the fourth appears to dwell among consonances. But the basic feeling of consonance and dissonance arises from the interval between any partial and its fundamental, not a neighboring partial. If the fundamental is C, a fourth above is an F—a note that is nowhere present among the lower partials. In other words, an F is "foreign" to the C's harmonic series, and the interval C–F isn't as consonant, therefore, as C–G or C–E.

The ear is most interested in the relationship between the lowest note of a chord and the notes above it, rather than the relationships among the higher notes themselves. This explains why the ear perceives the chord C-E-A as relatively consonant and the chord C-F-A as relatively dissonant. Both chords contain the interval of a fourth (E-A and C-F

EXAMPLE 16.12. The Picardy third

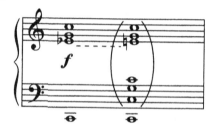

respectively), but the ear "reads" the chord from the bottom note up: It perceives the first chord as the combined intervals of C-E and C-A (both consonant), and the second as the intervals C-F and C-A (one dissonant, the other consonant).

In the hierarchy of the harmonic series, the third harmonic is the most important after the fundamental. If the fundamental is a C, the third harmonic is a G. The relationship between the chords of the tonic and the dominant is the defining factor in tonal music. If the tonic chord is C, the dominant chord is G. The tonic-dominant relationship, then, is the functional mirror of the acoustic relationship between the fundamental and the third harmonic. This relationship underpins the circle of fifths, which in turn underpins the whole of harmony and of tonal music. By different means, the harmonic series underpins the Church modes and the whole of modal music. And if you listen to Classical Indian music, the harmonic series is never far from how the sitar is tuned, how the ragas are constructed, and how singers sound their voices.

In sum, the harmonic series underpins virtually the entire edifice of music.

Modern composers have often exploited the harmonic series as an explicit compositional tool, for instance, using combinations of fundamentals and partials as colorist devices at the piano. Certain composers have used it as a structural (that is, not purely coloristic) compositional device. Karlheinz Stockhausen's "Stimmung" for voices is a seventy-minute piece consisting of nothing but partials spun from a single fundamental, B-flat. But the effect of the harmonic series in compositions dates from much earlier. Here is a single example, somewhat banal but illustrative. The fifth partial of any fundamental is the major third above the fundamental, transposed two octaves higher—for instance, the fifth partial of a C is an E. If you play a C-minor chord, which contains an E-flat, the minor third will clash with the fundamental's fifth partial, which is the E natural. You can hear the clash by playing and holding the chord in example 16.12 on a well-tuned grand piano. In the last chord of a minor piece resonating in a church, the clash can be rather uncomfortable. On this account, composers in the Baroque era would often end a minor piece with a major chord—a compositional device called (for unknown reasons) the *Picardy third*.

PRACTICAL APPLICATIONS

The harmonic series is such an all-encompassing phenomenon in music that we can scratch only its surface here. The following applications are way stations on an infinite journey.

1. RESONANCE AND PROSODY

Take an object to use as a pendulum—a cello or violin bow, for instance. Hang it from your index finger and tap it, letting it swing freely in the air. Tap it firmly, and the bow swings in a wide arc; tap it lightly, and the bow swings in a narrow arc. Tap the bow into movement and let it swing for a while. When the oscillation starts becoming narrower, refresh it by giving the bow another little tap. If the bow is coming *toward* you hand when you tap it, you create a barrier to the bow's natural oscillation. If the bow is going *away* from your hand when you tap it, you simply help it go where it's going already. Depending on your timing and the intensity of your energy, then, you can either jolt a pendulum out of its oscillation or renew its oscillation smoothly with a minuscule expenditure of effort. This is also true of the oscillations of sound. The harmonic series (which is the basis of resonance) and prosody (which is the organization of timing) can and must collaborate to give you the ability to make big, free sounds with little muscular effort.

This exercise is illustrated in video clip #61, "Harmonic Series IV: At the Cello."

Open your ears to the resonance of your instrument or voice and the room in which you're practicing. Play or sing the first note with the needed energy, and let it resonate. Then strike your next note with its own needed energy, while remaining attentive to the vibrations of the preceding note. Do so for the entire text, not letting any note jolt the vibrations of the preceding note. You may need to play or sing your piece well under tempo first, so that you have the time to sound a note, feel its vibrations, and sound the next note. With practice, you'll become able to think, act, and sense the consequences of your act instantaneously.

Ansel Adams, the great American photographer, was also an accomplished pianist who could have chosen to pursue a career as a concert artist. In his autobiography he describes to perfection the relationship between harmonics and timing. The secret—and the difficulty—lies in your being attuned to the present, to the past, and to the future at the same time:

> Consider a struck note; the first impact sound is followed by a complex series of harmonics. In this chain of harmonics there are links and profiles of completion, suggesting the ideal moment for the impact of the next note. However, the miracle dwells in the anticipation of the correct moment of impact of the following note; if we acted on perception of this moment, we would, because of the brain/nerve/muscle lag, be late in action and the theory of legato blasted.[1]

The psychological and aesthetic implications of this exercise are bigger than this simple description implies. An intense emotional involvement in singing and playing can cause sound oscillations to jolt out of their smooth paths. The exercise requires that you step back from "doing" and from pouring your heart out; open up your awareness; and allow optimal sound waves, rather than the expression of your emotions, to become the most important thing in your music making. Paradoxically, the exercise may lead you to express yourself more fully than ever in your life. Your sounds will become freer and more vibrant, and they'll emanate from your deep intimacy with the musical text itself.

2. CHORDS OF CHORDS

A normal musical sound is a kind of chord consisting of a fundamental plus its many partials, some clearly audible, some not. When two pitches or more are played or sung together, interactions take place between the pitches' fundamentals and also between all their partials, creating a complex "chord of chords."

Imagine a cellist and a violinist performing a passage in which the cellist plays a low C and the violinist a G two octaves plus a fifth above it. The violinist's pitch corresponds to the sixth harmonic of the cellist's C. The violinist, then, is doubling up a pitch that's already present in the cello's fundamental. There are at least three ways of balancing the two sounds:

1. The cellist takes the lead and plays the low C loud and focused, and the violinist fits the high G into the cello's palette of clearly sounded harmonics.
2. The violinist takes the lead and sounds the high G loud and focused, and the cellist plays the low C more quietly.
3. Both players sound their notes as focused and present as they can.

Choice 1 leads to a darker sound, with the fundamental in the foreground and the partials in the background. The justification for playing a loud C and a soft G is that the G is already contained in the C and doesn't need further iteration, which would make for "too much G."

Choice 2 leads to a brighter sound, in which the partials move to the foreground as the fundamental moves to the background. The justification for playing a softer C is for the cello not to rob the violin of its chance to shine and shimmer.

Choice 3 means the fundamental is very present but so are the partials above it, creating a dense and rich sound—possibly too dense and rich depending on context.

Needless to say, these technical and interpretive decisions can be made quickly, intuitively, and creatively once the players involved develop the necessary awareness.

3. AT THE PIANO

Pianists are permanently called upon to make choices about fundamentals and their harmonics. Should you let your left hand take a preponderant role, on the assumption that by sounding rich fundamentals it frees the right hand from the need to shout out its notes? Or should you play a softer left hand so as not to overwhelm the right hand?

Historically, the preference for pianists has been to favor the right hand over the left. The piano's lower strings are so long that they cross over the higher strings. Low notes strongly struck vibrate above the higher strings, potentially interfering with their vibrations. By tamping down the left hand, however, you risk creating an awkward situation. The left hand says, "I'm a little shy and ungrounded," and the right hand absorbs and mimics the feeling. How to balance out the need for the left hand to be present with the need for the higher notes not to be overwhelmed?

Overplay the left hand willingly, until the hand becomes comfortably grounded. This requires the temporary suspension of your aesthetic preferences, since the lower notes may appear too loud to your ears. Play a passage a few times in a row, moderating the left hand's weight little by little. The left hand will retain its feeling of ease as it passes from forte to mezzo forte to mezzo piano until it reaches the dynamic level you wish to give it.

If you haven't spent a lot of time paying attention to the harmonics at the piano, you'll tend to favor "doing" at the expense of "sensing." Play and hold an isolated chord from a passage, giving full weight to both hands. Receive the vibrations coming from the piano without judgment. Play the chord again, dampening the left hand; then play it dampening the right hand instead. Within each hand you can heighten one or more notes. In a ten-note chord you may have dozens of possible voicings, each with a subtly different energy and emotion. Repeat the procedure many times for many different chords, and you'll start using vibration as your single most important means of expression. It's entirely possible that you'll develop voicing preferences different from those you had when you favored the right hand by default!

THE BATTLE OF INTONATION

If the mathematical relationship between two pitches sounded together is simple, the interval's oscillations will be smooth; if the relationship is complex, the oscillations will be jagged. The ear tends to prefer smooth oscillations to jagged ones, but it's mathematically impossible for all intervals to be equally smooth. If you tune your instrument to play a diatonic composition in C-major with smooth oscillations, for instance, many other keys—E-flat major, for instance, or F-sharp minor—will sound inevitably jagged.

Intonation, in other words, is the art of oscillatory compromise between the ideal (which means optimally vibrant intervals) and the possible (which means at least some, if not all, intervals not optimally vibrant). The equal temperament of the modern piano, for instance, is a compromise from top to bottom. The octave is divided into twelve semitones of equal size, and every interval struck at the piano slightly deviates from the optimum vibrations of just intonation, except for the octave itself. To give two examples, a fifth in an equal-tempered piano is about one-fiftieth of a semitone lower than a just fifth, and an equal-tempered major third is about a sixth of a semitone higher than a just major third.

Equal temperament came to the fore in Western music in the eighteenth century, and as it arose it met with tremendous resistance from composers, performers, and listeners who all felt that most of its intervals were simply out of tune. Today most people grow up with equal temperament as a given, not even aware that it's a compromise by definition, and only one out of many possible compromises.

The battle between the ideal and the possible in intonation is a battle between the natural and the cultural—or, to put it otherwise, between the absolute and the relative. The cultural elements are relative: What sounds in tune to the ears of an average Western listener will sound out of tune to the average Tibetan listener, and vice versa. The one absolute element in the battle of intonation is the nature-given harmonic series. Its components never change. The frequency ratio between a partial and a fundamental, or between a partial and another, is measurable and predictable. What makes an octave "consonant" is its smooth oscillations, which come from a mathematical relationship between the notes involved. What makes a minor second "dissonant" is its jagged oscillations, behind which there also lies a mathematical relationship.

The most constructive way to conceive of intonation is not as a goal by itself but as a means to resonance, of which the harmonic series is the underpinning. The harmonic series is like a well of pure water. Intonation is like coffee, tea, consommé, or whiskey: something you brew, starting with pure water and spicing it according to taste.

Let's imagine a violinist who lives by this principle. When practicing, she starts by playing open strings singly, looking for the richest vibrations possible. She goes on to the most consonant intervals: open strings in double stops, sounding the interval of a fifth; or an open string plus an octave above it, fingered on the next string up. She understands that if she tunes a fifth to maximize its resonance, she'll have to compromise on her thirds and fourths. It's a fact of life, and she's made her peace with it. When she works on imperfect consonances such as thirds, sixths, and tenths she manipulates her intonation a little to *approximate*, not to match, the resonances of open strings and perfect consonances. She moves on to perfect fourths, then on to more dissonant intervals such as seconds, sevenths, and ninths, never forgetting that her goal is resonance and that achieving it will involve many compromises. Employing both conscious choice and acquired intuitive reflex, she tunes her playing differently when she plays a cappella, with a piano, or in a string quartet. And because she's at peace with the inevitable compromises of intonation, she actually enjoys adapting her playing to the needs of each musical situation.

In the next chapter we continue our discussion of the harmonic series, now concentrating on the voice.

CHAPTER 17

THE HARMONIC SERIES AND THE VOICE

THE VOICE AS A PATH TO THE DIVINE

The harmonic series is a permanent feature of your voice. Every word you say and every note you sing resonate with a specific range of partials. It may be difficult to become aware of the phenomenon and more difficult still to control it consciously, but exploring it will lead you to some unexpected, wondrous places—whether you're a singer or instrumentalist.

In Tibetan chant the harmonic series is perceived as a portal to the Divine. Vocal techniques heighten the overtones until they become as clearly audible as the fundamentals, so that the voice becomes capable of singing not a note but a chord. This is *multiphonic singing*, also called *throat singing* and *harmonic singing*. Huston Smith (author of *The World's Religions*) was one of the first Westerners to encounter it:

> Sensed without being explicitly heard, overtones stand in exactly the same relation to our hearing as the sacred stands to our ordinary mundane existence. Since the object of worship is to shift the sacred from peripheral to focal awareness, the vocal capacity to elevate overtones from subliminal to focal awareness carries symbolic power. For the object of the spiritual quest is precisely this: to experience life as replete with overtones that tell of a "more" that can be sensed but not seen, sensed but not said, heard but not explicitly. "Heard melodies are sweet, but those unheard are sweeter." To consciously, explicitly hear those "unheard melodies" was the lamas' unique achievement.[1]

Multiphonic singing is also practiced in Tuva (an autonomous region in south central Russia), Mongolia, Sardinia, and many other places. YouTube has a wealth of interesting clips featuring it. To start your exploration, use the keywords "Tibetan chanting," "multiphonic singing," "throat singing," and "a tenore" (for the Sardinian style).

A healthy voice rings out with a rich wealth of upper partials. In fact, the harmonic series is both an indication of your voice's health and a means to improving it. The exercises in this chapter are useful in both general and specific ways. Generally, they'll improve your awareness, further opening your ears to the world of harmonics. Specifically, they'll give you better control of your voice and your whole self.

HOWLING

Every sung or spoken vowel triggers a particular mix of overtones. An "ah" and an "oh," for instance, sung on the same pitch and with the same dynamics, will produce different harmonics. This exercise helps you tune your voice to produce the richest possible harmonics through the manipulation of vowel sounds.

⏵ This exercise is illustrated in video clip #62, "Harmonic Series and the Voice I: Howling."

1) Sing a comfortable pitch anywhere within your vocal range, sustaining it on the vowel "oo" (as in "boot"). If you aren't a singer and believe you can't sing, use "legato speech." Speaking normally, say the word "boot" and lengthen the vowel "oo" for several seconds, holding its pitch steady. While singing or speaking, change the vowel from "oo" to "ee" (as in "beet"). The change can be immediate, much as you turn a switch on and off; or gradual, much as you calibrate hot and cold water in the shower. The more gradually you change the vowel, the more benefits you'll draw from the exercise. If you make the change gradual enough, you'll hear a steady climb up the harmonic series as you pass through intermediate vowels on your way from "oo" to "ee."

2) Curl your tongue backward, letting the tip of the tongue touch the roof of the mouth lightly. Test your tongue's mobility and make it travel back and forth inside your mouth, sweeping the roof of your mouth toward the upper teeth, then toward the throat. Now hold the curled tongue still, in any one position in which you feel comfortable. While holding the tongue, test the mobility of your lips and jaw, separately and together. Make sure that lips and jaw aren't frozen in place when you curl your tongue.

3) While curling the tongue, sing the vowel "oo" in the middle-to-upper reaches of your voice. Vary the dynamics from very soft to very loud. Vary the pitch, raising and lowering it first by small amounts like a semitone, then by larger intervals. Then vary the pitch and the dynamics at the same time, with the tongue always curled. These vocal variations might make it sound as if you were howling.

4) Choose a specific pitch and dynamics, and hold it for a while. Without altering the pitch, vary the curling of your tongue and the shape of your lips. If you pay close attention to the sound you make, you'll notice that the changes in the tongue and lips alter the sound significantly. Pay closer attention still, and you'll notice that upper partials appear and disappear according to the shape of your mouth.

5) While holding a specific pitch and dynamics, change the vowel gradually from "oo" to "ee," then back to "oo." The change in vowel may or may not involve the lips, and may or may not involve the tongue. However you change the vowel, its harmonic series will be directly affected, with some upper partials coming and going depending on the shape of the vowel. A whistle may sound at the same time that you sing (or howl, if you prefer to call it so!). The whistling is a strong upper partial that kicks into place on account of a particular combination of lips, tongue, pitch, dynamics, and vowel.

6) If you make a sound that feels especially rich to your ears, put a fermata on it and change its dynamics with a crescendo and diminuendo. If you "feed energy" into the sound

without squashing it, your howling becomes tremendously loud and piercing—not because of muscular effort but on account of the harmonic series.

On a superficial level you're just learning to howl. The exercise, however, is much richer than it seems. It merits further discussion.

WHAT YOU LEARN THROUGH HOWLING

Imagine a canister full of gas. If you heat the canister, the gas inside will expand and push against the canister's inner walls with ever-increasing power. Canned and heated gas, in other words, has more power than gas that isn't canned or heated. Let's call this *compressed energy*. The compressed energy of the expanding gas can be put to a constructive use—for instance, to propel a rocket.

One of the reasons why howling is so useful is that it teaches you how to compress energy, in this case, the energy of the voice itself and the breath you use to activate it. There are at least three factors at play:

1) The tongue creates a barrier to the free flow of voice and breath, and their energies become like gas inside a canister: because they can't escape, they become stronger.

2) If you busk in a subway corridor, in an open park, or underneath an arched gate, you'll immediately feel how different spaces have different acoustic properties, some more resonant, others less so, some concentrating the vibrations of sound, others dispersing it. The same principle applies to your vocal organism: You change its acoustic properties when you change its shape. The curled tongue is only one element in howling; the lips, soft palate, cheeks, uvula, and throat all come into play. With practice you learn how to use the whole mouth cavity to shape your voice and compress energy, using your ears' sensitivity to the harmonic series to guide you.

3) Some vowel sounds facilitate the compression of vocal energy, while others allow energy to disperse too easily. In howling you learn how to manipulate the shape of your vowels, and in time you develop the ability to choose vowels with compressive capabilities across your entire vocal range, in singing and in speaking.

Once you get the hang of compressed energy you can trigger the phenomenon without curling the tongue back at all. The tongue helps you start your exploration, but it's strictly unnecessary for it. Vocal control ultimately arises in the throat, and the tongue is only an adjunct to it.

If you howl high up on your voice, you strengthen your falsetto register. It has the counterintuitive but logical effect of indirectly enhancing your chest voice, which seizes upon the strengthened falsetto as a reliable collaborator. Then the chest voice can "pull" while the falsetto "holds," and their opposition is beneficial to the voice as a whole.

When you perform the curled-tongue exercise on the lower notes of your voice, you strengthen your chest voice. While doing it you might sound like a bull or a cow mooing, rather than a wolf howling. Both the mooing and howling might displease your ears, but they're useful intermediate steps toward complete vocal control.

You may remember from chapter 11 that F. M. Alexander postulated that the orientation of the head and neck affects the whole body, working as a sort of "primary control" in coordination and movement. At the risk of oversimplifying the principle, let's say that if you scrunch your head and neck, your whole body suffers; and if you energize your head and neck, your whole body benefits. Howling—or, more precisely, working on vocal harmonics—seems to be a very effective way to direct your head and neck from the inside, as it were. While vocalizing in the manner prescribed, you naturally shape and reshape the mouth cavity. Lips, tongue, uvula, soft palate, and throat all come into collaboration, and the voice itself becomes a source of well-directed energy. Your neck lengthens and your head seeks its own poise without your doing anything beyond the vocalizing itself. And because the head and the neck determine your overall coordination, your whole body becomes stable and open. In short, the harmonics direct the voice, the voice directs the head and neck, and the head and neck direct the body. It happens more instantaneously than implied by this description; although one thing follows the other, they all take place at the same time.

Vocalizing with harmonics is directly useful for singers, of course, since it "places" the voice. (The quotes indicate that the term is a bit ambiguous, and I employ it here for the sake of brevity.) It's also useful for wind and brass players. A horn player howls or vocalizes for a while and finds the ideal space for her mouth and throat—as witnessed by the powerful vibrations of her voice. Then she keeps herself "spacious" and plays a note on the horn, perhaps the very same pitch on which she's been howling. It has the effect of "tuning the player to the instrument" and creating a particularly rich sound.

String players and pianists can also tune themselves to their instrument. I play an open string at the cello and vocalize at the same time, choosing a pitch along the open string's harmonic series and holding the pitch steady. Suppose I play a G: I can sing the G itself (which is the first harmonic), the G an octave above it (the second harmonic), the D a twelfth above it (the third harmonic), the G two octaves above it (the fourth harmonic), and so on. Provided I'm sensitive to the cello's vibrations and to the spaces inside me, the collaboration between the cello and the voice enhances my overall resonance and helps me project my sound outward.

You don't need ever to howl, sing, or vocalize; all you need is the latent capacity to do so. Then you remain as poised and internally spacious as when you actually howl.

SING TO THE PIANO

For the next exercise you need a well-tuned piano, upright or grand, with its lid open.

1) Stand next to the piano. If it's an upright, lean your head down toward the piano's inside; if it's a grand, lean your trunk over so that your face is close to the piano's resonating board. Sing a short note in mezzo forte or forte dynamics, in a pitch that is comfortable for your voice, using the vowel "ah." Regardless of the note you sing, the piano will vibrate sympathetically: Waves of vibration will arise from the piano as if you had played an actual note on it. You'll set up sympathetic vibrations whether you sing,

EXAMPLE 17.1. The first six harmonics

speak, whistle, or shout. A short, loud, healthy sound is a good way of optimizing the vibrations. Using the pedal will multiply the vibrations.

2) Now press down the piano keys for the low C's first six harmonics (example 17.1).

You don't need to play these notes; it's enough just to hold the keys down. Again, sing a short note into the piano, but with the specific pitch C. Sing the most comfortable C in the lower part of your voice. If a higher C is more comfortable, however, use it instead. The sympathetic vibrations from the piano will be stronger and more noticeable than before, since you've created a coincidence between your pitch and the piano's pressed keys.

Keep the pitch steady and vary its length and dynamics. Every time you sing the note, stay attentive to the piano's vibrations. At first, in order to really feel the vibrations, you may need to stop singing altogether: Sing a note, stop and listen; sing another note, stop and listen. Soon you'll develop the capacity to sense the vibrations from the piano at the very same time you sing, rather than by intermittent alternation.

Many factors affect the piano's sympathetic vibration: the intonation, intensity, and length of your note, but also the type of vowel you use. You can vary your "ah" by imagining that it comes from an Italian, an Australian, an Indian, and so on. Each vowel will have its own richness of vibrations. At some point you might start preferring some vowels over others, sensing that they trigger richer vibrations. Before you develop aesthetic judgments and preferences, however, it's better for you to explore your vowels freely. If you settle too soon on a vowel as your favorite one, you may neglect to discover the true fullness of your vocal capabilities.

3) When you manage to produce a free-sounding vowel in tune with the piano, put a fermata on it and perform a series of crescendi and diminuendi. When making it louder, fight the temptation to "muscle" it. You'll obtain optimal vibrations from your voice and the piano by using well-balanced vocal energies, rather than sheer muscle power.

4) Still holding down the same keys as before, start varying the vowel itself. Sing "ah," "eh," "ee," "oh," "oo," and any other vowel you wish. Start changing your pitch, from C to G and back again. Then add an E and improvise a simple tune using those pitches (example 17.2).

Singing into the piano has the merit of making the phenomenon of sympathetic vibrations clearly perceptible, but the phenomenon takes place whenever and wherever you sing

EXAMPLE 17.2. A short melody in C major

EXAMPLE 17.3. Johannes Brahms: Sonata for Violin and Piano, opus 78 in G Major, first movement

or play. Broadly speaking, the exercise awakens you to the acoustic properties of every environment in which you make music and to the possibility of setting up a collaboration between you and the environment. Your foregoing C-major improvisation is only a starting point, a simple template. Look at the following excerpt from the mainstream literature. The piano and the violin collaborate sympathetically much like the piano and your voice did (example 17.3).

BA-DAM!

The next exercise is an elaborate variation of the Father and the Daughter exercise in chapter 14. Reread the section in question to prepare for the new exercise.

🔊 This exercise is illustrated in video clip #63, "Harmonic Series and the Voice II: Ba-Dam!"

1) Sing the vowel "ah" in a comfortable pitch, relatively low in your voice, in mezzo forte or forte dynamics. Give it the elasticity that comes from a latent crescendo and diminuendo.

2) Say the nonsense syllables "ba-Dam!" several times in a row, with an iambic impetus of preparation/STRESS, or upbeat/DOWNBEAT. Vary their speed and dynamics, and vary the consonants from tender to explosive. Besides the voice and breath, these two syllables engage the lips, tongue, jaw, and soft and hard palate in alternation and combination. You have no choice but to use your lips for the "b" and your tongue for the "d." Hum the "m" in "Dam" for a brief moment, and you'll tickle both the soft and hard palate. If you speak in a normal way, you'll move your jaw at least once, as you sound the "b" (although it's technically possible to say "ba-dam!" without moving your jaw altogether).

Ideally, the consonants won't disturb the vowel's vibrations; your "ah" ought to be as free preceded and followed by consonants as it is all by itself. This takes practice. Once your mouth is thoroughly expert in saying "ba-dam!" without disturbing the vowel, sing the syllables in a region of your voice where you're comfortable with a low pitch and loud dynamics.

3) Sing the vowel "oo" (as in "boot") high up in your voice. Vary the dynamics from triple piano to mezzo forte. Vary the pitch within a narrow range, making it rise and fall by a second or a third. Vary both the pitch and the dynamics at the same time, as if the vowel were an elastic band that you could pull and twist at will.

4) Say the following syllable sequence:

Ba-DAM, ba-DAM, ba-DA-da ba-**DAM!**

Example 17.4 lays it out in $\frac{12}{8}$ time.

This snippet has a wealth of rhythmic and prosodic elements: the beat and meter; a variety of note groupings, some with two, others with three syllables; the interplay of preparation, stress, and release; a hierarchy of rhythmic levels of syllable, word, and sentence. The measure is organized as "2, 3, 4, **1**!" where 2, 3, and 4 point dynamically toward the **1**, which is both a destination and the point of departure for the next iteration of the sequence. Rhythmic impetus animates your voice and gives it power and flexibility. Energy accumulates as you pass from beat to beat and reach the downbeat of the next bar.

5) Having become comfortable saying the above sequence, now sing it, in that region of your voice where you can comfortably produce a low note with forte dynamics. Sing the sequence once, twice, or as many times in a row as your breath allows for. Take a quick breath if you run out, and start again. The most natural and logical place for your breath is right after the downbeat ("DAM!"). Then your breath will be both biological and linguistic (example 17.5).

6) Go back to the vowel "oo." Sing it high in your voice, and sustain it for a while. Underneath the long note, imagine a steady pulse and a $\frac{12}{8}$ bar of four beats. Then use the

EXAMPLE 17.4. The spoken "ba-DAM!"

ba- DAM,   ba - DAM,   ba - DA - da   ba - DAM!

EXAMPLE 17.5. The sung "ba-DAM!"

ba- DAM,   ba - DAM,   ba - DA - da   ba - DAM!

EXAMPLE 17.6. The falsetto

EXAMPLE 17.7. Using vowels to bridge the registers

ah - oo - ah

EXAMPLE 17.8. A complete vocal exercise

"elastic band" effect of changing dynamics, timing the stretches and releases of your vocal power to fit the steady pulse (example 17.6).

7) Sing a large interval, with the bottom note on the vowel "ah," the top note on the vowel "oo." Connect the two vowels with an unbroken legato, taking time to go from one note to the other and down again. Use the two vowels to sing the interval of an octave. Then sing a twelfth (an octave plus a fifth), legato (example 17.7).

8) Now put together the previous three steps. Sing the sequence of "ba-dam's" in your chest voice, on a comfortable C, and leap to a G a twelfth above it at the end of the sequence, using the vowel "oo" in your falsetto. Coming back down from the high pitch, sing the passage from "oo" to "ah" legato, without a consonant (example 17.8).

The low note on the vowel "ah" engages the chest voice; the high one on the vowel "oo" engages the falsetto. When passing from one to the other, you establish an opposition between the two of them, strengthening both registers at the same time.

Once you reach the falsetto, the rhythm of the exercise changes. It allows you to inhabit your falsetto and own it. Shape and reshape it, invigorate it, challenge it: "Are you in place? Are you strong? Show me! I'm going to pull you here and there, and I want you to resist me." While holding the long note, you can alter the pitch a little if you want, up to a semitone or so. Altering the pitch becomes a renewal of energy: You feed the falsetto by pulling away from the pitch and coming back to it.

Any one note that you sing contains the harmonic series. If your fundamental is a C, the sound you make contains the C itself; the C an octave above it; the G a twelfth above the fundamental; the C two octaves above; the E two octaves and a major third above it;

and so on. Train yourself to navigate these intervals at will, leaping from the fundamental to the second harmonic (the octave), to the third harmonic (the octave plus fifth), to the fourth harmonic (two octaves), to the fifth (two octaves plus a major third).

The exercise will help you widen your vocal range. Depending on your abilities, you may be able to make sounds across three octaves, some days even three and a half octaves or more. Although you don't need a wide range for most of your vocal needs, to have a latent wide range at your disposal enhances the use of your habitual voice, indirectly contributing to your good health whether you're a singer or not.

You can do the exercise with many different dynamics: forte for the chest voice, forte for the falsetto; forte for the chest voice, piano for the falsetto; piano for both. Each combination will have its risks and dangers, its merits and demerits. Find out for yourself what these may be!

The rhythmic motor of the exercise is so strong that you may be tempted to dance to it. But if the body remains still and actually opposes these rhythmic pulls, it'll contribute to the efficacy of the exercise and the voice's power. Resistance and mobility together are stronger than mobility alone. The voice moves, the breath moves, the rhythm moves… and the body provides them with welcome resistance.

Leaping over an octave is easy for everyone; an octave plus a fifth is a greater challenge to voice and ear; two octaves requires a healthy and supple voice; distances larger than two octaves requires virtuosity (if your voice is healthy) or foolhardiness (if your voice is uncoordinated).

Several factors make the leaps easier. The construction of the exercise plays a part; your attitude as you perform it plays a bigger part.

1. The leaps are easier if you use a well-tuned piano to help you find both the intervals and the vibrations you are aiming to produce.
2. The leaps are easier if you launch them with sufficient rhythmic impetus, in which case rhythm itself does some of the work for you.
3. The leaps are easier if you find a good combination of vowels and dynamics. Leaping from a low "ah" to a high "oo," for instance, is much easier than leaping from a low "oo" to a high "ah."
4. The leaps are easier if you sense that the high sounds you're aiming for are already present in the fundamentals you start with. If you tune yourself to the vibrations of the fundamental, leaping to a pitch that corresponds to an upper partial means traveling to a place announced and sounded by your voice already.
5. The leaps are easier if you keep head, neck, back, and the whole body in a state of latent resistance rather than a state of relaxation.
6. The leaps are easier if the inner animal and the opportunist work together. Reread the relevant section in chapter 14.
7. The leaps are easier if you aren't afraid of making mistakes or sounding like a fool. This doesn't mean you should do things badly and not care; it means you shouldn't refuse to do something constructive because of misplaced aesthetic judgments.

With a little imagination you'll be able to adapt the exercise to many areas of your music making. Brass players can perform the exercise directly at their instruments, using the tune's rhythmic and melodic construction and simply employing their embouchure to pass from the fundamental to the chosen upper partial. You can also decide to keep the exercise's essence, and discard its framework. At the piano, for instance, improvise rhythmically charged tunes alternating fundamentals with their upper partials. Practicing the exercise in many variations over time will allow you to put the harmonic series and prosody at the service of each other—that is, to integrate sound and rhythm until they become inseparable partners in a divine marriage.

CHAPTER 18

THE MESSA DI VOCE

Virtuosity of Contact

THE ULTIMATE EXERCISE

On March 5, 1760, Giuseppe Tartini wrote a letter to Maddalena Lombardini, in response to her request for advice on playing the violin. Tartini (1692–1770) was one of the master teachers of the eighteenth century, and his words are worth heeding:

> Your main study should be the use of the bow, in order to make yourself mistress in the expression of whatever can be played or sung. . . . First, exercise yourself in a messa di voce upon an open string, for example, upon the second, which is the D string. Begin pianissimo, and increase the tone by slow degrees to fortissimo; and this should be equally done on the down-bow and the up-bow.
>
> Set out on this exercise at once, and spend at least an hour on it every day, though at different times, a little in the morning, and a little in the evening; and keep constantly in mind that this is, of all exercises, the most difficult and the most important.
>
> When you master this exercise, every degree of pressure upon the string will become easy and certain; and you will be able to execute with your bow whatever you please.[1]

In short, Tartini says the messa di voce is the most difficult and important of all exercises, the mastery of which enables a player to do whatever she pleases with her bow. Why is this so, and how does the messa di voce relate to the prosodist's art?

We must make a detour all the way back to the invention of opera.

In the late 1500s a group of Florentine musicians, poets, and thinkers came together in a society called the *Camerata*. Their experiments, originally meant to revive the music of ancient Greece, led to the gradual development of a new musical form, the opera. Until then, most vocal music was polyphonic. Voices blended smoothly in long contrapuntal lines of a meditative nature. From its beginnings, opera concerned itself with dramatic action, the primacy of words, and the thoughts and feelings of individual characters, all of which encouraged monody as opposed to polyphony.

In polyphony, singers used a limited range of pitch, dynamics, and expressive devices. In monody, solo singers could widen all these ranges, and were indeed required to do so by the composers of the new style. Expressive effects in opera included trills, mordents, appoggiaturas, slides, vibrato, and the messa di voce—a gradual crescendo followed by a decrescendo on a long note. The term comes from the verb *mettere*, "to place," and may be translated as "the placing of the voice." It mustn't be confused with *mezza voce*, which means "half voice."

Giulio Caccini (1551–1618), a member of the Camerata, was the first person to write about the messa di voce and to systematize its use, in a collection of arias and recitatives published in 1602 and titled *Il nuove musiche*, "The New Music." Caccini also discussed variations on the basic ornament, such as the *esclamatione viva* (starting a note forte, then diminishing and swelling it), and the *esclamatione languida* (first swelling the note, then diminishing it again, to finish with a second swell).

It became standard for performers of the era to execute an *esclamatione* on most notes of suitable length. In Baroque manuscripts, written crescendi and diminuendi are almost always absent; as with other ornaments, composers and performers alike assumed the effect would be applied automatically, whenever appropriate.

The difficulties of executing a perfect messa di voce quickly became apparent to singers and instrumentalists. Baroque treatises and manuals underline its importance and propose numerous exercises for its study. After Caccini's first mention of it, we find the messa di voce adapted and discussed, among many others, for brass by Girolamo Fantini (1638), for strings by Christopher Simpson (1659), for woodwinds by Johann Joachim Quantz (1752), and even for the keyboard by François Couperin (1717). (The messa di voce on a keyboard instrument is a special case that we'll study later in the chapter.)

The messa di voce poses great challenges because it addresses the central problem in sound and coordination: the apportioning of energies and the interplay of tension and relaxation. To execute a perfect messa di voce is to employ your energies perfectly. Let's imagine Tartini's correspondent, Maddalena, practicing her messa di voce on a sustained note. When she tries to swell the sound, she leans too hard on the string and crushes it; she uses too much bow too quickly and arrives at the tip of the bow too soon; she concentrates on the crescendo and neglects rhythm and intonation. To avoid choking the instrument, Maddalena pulls the bow away from the bridge and toward the fingerboard. Her sound becomes "pretty," but it lacks power and the capacity to project in a concert hall. Consciously or unconsciously, she tries to compensate for the lack of power by tensing her neck and shoulders. The difficulties of performing a decrescendo are even greater. Maddalena tends to change both the dynamics and the color of sound whenever she performs a decrescendo, "letting go" of the sound's core and making it feeble and unsubstantial.

If it's challenging to maintain dynamic control over a single, long note, imagine how hard it is to master dynamics while changing bows, crossing strings, or using double stops. All technical and musical events contained in every phrase constitute provocations to your capacity to execute a messa di voce. Conversely, mastering the messa di voce means having the means to navigate all technical and musical events.

THE MESSA DI VOCE REDEFINED

Instead of defining the messa di voce as "a crescendo followed by a diminuendo," let's call it "a change of dynamics that causes neither a change of tonal color nor a change of vocal or instrumental mechanism." You perform a crescendo or a diminuendo, or both in succession or in alternation; your technique remains steady and controlled, and your sound quality remains constant. Seen under this light, the messa di voce reveals its true significance, for it represents a virtuosity of contact between player and instrument or between singer and voice.

The impresario and voice teacher Domenico Corri (1746–1825) once defined the messa di voce as "preparing the voice for a crescendo,"[2] which is very different from actually performing a crescendo. The ideal preparation to an action normally ensures an ideal outcome. A basketball player sometimes is sure that a shot will go in even before she throws it, for she feels that the preparation for the shot was ideal. If you prepare the voice for a crescendo but don't actually execute it, your messa di voce becomes latent, held in reserve at your disposal for you to use it or not. "Every note," the flutist Johann Joachim Quantz wrote in 1752, "whether a quarter, eighth, or sixteenth, must have its *piano* and *forte* in itself, as far as the time permits."[3] You might not have the time to execute a crescendo or diminuendo on a short note, but you can have the capability to do so in reserve. The ultimate virtuosity of contact, *latent messa di voce* is permanently present in the ideal instrumental or vocal technique.

Imagine two parents walking down the street, each holding one hand of their small child. Every few steps they swing the child far forward and up in the air, only to release the child back and down, without dropping her or hurting her arms. In dancing, in swinging a child, in riding a horse, in stroking a cat, intimacy and control both depend on a continuous yet variable contact that is elastic, resistant, and rhythmically organized. This is messa di voce in tangible form.

The messa di voce doesn't require actual physical contact between partners. Werner Thärichen, a timpanist with the Berlin Philharmonic, describes the first time he played the Prelude from Richard Wagner's "Tristan and Isolde" under Wilhelm Furtwängler in 1947:

> The Prelude starts with an upbeat played by the cellos. Furtwängler lowered his right arm very slowly. Apprehensively, I asked myself: With gestures like those, how would we manage to play our respective entrances? I waited, unable to determine the moment when, out of nothing, a powerful sound, intense and infinitely warm, arose from the cellos. And the build-up of intensity! At the climax of the Prelude, I had to play two bars in tremolo, crescendo. Never had I dreamed that two bars could last as long as those. How long I had to wait before the liberating strike! The sound of the chord at the climax of the phrase exploded with a violence impossible to explain by loudness alone. Furtwängler leaned backwards, as if he found it difficult to receive the sound waves he had just provoked.
>
> …And then came the descent after such a summit!
>
> This had nothing to do with a gradual release or diminution of intensity. On the contrary: it was the gripping extension of a great moment. His left hand was open as if he

presented us with a precious object, and he kept his hold on the object even when the score indicated a decrescendo and the instrumentation became ever thinner. He did not want to abandon his sound, and he augmented the intensity even while reducing the volume. That after such an intense experience, music could still be so vividly present during the measure of silence that followed—to the point where I dared not breathe and my skin broke out in a cold sweat—was a completely foreign realization to me, despite my many years' experience with orchestral playing.[4]

This is a description of ideal messa di voce. Two aspects of it merit highlighting. First, a decrescendo indicates a lessening of volume, not intensity. Second, there can't be an ideal messa di voce without a rhythmic construction. This will become clearer as we ponder how to produce the messa di voce at the keyboard.

THE MESSA DI VOCE AT THE KEYBOARD

Performing a messa di voce at the harpsichord or the piano may seem impossible, for once you strike a key, a crescendo is out of the question. I believe this is a misunderstanding of the deeper meaning of the messa di voce. We need to take another detour, this time to study the two master pianists of the nineteenth century, Frédéric Chopin (1810–1849) and Franz Liszt (1811–1886).

Chopin was steeped in opera. Among his compositions are pieces on themes from Ferdinand Hérold's *Ludovic*, Giacomo Meyerbeer's *Robert le Diable*, and Mozart's *Don Giovanni*. He met, heard, or accompanied singers such as Maria Malibran, Jenny Lind, and Pauline Viardot, exemplars of the vocal freedom and power that characterized the bel canto era.

Richard Hudson, in a study of rubato, discusses how Chopin absorbed the lessons he learned from his beloved singers. "Chopin felt that his playing style was modeled on the great singers, and he taught his students that the best way to learn how to perform the long, singing melodies was to listen to and imitate the singers."[5] It's tempting to consider Chopin's compositions as fundamentally pianistic in nature, but their elaborate pianism shouldn't distract us, as listeners and players, from what Chopin meant to achieve: to make the piano sing. "In addition to incorporating the vocal *cantabile* style and its sense of declamation and phrasing," Hudson writes, "Chopin also seems to have borrowed some specific ornamental techniques from the vocal style," including portamento, on-beat performance of trills, several types of appoggiaturas, and "the vocal ornament in which a small note before the beat repeats the pitch of the preceding note."[6] In composition as well as in performance, Chopin also emulated the bel canto singers' sense of rubato.

It's inconceivable that Chopin would integrate so many vocal facets without embracing the messa di voce. I believe the messa di voce lives in Chopin's music and in the piano music written by his contemporaries and successors in at least four different ways. To understand this, we turn our attention to Chopin's friend, Franz Liszt.

Liszt's involvement with singing and singers was even more extensive than Chopin's. As Kapellmeister in Weimar from 1848 onward, Liszt championed the music of Berlioz and Wagner, conducting the first performance of *Lohengrin* in 1850. Wagner eventually became Liszt's son-in-law, and their mutual artistic influence constituted one of the forces that shaped the music of the nineteenth century.

Liszt's ideal of piano playing was, like Chopin's, vocal in nature. Intriguingly, the historical record seems to indicate that Liszt was able to make his piano sing long lines thanks to the influence not of a singer but a violinist: Niccolò Paganini (1782–1840). In a study of Liszt's pianism, Bertrand Ott writes the following:

> It is well documented that the era of the definitive transformation of Lisztian playing was the period following the concerts of Paganini in Paris in 1831 and 1832. (Liszt was twenty years old.)…Liszt realized one day that the mechanism of Hummel, Cramer, and Clementi as applied by Czerny [Liszt's teacher in Vienna] was not really adequate for the gripping ardor and lyricism proposed by Paganini.[7]

The Paganini of popular legend is a devilish trickster distinguished by his feats of dexterity. Upon hearing Paganini, however, discriminating listeners were struck not so much by his technical or theatrical flair but by his musical, singerly expressivity, which provided Liszt with the means for his pianistic metamorphosis.

Two nineteenth-century violinists achieved renown equal to Paganini's, the Norwegian Ole Bull and the Belgian Henri Vieuxtemps. Bull described Paganini's playing:

> Without knowledge of the Italian art of singing, it is impossible to properly appreciate his playing. Contemporary with Pasta, Pizzaroni, Rubin, Malibran, Paganini rivaled them, singing on his violin melodies, many of which had been sung by those artists and astonishing even *them* more than the public.[8]
>
> …Paganini especially excelled in giving life to the simplest melodies, in giving to his tone the quality of the human voice; in contrasts of light and shade, and expression, now plaintive, now brilliant and gay, now fantastical.[9]

Robert Schumann, in a review of a recital by Vieuxtemps, describes hearing Paganini for the first time:

> When I first heard [Paganini] I rather assumed that the sound would be unique right from the start. Nothing of the kind! He began with a tone so thin, so small! Then effortlessly, almost imperceptibly, he cast his magnetic charms. They oscillated from artist to listener, from listener to artist, becoming ever more wondrous, more intricate, while the listeners pressed together in a bond of common fascination. He bound them ever tighter until they had become as one, to face him as a single entity and to receive from him as one from another.[10]

In sum, Paganini's messa di voce contributed mightily to how he connected with the public. "Partly because of the brilliant violinist," Ott writes, "Liszt changed his touch and, in all likelihood, strengthened the axes of his arms and his general posture." Lina Ramann, a pupil of Liszt's, made an observation that helps us understand what Ott means. "The starting point of this new technique inspired by Paganini rests on the practice of great tensions and the rebounding possibilities of the hand."[11]

To create tonal impact, most pianists attempt to relax their arms and employ the dropping weight of the arms and hands in a vertical gesture, down toward the keyboard. The continuity of legato in a singing line, however, requires not vertical gestures, but horizontal ones. And they must be animated by a kind of tension, not relaxation:

> The extraordinary agility and the lightning shifts of Paganini that first and especially fascinated Liszt gave him the idea of a new technique based first of all on movement, and then on ease, lightness, jumps, and rebounds. To imitate at the piano the swift changes and lyric flights of a violinist presupposed a transposition, since the physical aspects of the two instruments are, of course, incompatible. But through musical imitation Liszt found the gesture that made it possible to play the piano with suppleness and in space like the motion of a violin bow.[12]

In other words, a pianist who wishes to make her piano sing would do well to imitate a violinist's bowing arm, all the while keeping in mind that the violinist who makes her violin sing does so by imitating a singer. Emulate Liszt, who emulated and surpassed Paganini, who emulated and surpassed the great singers of the bel canto era.

THE MESSA DI VOCE AND PROSODY

The ideal technique draws its energies from the energies embedded in the music itself. The musical text may be seen as a set of instructions, some implicit and others explicit: "Here there is tension, now relaxation; tension again, relaxation again." Two or three notes belong together in a burst of harmonic, melodic, or rhythmic tension. They may be immediately followed by a minuscule moment of relaxation, before a new burst of tension. The smallest building blocks must be fitted into a grid of larger units—measures, phrases, entire sections—that are equally subject to laws of tension and relaxation. The messa di voce, in itself an exercise in tension and relaxation, becomes the means whereby the interplay of musical tension and relaxation is physically sounded, the elastic glue that binds rhythmic building blocks together.

Ott points out that many pianists, having struck a note, continue to depress the key even though the note, once struck, can't be controlled or changed in any meaningful way apart from its duration. To depress a key longer than necessary may seem like a waste of effort, but Ott explains there exists a type of energy "that is preparatory to the tonal function and which consequently economizes the muscle effort required for the tonal function itself. . . . Keeping depressed a key that has already played therefore has the role of an indispensable preparation for the articulation of the following note."[13] Depressing a piano key in this spirit implies not a relaxation of the weight of the arm into the key but a skillful suspension of the arm that readies it to strike the following note. "*Music is continuity*," Ott points out; "one does not play the piano by juxtaposing notes without a muscular and musical organic link."[14] This organic link is the ultimate purpose of the virtuosity of contact that the messa di voce represents. The messa di voce is an agent of timing as much as of dynamics.

Ott writes that touch "is not embodied in a simple note or a single chord but in musical agogics taken as a whole. . . . [A] beautiful sound that is isolated and static, because it is outside a musical momentum, will not necessarily be of the same quality when it is blended in the continuity of a work."[15] Heinrich Neuhaus, whose piano students included Sviatoslav Richter, Radu Lupu, and Emil Gilels, concurs:

> [W]hat gives us the impression of a beautiful tone is in actual fact something much greater; it is the expressiveness of the performance, or in other words, the ordering of sound in the process of performing a composition. . . . With a really creative artist and pianist "a beautiful tone" is a most complex process combining and ordering the relationship of tones of varying strength, varying duration, etc., etc., into a single entity.[16]

François Couperin, in *L'art de toucher le Clavecin*, explains how timing may be used at the keyboard to create if not the effect of messa di voce, then an illusion of it.

> As the sounds of the Harpsichord are determined, each one specifically, and consequently incapable of increase or *diminuendo*, it has hitherto appeared almost impossible to maintain that one could give any "soul" to this instrument. However, by investigations which have lent assistance to what little native talent Heaven has granted to me, I shall endeavor to show by what means I have managed to gain the happiness of touching the hearts of people of good taste, who have done me the honor of listening to me; and of training pupils who, perhaps surpass me.
>
> The feeling or "soul," the expressive effect, which I mean, is due to the (cessation) and (suspension) of the notes, made at the right moment, and in accordance with the character required by the melodies of the Preludes and Pieces. These two agréments, by their contrast, leave the ear in suspense, so that in such cases string instruments would increase their volume of sound [that is, execute a messa di voce], the suspension (slight retardation) of the sounds on the Harpsichord seems (by a contrary effect) to produce on the ear the result expected and desired.[17]

I wrote earlier that there are at least four different ways of applying the messa di voce at the keyboard. Let's call them *imagining*, *trilling*, *shaping*, and *timing*.

1) The power of the imagination is such that you can see, hear, smell, and touch something that doesn't exist. Charles Rosen opens *The Romantic Generation* with a discussion of this very issue:

> We put our aural imagination to work as a matter of course every time we listen to music. We purify the music by subtracting what is irrelevant from the undigested mass of sound that reaches our ears.
>
> . . . We also add to the sound whatever is necessary for musical significance. During every performance we continually delude ourselves into thinking we have heard things which cannot have reached our ears.[18]

Rosen cites Beethoven's piano sonata, op. 111, where the ear, thirsting for a particular experience, lengthens and sustains what is in fact a short-sounding note (the B-flat at the

EXAMPLE 18.1. Ludwig van Beethoven: Sonata for Piano #32, opus 111 in C Minor

EXAMPLE 18.2. Ludwig van Beethoven: Sonata for Piano #27, opus 90 in D Minor

end of measure 5 in example 18.1). "We create the necessary continuity that does not actually take place—or, rather, the expressive force of the music causes us to imagine as actually existing what is only implied."[19]

It's impossible to create an actual singerly legato on the piano, and yet pianists play with the innermost conviction that they can do so. Their conviction conjures up the legato well enough for the listener to share the pianist's delusion. If the imagination creates an impossible legato, there's no reason why it would fail to create an impossible crescendo. Composers themselves invite pianists to do it; Beethoven, for instance, indicates a crescendo on a sustained note in his piano sonata, opus 90 (example 18.2).

"[I]magination and desire are ahead of the possible results," Heinrich Neuhaus wrote. "A deaf Beethoven created for the piano sounds never heard before and this predetermined the development of the piano for several decades to come."[20]

2) The smooth execution of sustained crescendi and diminuendi on a long trill might give the pianist an inkling, at least, of what a singer feels while swelling and diminishing a long note. You may argue that the inkling of a feeling is far removed from an actual experience. And yet, reading a novel or watching a movie you can feel the terrors and joys of a fictional character as if they were your own terrors and joys.

3) Picture a crescendo over five notes of varying lengths. For the passing from note to note to be smooth and coherent, each of the notes must be pregnant with the dynamic qualities of the notes preceding and following it. The shape of each note and the shape of the space between notes can become sufficiently pregnant to create the appearance of messa di voce.

4) The final form of the keyboardist's messa di voce is that advocated by Couperin. Imagine an instrument that gives you absolutely no control of dynamics whatsoever. You'd still be able to create the illusion of dynamic change through timing. Simply put, two notes played close together in time have less silence between them than two notes played farther apart. The more silence (that is, the more time) between two notes, the more decrescendo you hear on the first note. Inversely, if you crowd two notes together, you might begin to imagine that you hear a crescendo on the first note.

In sum, the keyboardist's messa di voce starts with the imagination and proceeds beyond it, bypassing reality altogether but being none the worse for it. In the end, what would you rather hear—an imaginative pianist or a dull singer?

THE DEMISE AND REBIRTH OF THE MESSA DI VOCE

Although Vincenzo Bellini indicated *con messa di voce* over a line in his opera *Norma* as late as 1831, the term (and the concept behind it) gradually sank into oblivion during the nineteenth century. The Baroque and Classical tastes favored the flexibility of tonal effects exemplified by the messa di voce, while the emerging Romantic fashion aimed for a more even sound. The concave violin bow developed by François Tourte in the late 1700s lent itself only too well to the newfangled legato technique, distracting string players from the pleasures of swelling and diminishing.

In 1855 Manuel Garcia invented the laryngoscope, thanks to which he could more or less see the vocal mechanism in action. His invention had the unfortunate consequence of leading teachers and singers to become concerned with seemingly measurable aspects of vocal coordination. With the messa di voce, you use subtle energies to spin your voice as you would cotton candy; in the modern era that Garcia unwittingly founded, you try to "use the right muscles." Simplifying a bit, we can say that one technique is based on "allowing," the other on "doing."

Many pianists have abandoned the singerly ideal in their conception of sound and technique. Some claim the piano is a percussion instrument, which isn't wholly false from the point of view of engineering. The engineering argument is illustrative of the modern paradigm, centered on mechanics, technology, the control of measurable effects, and the visible above the audible. The title of one of Charles Bukowski's poems stands as an apt metaphor for the modern aesthetics: "Play the Piano Drunk Like a Percussion Instrument until the Fingers Begin to Bleed a Bit."

I return to Giuseppe Tartini and his audacious claim: The messa di voce "is, of all exercises, the most difficult and the most important." "With mastery of the messa di voce," the equally audacious Cornelius L. Reid writes, "all physical difficulties of a technical nature should be nonexistent. The singer now has the means to overcome all reasonable difficulties and to control his technique, rather than have his technique control him."[21]

In the next chapter I propose a number of exercises to help you embrace this old principle and make it new again.

CHAPTER 19

PRACTICING THE MESSA DI VOCE

CONTACT, FRICTION, COORDINATION, AND SOUND

To define messa di voce as a virtuosity of contact (as we did in the previous chapter) is useful, because then we know we need to become "contact experts." I still remember a car ride thirty years ago, when my cello teacher drove me from his house in the suburbs to the university downtown. He'd speed up and slow down, turn left or right at high speed, or brake suddenly, and none of his actions ever caused me to be jerked in my seat. He stayed "on the road," as it were; he never swerved or flew off the road's surface. My teacher seemed to have a feeling for the contact of his car with the road, and of his body with the car, and of his mind with his body.

The way he drove showed complete mastery of the messa di voce.

The contact between the car and the road has many elements, including the road itself (mud, asphalt, gravel), the state of the road (dry, icy, bumpy, smooth), and the car's tires and suspension mechanism. The tires alone are variable in many ways. They can be old or new, well threaded or not, inflated or deflated, tightly fitted to the wheels or not. Changes to any one of these elements would alter the contact between the car and the road to some degree. The possibilities are huge: driving on deflated tires; driving on a gravel road after a storm; driving on a gravel road after a storm with one overinflated tire, two partly deflated ones, and one bald one.

Most aspects of your daily life contain highly variable elements of contact. Feet, socks, shoes, and pavement collaborate to make your walking comfortable or uncomfortable. Do the following exercise: One foot bare, the other wearing a sock, walk around your house and caress different surfaces with your feet, one at a time. Stand on a rug next to a wooden floor. Slide your bare foot in little circles on the rug, then on the wooden floor. Now change feet and employ the sock-clad one in the same manner. The contact between the foot and the surface varies from foot to foot and from surface to surface. Use your feet to touch rug, tile, wood, linoleum, leather, cotton, and so on.

What does it feel like, not just at the level of the foot, but along the leg, at the hips, in your back, neck, and head?

The contact between the foot and the floor creates friction, which the dictionary defines as "the resistance that one object or surface meets when moving over another." Friction affects the coordination of your whole body, from the foot upward all the way to your head. It may not seem so at first, when you're too focused on the surface contact to perceive the effects of friction beyond the sole of your foot. Spend enough time sensing friction, however, and you will start feeling its effects up and down the body.

Contact creates friction, and friction affects coordination. By itself, friction is a neutral force. It becomes good when it's the right type and amount for your needs, and it becomes bad when it's excessive, insufficient, or otherwise costly to your coordination.

Let's look at some of the frictional elements that affect cello playing. With a little imagination you can make a list of the frictional elements in your own field of music.

1. Cellists apply rosin to the bow hair. It works like a kind of glue, augmenting the adherence of the bow hair on the string. Too much rosin and the bow gets stuck on the string; too little, and the bow skates.

2. The bow hair can be made tighter or looser. If the hair is too loose, it offers no resistance to the string. Tightening the bow hair also affects the bow's wood stick, making it more or less taut and affecting the overall friction of the bow against the string.

3. Cello strings vary in thickness. The top string is relatively thin, the bottom one thick. The thicker the string, the more friction it offers to the bow. The strings can be made taut or loose; the pitch goes up as you tauten a string and down as you loosen it. A loosened string may not offer sufficient friction to be playable. The normal cello tuning is (from top to bottom) A D G C. There are pieces in *scordatura*, in which the cello is required to be tuned differently: G D G C, for instance (for J. S. Bach's Fifth Suite for Solo Cello), or A D F-sharp B (for Zoltán Kodály's Sonata for Solo Cello). These tunings affect the strings' friction.

4. You can draw the bow close to the bridge, close to the fingerboard, or anywhere in between. The closer to the bridge, the more friction the string offers to the bow.

5. When you start drawing a bow, your hand and arm are close to the bridge, and their weight bears down on the string more directly. As you draw the bow, the hand necessarily moves away from the bridge and the string, and the arm and hand weight bear less directly down on the string. The closer your hand is to the string, the more weight you have at your disposal; the more hand and arm weight you use, the greater the friction between the bow and the string.

6. At the cello you can play open strings (without using the left fingers) or stopped strings (in which one or more left fingers lean on the string to create different pitches). The open string offers less friction than a stopped one and vibrates more freely. The higher the pitch you play, the shorter the vibrating string actually becomes; the shorter the string, the more friction it offers.

To sum it up, friction is the be-all and end-all of string playing. To play the cello is to "play friction." The principle is universal: Friction is an integral aspect of playing the piano, the oboe, the harp, and so on. It's also essential in singing, where the breath and the vocal folds meet and create friction.

To become an expert on friction and control the messa di voce, you need to balance your actor, receptor, and witness functions.

ACTOR, RECEPTOR, WITNESS

This exercise is illustrated in video clips #64, "Actor, Receptor, Witness I: An Introduction," and #65, "Actor, Receptor, Witness II: An Application."

We all play three roles in every moment of our lives. As *actors* we move, speak, push and pull, make decisions, and otherwise engage in any number of activities animated by our goals and desires. As *receptors* we use our senses to listen, smell, touch, get pushed and pulled, and react emotionally to other people. As *witnesses* we observe everything going on around us, analyzing, synthesizing, describing, explaining, and understanding the world in which we live.

It's nearly impossible ever to stop being an actor. Even when asleep you're an actor of sorts, snoring and leaning your body against your lover's. It's also impossible to stop being a receptor. Biology makes sure that our senses permanently receive information, from the external world and from our own inner selves. Your witness function requires that you be conscious, but some people would argue that while asleep you still witness a great many things. Proof of it is that upon waking up you can describe one or more dreams in detail.

The three roles are a permanent fixture of your life, but a completely harmonious interplay of all three is difficult to obtain. An actor can be so vigorous as to overwhelm the receptor. Some receptors are insensitive, others sensitive to the point of paranoia—which is no better. A witness may be handicapped by judgment and emotion, or even a simple lack of vocabulary: How to bear witness if you don't know how to articulate what you see and hear?

Your actor does any one thing. The action has consequences and effects that reverberate all around you. Your receptor senses these effects, and your witness analyzes the information your receptor has gathered. Then you act again, perhaps in a slightly different manner because of what your receptor and witness told you. The cycle of action, reception plus witness, and new action never stops, and the passage from one to the other can be lightning fast. Often the three happen at the same time.

It's not possible to receive every last bit of information from every last action. Sensory overload is actually dangerous, so we all have means of diminishing the sensitivity of our receptor functions. The difficulty lies in keeping your receptor alert and adaptable, neither sluggish nor thin-skinned.

The ideal witness has no feelings, expresses no preferences, and passes no judgment. The witness says, "I'm using a MacBook Pro laptop computer as I type." The receptor says, "I love my computer." Your witness's capacity to observe neutrally is essential, since it'll moderate your receptor and guide your actor, helping you make fewer mistaken judgments. If your witness function doesn't guide you dispassionately and help you pick the right guy out of the lineup, then you risk sending an innocent man to the electric chair.

A good actor balances "doing" and "allowing" within the same gesture. Playing with a yo-yo illustrates the point. The actor actively throws the yo-yo; then the actor backs off and allows the yo-yo to go down and up again; then the actor becomes a little more active again and refreshes the yo-yo's oscillations with a pull on the string, timing the pull according to the information gathered by the receptor. If the actor "did" incessantly, the yo-yo's oscillations would soon come to a halt.

Meditating on your actor, receptor, and witness functions is always useful, but with the messa di voce it's downright obligatory. The messa di voce requires that your actor be able to "do" and to "allow" as needed, perhaps both at the same time, otherwise the actor's eagerness will kill the very oscillations you're supposed to nourish. The receptor senses the friction at your disposal. Guided by the receptor and the witness, the actor starts the oscillations of sound with an affirmative gesture, backs off a little and allows resonance to do its job, and then refreshes the oscillations with a well-timed, well-gauged input of energy.

THE BASIC EXERCISE

Kata are simple postures and training exercises used by martial artists. To perform a *kata* you stand in a certain way and punch or kick the air in front of you—again and again, a hundred times in a row. Why does a karate sensei practices his or her *kata* with an obsessive devotion that leaves the uninitiated baffled?

The sensei knows that the exercise isn't as simple as it seems. A *kata* is a meditation on freeing your mind of parasitic thoughts, finding your balance, apportioning your energies, and timing your punch or kick. It's a psychophysical exercise, not a purely physical one, and it has metaphysical dimensions. Mastering the *kata* allows the practitioner to master all other techniques. In sum, the *kata* is all-encompassing and all-empowering.

Similarly simple exercises provide the foundation for many human endeavors, from ballet to basketball, from horseback riding to writing poetry. Johann Sebastian Bach wouldn't have created his masterpieces if he hadn't mastered counterpoint, and he wouldn't have mastered counterpoint if he hadn't completely and totally mastered first-species counterpoint—which to the uninitiated looks like putting two little notes together. It's safe to assume Bach practiced his first-species counterpoint with great discipline and perseverance.

The messa di voce starts with an exercise as simple as the most basic *kata*, the most basic counterpoint exercise, or the most basic *plié*. Play or sing a long note, and make it swell and diminish (example 19.1).

EXAMPLE 19.1. A messa di voce on a single note

There are dozens of ways of practicing the messa di voce, and you should explore them all. Nevertheless, the basic form, sacred in its simplicity, will always remain the most useful and pertinent of all exercises. Mastering it means the ability to connect with your voice or your instrument on any note and all times, including the very first note you sound in your day's work—and on all notes you perform publicly on stage. Like the *kata* and the *plié*, the messa di voce requires constant practice. It might take you a long time even to understand and appreciate all of the exercise's implications.

We'll look at the relationship between consonants and vowels in singing and playing, rhythm in the study of messa di voce, and other practice strategies. They all flow from the basic exercise, which is an infinite well of possibilities.

CONSONANTS AND VOWELS

To some degree, everything you play and sing is comprised of an alternation of consonants and vowels. This is obviously the case in singing, but it's also true in instrumental playing. Tonguing at the flute makes literal use of consonants, while bowing at the violin or plucking notes at a guitar makes a more figurative use of it.

Revisit the exercise called Coincidence, which we studied in chapter 5. It helps you coordinate intention and gesture in an absolutely precise moment in time. Your consonants (and, more broadly, the starts to all your notes) will become cleaner and more controlled if they're borne of the precise coincidence of intention and gesture.

Play or sing a scale of short notes separated by silences, andante con moto. Play the first note, and listen to it without passing judgment. Play the second note, listen to it, and make a dispassionate but immediate judgment: too rushed, too sluggish, too heavy, too light, or just right. Use the technical information you gathered about the second note and apply it to playing the third note, choosing either not to pass judgment on it or to make a snap assessment of its qualities. Little by little you'll become an expert not on consonants, but on being in the moment, thanks to your actor, receptor, and witness functions.

A consonant and the vowel that follows it are so close together that the energy you spend to articulate the consonant will inevitably affect the vowel. Immediately after feeding the consonant its energy, "put the brakes on," so to speak, preventing the energy from dispersing. Not only must the consonant be economical; its follow-through—which starts the microsecond after you release the consonant—must also be economical, or the vowel will suffer.

Play another scale of very short notes. Insert a fermata on a note chosen at random, lengthening the vowel-like portion of the note and executing a messa di voce upon it. You'll know you've played a healthy consonant when its corresponding vowel's messa di voce is easy to control.

Play yet another scale of short notes, in which every consonant has a latent messa di voce on the vowel following it. Now approach all passages in your repertoire with the same skill.

VOCAL REGISTRATION AND THE MESSA DI VOCE

In chapter 14 we studied two vocal registers called the *falsetto* and the *chest voice*. Sing a single note, low in pitch and loud in dynamics, on the vowel "ah" (as in the word "car"). Now sing a single note, high and soft, on the vowel "oo" (as in "boot"). You'll engage your chest voice preponderantly when singing the low "ah" and the falsetto when singing the high "oo." This shows that you can access and manipulate the vocal registers through the use of different vowels, pitches, and dynamics.

The point where one register's pitch range ends and the other starts is called the *break*. Its location is variable depending on the condition of your voice and how you use it, but it lies (for women as well as men) in a compass of several semitones around E above middle C. Example 19.2 is a schema established by Cornelius L. Reid, showing the registers, their respective pitch range, and the vowel and dynamic scope most likely to trigger their innate qualities.

Let's call the registers' basic actions *pulling* and *holding*. One register holds its ground, and the other pulls against it, in an elastic and ever-changing opposition of forces. As you pass from note to note, from vowel to vowel, and from forte to piano and back again, the registers' interplay of pulling and holding changes constantly.

Sing a note on the vowel "ah." While holding the pitch, change the vowel to "ee." This will alter the balance between the two registers in some way. Sing a low note on the vowel "ah," and pass to a note an octave above on the vowel "ee." The balance registration will change more significantly. Sing a note on the vowel "ee" right around the break—on an F, for instance. Make it swell and diminish. You'll use a certain register balance singing quietly and another balance singing loudly, making the falsetto and the chest voice dialogue and collaborate. The art of vocal registration is subtle and difficult, and it'd take a whole other book to lay it out in detail. What we can state unequivocally is that it's not possible to be a good singer without a good control of the messa di voce.

In advanced stages of training, Reid writes,

> the performance of the messa di voce must be practiced continually until there is an exact matching of both the quality and intensity at the point of transition. After this technique has been mastered the "break" disappears, and the singer is able to pass freely from one register to the other, from soft to loud and from loud to soft, without difficulty.... This is the singing style known as Bel Canto.[1]

EXAMPLE 19.2. The vocal registers

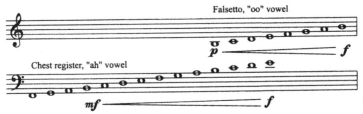

EXAMPLE 19.3. The expanded vocal registers

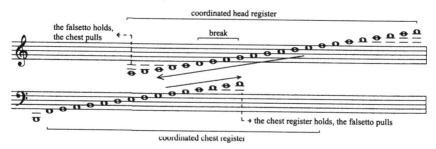

Example 19.3 is another schema established by Reid. It illustrates the collaboration between the registers and its result upon the vocal range.

When performed in the manner Reid advocates, the messa di voce is the ultimate voice-building exercise. It isn't the only way in which singers can use the messa di voce, since in the vocal repertoire there exist limitless possibilities for swelling and diminishing tones that lie comfortably away from the break between the registers. In other words, singers can practice the messa di voce on all notes, but when they practice it on certain pitches and vowels, they're using it in a singularly rewarding manner.

THE MESSA DI VOCE AND THE HARMONIC SERIES

What happens when you change the quality of contact between you and your instrument or voice? Your sound changes right away. Take cello playing as an example. The sounds a cellist makes by drawing the bow closer to the bridge are necessarily different from the sounds made closer to the fingerboard. The resistance of the string is much greater close to the bridge than close to the fingerboard. Resistance condenses energy, like boiling water in a pressure cooker or heated gas inside a metal canister. To some degree, then, resistance is helpful in sound production. This is a universal principle: It applies to string playing, but also wind playing, piano playing, singing, and all other areas of music making.

Partly because of resistance or the lack of it, harmonics are much richer when the bow is drawn closer to the bridge, and poorer when the bow is drawn closer to the fingerboard. Sounds rich in harmonics can be painful to the ear up close, but they're brilliant and warm from a certain distance onward. When you stand next to a singer whose voice is rich in harmonics, your ears might hurt even if the singer sings pianissimo. The sound has a core to it that musicians refer to as "golden," "silvery," "like a red thread," or "like the sharp edge of a knife." The opposite of this is a sound that appears appealing up close but is flabby and inconsequential from a distance; invariably, such a sound has poor harmonics.

Your first goal in sound production shouldn't be aesthetic but functional: to play or sing with the freest, richest, and most condensed sounds, however harsh or even ugly they may seem at first to you or to a casual listener. Sounds that are condensed at the outset can be molded into every shape; you can even choose to mold these sounds into something shallow and thin. But sounds that are thin at the outset can't be molded into many shapes at all.

The messa di voce is a game of contact, and contact determines the harmonic spectrum of sound. We might say that the messa di voce is the dynamic device through which you liberate the energies of the harmonic series. Their collaboration is mutually beneficial: You can use your ears' sensitivity to partials and overtones to improve your execution of the messa di voce, and your mastery of the messa di voce to condense your sounds and enrich them with vibrant harmonics.

MESSA DI VOCE AND RHYTHM

This exercise is illustrated in three video clips: #66, "Messa di Voce I: The Basics," #67, "Messa di Voce II: An Application," and #68, "Messa di Voce III: At the Flute."

Originally, the term messa di voce referred to an ornament in vocal music consisting of a crescendo and a diminuendo on a long note. Among possible variations on the basic effect were the *esclamatio viva* (starting a note *forte*, then diminishing and swelling it), and the *esclamatio languida* (first swelling the note, then diminishing it again, to finish with a second swell). Visualize and memorize these variations by studying the following list:

Messa di voce: < >
Esclamatio viva: > <
Esclamatio languida: < > <

I've been using the term more broadly to include all variations in dynamic within a single note (or, in the case of the piano, over two or more notes or over a trill). As I see it, mastery of messa di voce means the mastery of all dynamic changes.

There's an art to practicing the messa di voce. Consider the following:

1. Passing successfully from dynamic to dynamic is challenging.
2. Controlling your singing or playing in soft dynamics is harder than controlling it in moderate or loud dynamics.
3. A decrescendo tends to be harder than a crescendo.

Logically speaking, the easiest forms of the messa di voce are those that avoid the softest dynamic ranges and the biggest changes of dynamics. For instance, it's much easier to pass from forte to mezzo forte than it is to pass from piano to pianissimo. The original messa di voce effect entailed passing from very soft to very loud and to very soft again, but you'll learn it faster and better by concentrating on the easier dynamic passages first. A practice session might go like this:

1. Forte, mezzo forte, forte
2. Mezzo forte, mezzo piano, mezzo forte
3. Forte, fortissimo, forte
4. Mezzo forte, poco forte, mezzo piano, piano

5. Piano, pianissimo, piano
6. Fortissimo, forte, mezzo forte, poco forte, poco piano, piano, pianissimo
7. Pianissimo, piano, poco piano, poco forte, mezzo forte, forte, fortissimo, forte, mezzo forte, poco forte, poco piano, piano, pianissimo

A single long note outside a metric context has its own inner rhythm, which may be a metronomic pulse underneath the note, a pulse with rubato, or a surge of energy with no metronomic logic. Blow your breath gently at a burning candle, making the flame change shape without extinguishing it: There'll be a nonmetronomic rhythm to your thought, your breath, and the interaction between your breath and the flame. You can do the same thing when you practice a single crescendo or diminuendo on a long note.

On a long note, perform two, three, or more cycles of crescendo and diminuendo, metronomically or not. Make some cycles louder, others softer, and arrange them into larger groups of two or three cycles each. Each cycle becomes a syllable, and each group a word. Thus starts the collaboration between messa di voce and phrasing (example 19.4).

Insert the changing dynamics into a musical setting. Play or sing the scale in example 19.5, using the *esclamatio viva* to add rhythmic vitality to the short notes.

Let your imagination take flight, and turn the scale into an improvised melody. Use the same mixture of messa di voce and prosodic awareness to all passages and phrases in your repertoire (example 19.6).

You're now ready for the final, decisive exercise. Play or sing a long note with an even sound quality. Using the knowledge you accumulated so far, ensure that you can, at any moment, execute a crescendo or a decrescendo, or both in quick succession, or a sforzando followed by a piano subito and then a long crescendo, or any combination of dynamics. This is *latent messa di voce*, at your disposal at all times whether or not you actually vary the dynamics of any note (example 19.7).

EXAMPLE 19.4. Multiple dynamic changes

EXAMPLE 19.5. A scale with dynamic changes

EXAMPLE 19.6. An embellished melody with dynamic changes

EXAMPLE 19.7. The latent messa di voce

The practice of the messa di voce raises an interesting question about breath control. The messa di voce deals with friction, contact, and the opposition between forces—for instance, the opposition between the bow and the string, or between the breath and the vocal folds. Take a rubber balloon and inflate it. Hold its spout in your fingers and let air out slowly. The balloon will wheeze and whistle. By varying the spout's aperture, you create more or less friction, thereby affecting the outflow of air, which can become extremely economical if you handle the spout just so. The human voice works in a similar manner, as do all wind and brass instruments: the sound-making mechanism of vocal folds or embouchure plays the role of the spout and controls the outflow of air. Ultimately, then, it's the voice that controls the breath, not the other way around.

As I see it, mastering the messa di voce frees you from the need to pursue breath control in any way, shape, or form whatsoever. If you don't agree with me, however, you can still enjoy practicing the messa di voce!

NEVER TAKE YOUR MESSA DI VOCE FOR GRANTED

In some ways, the messa di voce is the aural manifestation of a universal phenomenon. Everything in life involves contact in ever-changing forms—as illustrated by my anecdote about my teacher's driving, his contact with the car, and the car's contact with the road. Holding hands with your beloved is a form of contact. You vary it by increasing or decreasing the touch's firmness, intertwining fingers in different combinations, twisting the hand a little, pulling on it, or pushing on it. Contact means intimacy, and variations of contact enhance, deepen, and broaden intimacy. Contact has an archetypical and metaphysical dimension. The unborn baby lives inside the womb in permanent intimacy with the mother. Together, mother and baby perform a primordial messa di voce: Their breath, circulation, and energy swell and diminish, in cycles of convergence and divergence. From birth onward, everything we do is but a quest to reproduce, remember, or otherwise recreate this contact, if not in its physical manifestation, then in its metaphorical one.

This is how important, how vital the messa di voce is for all musicians: It's the play of life itself. It's a mistake to neglect practicing it.

Insert short bursts of messa di voce in everything you practice. Suppose you're studying a Beethoven sonata. Perform a couple of crescendi and diminuendi on a sustained long note, then play the sonata's opening phrase a couple of times. Suppose the phrase consists of a series of rolling arpeggios. Play the first arpeggio, insert a fermata on its top note, and execute a messa di voce upon it. Do this for every arpeggio, then play the phrase as written, with latent fermatas and latent messa di voce on any note of any arpeggio. Suppose the phrase climaxes on a trill. Play the note without the trill, swelling and diminishing it. When you feel perfectly connected with the long note, add the trill without losing your connection. You can work this way for every piece in your repertoire. I'd go further and say you *must* work this way.

Do this for a few days and weeks, and undoubtedly you'll see, hear, and feel wonderful results. But do it for years and the results will be dramatic. You don't even have to devote yourself to the messa di voce out of duty; you can do it wholly out of pleasure. The vibrations of your instrument or voice when you perform a good messa di voce make daily practice a treat, not an obligation. Start every practice session with variations on the messa di voce, and you'll always look forward to practicing, day after day, for the rest of your life.

CHAPTER 20

IMPROVISATION

A Lifestyle

THE IMPROVISER'S PSYCHOLOGY

Improvisation means different things in different contexts. Entire musical languages are based primarily or wholly on improvisation. Our purpose in this chapter, however, is not to learn how to improvise in a specific musical language, but how to use improvisation as a sort of lifestyle—or, more precisely, a state of body and mind you can enter at will in order to achieve any goal.

Many classically trained musicians are afraid of improvisation, considering it a foreign skill permanently out of their reach. They argue that they can't improvise, will never become able to improvise, don't like improvising to begin with, and don't need to improvise anyway. They're wrong on every count.

Most adults don't need to learn how to improvise; they need to *remember* how to do it, for they were born with an instinct for improvisation. The child sits at her mother's piano and starts improvising as a matter of course, inventing, exploring, and "playing." Or the child walks into an enclosed courtyard with resonant acoustics and starts vocalizing improvised sounds, for the sheer pleasure of hearing her own voice. We all did so until good manners, conservatory training, and the fear of other people's opinions stopped us from inventing. Judgment and fear—not lack of knowledge or talent—are the real obstacles adults face when improvising.

To talk is to improvise: You open your mouth and you speak, not knowing exactly what you're going to say, plucking words and sentences from a huge database you've built over the years. Music is a language much like your native tongue. Your mind contains a vast database of musical information, some of it analytical and reasoned, some of it sensorial and intuitive. Right now your database is already sufficiently developed for you to extract an infinite number of good tunes out of it. It's always possible to enlarge your database and access it more efficiently, but that doesn't change the fact that you already have everything you need to start improvising.

Improvisation is like a planet, full of countries, cities, communities, and neighborhoods. Musicians who are afraid of improvising think they must conquer the planet at once, when in effect the planet is there to be visited, explored, and enjoyed neighborhood by neighborhood. To play five random notes on the piano is to improvise. To whistle a thoughtless tune is to improvise. To sing a C-major scale and change its direction in mid-flight is to improvise. All accomplishments start with a simple step, and some accomplishments don't need to be any bigger than *taking* that step.

The psychological difficulty in improvisation is to let go and to let be. Sounds and notes come out, and you let them. Time whizzes by, and you let it be. Those two or three notes you have just made? They aren't so important anymore, because right now these *other* few notes you're making are the only ones that matter! Let go, let go, let go!

Most important, you must let go of judgments of right and wrong. If Bach wrote down a B-flat and you played a B-natural, then you struck a wrong note. If you're unable to "right" your wrong note by turning it into an acceptable ornament leading back to the printed note, then your B-natural is absolutely wrong within the world in which the Bach minuet is habitually performed and appreciated. In many improvisations, however, there can be a free debate about right and wrong; in some styles of improvisation, it's considered that *nothing* is ever wrong.

In improvisation you never know how things are going to turn out. Every note is a risk of sorts. The master risk taker can take bold risks and survive. Until you become such a master, you must be willing to improvise ugly, ridiculous, or even disgusting tunes. This is an integral and unavoidable part of the learning process, and you might as well embrace it.

Work on your database of music knowledge every day, making it broader, deeper, and more easily accessed. In the meantime, tap into your database as it is and start improvising from where you are. All you need is to suspend judgment, put fear aside, and let the first note come out of your being.

We'll look further into the improviser's psychology and we'll study some practical ways of improvising, but first let's imprint upon our minds the importance of improvisation.

TEN REASONS TO LEARN HOW TO IMPROVISE

1) Improvisation is a function of good health, like breathing and walking—an innate ability that keeps you alive and well. Not to improvise is akin to not breathing.

2) Any unreasonable fear is a needless handicap. It's better to overcome the fear than live with the handicap. Further, the capacity to improvise is a source of power. Like all power, you don't ever need to exert it; it's enough that the power be latent. If you know you can improvise a last-minute dinner for eight, then you'll feel comfortable in your power to deal with unexpected guests even if such guests never show up.

3) Many pieces in your repertoire actually demand that you improvise ornaments, cadenzas, lead-ins, and so on. In such pieces improvisation is as obligatory as playing in tune and in time. This applies to much of Bach and Mozart, almost everything written before Bach, and many modern pieces.

4) Johann Sebastian Bach, Carl Philipp Emanuel Bach, Mozart, Beethoven, Liszt, Franck, Fauré, and many other composers were magnificent improvisers. It's better for you to be their junior colleague than not to belong in their company at all.

5) You can learn to improvise solutions to your technical problems in a composed passage. Indeed, you could learn how to improvise your entire technical apparatus. We'll study the principle in the section "Improvising an Existing Composition."

6) Life is made of the balance between order and disorder, and this means that a degree of disorder is an actual requirement in a healthy life. Improvisation in its disorderly aspects can help you balance your life.

7) A force is strengthened when it resists the pulls of its opposite. Improvising will indirectly improve your capacity to obey a canonic text faithfully, note by note.

8) The paradox of musical improvisation is that you don't fully control it, even though in some way you actually choose every note that comes out of you. Stephen Nachmanovitch puts it elegantly in his book *Free Play: Improvisation in Life and Art*: "The outpourings of intuition consist of a continuous, rapid flow of choice, choice, choice, choice."[1] The decisions you make—What note next? What about now? And *now*?—happen too quickly for you to ponder them one by one intellectually. Improvising quickens yours mind, rendering it supple and adaptable.

9) Improvisation can become a portal to the Divine. It allows you to enter an altered state of consciousness in which you receive, channel, or otherwise seize potentially life-changing songs and prayers.

10) Improvisation is tremendous fun!

TWO SIMPLE EXERCISES

For many musicians, improvisation is so scary that it seems literally impossible. "I don't even know how to start!" The easiest first step consists of sitting at a piano and plucking notes at random. The physical and musical aspects of the exercise are simple, the psychological aspects less so. Improvising is an act of disobedience—toward the canonical composers, the teachers who told you to follow their instructions, and your parents who scolded you for goofing off when you practiced your lessons. It may feel terribly wrong for you to do improvise. Besides, you might balk at making "ugly" music. And yet no two people agree wholeheartedly on what is beautiful or ugly. Your certainty that playing random notes in sequence or together is "ugly and wrong" is unwarranted; someone else may find them attractive and admirable. In time you, too, will grow fond of what you rejected at first.

This next exercise, a little less simple than the previous one, has the merit of taking you from complete randomness to a safe interplay of structure and improvisation.

1) Play or sing a one- or two-octave scale in a key such as C or G major, in $\frac{4}{4}$ time, in moderate speed (for instance, quarter note = 80) (example 20.1).

2) Play the scale again, now with the rhythm of a dotted half followed by a quarter (example 20.2).

3) Instead of playing the scale straight up and down the octave, change its direction in mid-flight for a few notes at a time. We'll call this effect *back and forth* (example 20.3).

EXAMPLE 20.1. A scale in quarter notes

EXAMPLE 20.2. A scale with a dotted half/quarter note pattern

EXAMPLE 20.3. "Back and forth"

EXAMPLE 20.4. A scale with freely alternating patterns

EXAMPLE 20.5. A scale with intermittent leaps

These three elements can be combined in four ways: scale in quarter notes, up and down straight; scale in dotted half/quarter notes, up and down straight; scale in quarter notes, back and forth; and scale in dotted half/quarter notes, back and forth. Alternate them freely, and you'll turn your scale into an improvisation (example 20.4).

Now as you play your scale, disrupt it with an occasional leap of a third, fourth, or fifth, creating a simple tune that has never been heard in the history of music—your own composition, unique and unexpected (example 20.5).

The improvised or embellished scales as just outlined can be varied in so many ways that you could easily spend an hour every day practicing them without getting bored. Your career as an improviser is now born!

IMPROVISATION AND PROSODY

Brazil's Northeast region, the *Nordeste*, has a long tradition of improvising bards, called *repentistas*. (Their name is derived from the Portuguese word for "sudden.") Repentistas work in pairs, telling tall tales, throwing lewd insults at each other, and teasing members of the public. On a visit to my native São Paulo some years ago, I found myself in a downtown square where two repentistas were performing for a crowd of passersby.

EXAMPLE 20.6. The prosody of Brazilian repentistas

The two repentistas faced each other about ten feet apart, one of them plucking chords on a guitar, the other shaking a tambourine. After every few verses they would walk slowly within the circle formed by the listeners and trade places, adding a visual and kinesthetic element to their performance. They improvised in a monochromatic voice over a narrow interval range, illustrated in example 20.6.

The repetitive patterns, the guitar and tambourine, the monochromatic singing, and the pacing back and forth collaborated to put the two repentistas in a creative trance, at the same time drawing the audience into their world. Most important, their rhythmic patterns were absolutely suited to the Portuguese language as spoken in Brazil, allowing for words, half-sentences, and whole sentences to flow easily from the repentistas's imagination. YouTube has a wealth of entertaining clips featuring street repentistas. It doesn't matter if you don't speak a word of Portuguese; you'd still learn a lot about prosody and rhythm. Use the keywords "repentista," "embolada," "Caju e Castanha" (two brothers who started performing together as little kids).

Behind the repentistas's prowess lies a universal principle: Prosody opens the door to improvisation. We think of the Homeric epics as compositions written by a single individual named "Homer." In truth they were born and developed within an oral tradition over generations. The epics are peppered throughout with recurring epithets for certain gods, heroes, and even objects. Whenever Achilles shows up, for instance, the poet adds a little adjective such as "brilliant," "godlike," or "swift-footed." Studying the *Iliad*, the scholar Milman Parry realized that there existed a highly organized system of metrical alternatives for these epithets. The system helped improvising bards create their own lines. Bernard Knox writes in his introduction to Robert Fagles's translation of the *Illiad*:

> The system, obviously the product of invention, refinement and elimination of superfluities over generations, could only be the work of oral bards, and in fact similar phenomena, though infinitely less sophisticated, are found in oral poetry, living and dead, in other languages.[2]
>
> …Whole lines, once honed to perfection by the bards of the tradition, became part of the repertoire; they are especially noticeable in recurring passages like descriptions of sacrifice, of communal eating and drinking. Such passages give the oral singer time to concentrate on what is coming next, and if he is a creative oral poet, to elaborate his own phrases mentally as he recites the formulas that he can sing without effort.[3]

You don't need to improvise lewd lines like the Brazilian repentistas or gigantic epics like Homer and his peers. You can, however, develop the skill of melding prosody and improvisation.

Choose a time signature and a phrase length—for instance, four bars in $\frac{3}{4}$. Use Rhythmic Solfège to snap the beat, conduct the bar, and scat a simple line of music, concentrating not on its intervals but its rhythms. Adopt a conversational tone, and let

Improvisation • 249

EXAMPLE 20.7. Conversational rhythm

your notes coalesce into word-like units. The beat, the measure, and the conversational tone will awaken your inventiveness (example 20.7).

Another technique is to extract the rhythms from an existing melody and add your notes to it. The more compelling a line's rhythms, the easier it is to add pitches to it. Take something like "Happy Birthday" or "Frère Jacques." Scat it without intervals, then sing it with new intervals. Do the same for pieces in your repertoire: strip the pitches from a line of Mozart or Stravinsky and ride the line's rhythms into melodic improvisation.

These steps will prepare you for the challenges in the next section.

SETTING UP IMPROVISATORY TASKS

Give yourself tasks of improvisation with specific parameters. The parameters can be a key or mode (G major, C minor, pentatonic); a time signature ($\frac{2}{4}, \frac{3}{4}, \frac{4}{4}$) or the absence of one; a mood or atmosphere (allegro, dreamy, sleazy); a specific composer's style (Mozart, Debussy, Ellington); or a multilayered task (a love aria in the style of Mozart, starting in E-flat major and modulating to the relative minor before returning to the tonic, andante moderato in $\frac{3}{4}$ time).

Suppose I ask you to improvise a tune with the key of D major as its sole requirement. If you start worrying about how difficult it is to create a masterpiece worthy of publication, you're choosing to worry for silly reasons, since you can just play an embellished scale in D major. Suppose the only requirement is the time signature of $\frac{3}{4}$. You can make your improvisation atonal, tonal, haphazard, incomprehensible, and so on; your *only* obligation is $\frac{3}{4}$! Suppose I ask you to improvise an eight-bar phrase articulated into two halves of four bars. To fulfill the obligation to the letter, say eight words out loud, at a deliberate pace:

Ba-DAM, ba-DAM, ba-DAM, DAM;
Ba-DAM, ba-DAM, ba-DIM, DOOM!

Success breeds success. Do easy things many times in a row, increase the difficulty of your tasks gradually, and your climb up the slope will be smooth.

Suppose I give you the task to improvise an eight-bar phrase in D major, in $\frac{3}{4}$ time. The intermediate steps have prepared you to attempt the task with confidence. The swing and pull of the time signature will be a big contributing factor to your success. Spend time establishing and nourishing its feel, and then launch the improvisation without hesitation, letting the meter work its magic on you.

Determine what you're trying to accomplish at any one point during a practice session, and see if you accomplish it better through improvisation. In "Carnival of the Animals," Camille Saint-Saëns created a menagerie that includes, among others, wild asses, a swan, an elephant... and "les pianistes," those laughable animals playing ferocious scales up and down the keyboard. What exactly are those pianists trying to do? "Warming up," they might say, or "working on technique." Most musicians practice their version of the thoughtless, joyless, senseless warm-up as finger exercises, licks, riffs, and vocalises. But the proper aim of warming up isn't to get your fingers or chops going, but to find those vital connections without which you can't make music—connections among all body parts, between mind and body, between you and music itself.

Ideally you'd sleep connected, wake up connected, and start your daily practicing connected from the first note onward. But if you find yourself disconnected in the practice room, skip the mindless repetitive exercises; instead, improvise a simple piece that allows for physical, psychophysical, and musical connections. Here are a few pointers:

1. High jinks early in the day aren't necessary, but establishing comfortable contact with your voice or instrument certainly is. Use the messa di voce on long notes and you'll find your contact.
2. Controlling slow motions is harder than controlling motions at moderate speed. The day's first improvisation will be easier if you perform it andante con moto instead of adagio.
3. A steady beat "carries" you, so to speak. You'll warm up more easily if your playing or singing is rhythmic.
4. Music has the capacity to alter your mood. One piece makes you nervous, another annoys you, and a third one leaves you sad. Your improvisations can have specific psychological goals: to fight lethargy or boredom, to calm down after a stressful rehearsal, to express and disperse anger, and so on. Your warm-up improvisation ought to caress your ears and your heart. Improvise in a soulful D minor, for instance, or a mode that reminds you of Gregorian chant and puts you in a meditative frame of mind.

In short, a good warming-up improvisation employs a steady beat in andante con moto, long notes that you swell and diminish, and an emotionally meaningful musicality.

Once you start immersing yourself in improvisation, you'll realize that every aspect of your daily practice lends itself to it. You can even improvise the actual pieces in your repertoire, as we'll soon see.

IMPROVISING AN EXISTING COMPOSITION

In one of his "Fictions" (a series of short stories that read like near-plausible nonfiction essays), Jorge Luis Borges (1899–1986) eulogized an imaginary writer, Pierre Menard. Menard's singular ambition was to write parts of *Don Quixote* without copying or imitating Miguel de Cervantes. His initial strategy was relatively simple, consisting of *becoming* Cervantes: "Learn Spanish, return to Catholicism, fight against the Moor or Turk, forget the history of Europe from 1602 to 1918...."[4] But then he decided this method, though impossible, was too easy. "Being, somehow, Cervantes, and arriving thereby at the

Quixote—that looked to Menard less challenging (and therefore less interesting) than continuing to be Pierre Menard and coming to the Quixote *through the experiences of Pierre Menard.*"[5]

In Menard's words,

> I have assumed the mysterious obligation to reconstruct, word for word, the novel that for [Cervantes] was spontaneous. This game of solitaire I play is governed by two polar rules: the first allows me to try out formal or psychological variants; the second forces me to sacrifice them to the "original" text and to come, by irrefutable arguments, to those eradications.[6]

Menard's approach to writing a book that is already written gives you a strategy to improvise a piece that is already composed, such as a Mozart piano sonata—and to do so while remaining yourself, instead of becoming Mozart.

The number of possible note combinations in all of music is infinite. Play any one note: a G, for instance. The next note can be anything you want: another G, a B, an F-sharp. How many ten-note combinations can you produce out of all the notes available to you? How many hundred-note combinations? By the time you arrive at a forty-minute composition in three movements, its mathematical possibilities are unfathomable. Out of that infinite universe, Mozart chose one particular combination as his sonata. When you start improvising his sonata from scratch, from the outset you have at your disposal an infinite number of note combinations. From them you can potentially draw a very large number of note combinations that are somehow related to Mozart's specific combination; a large number of combinations that sound very similar to Mozart's; and one combination that coincides, note for note, with Mozart's choices. Like Menard, you try out "formal or psychological variants," testing many Mozartian combinations out of the infinite possible ones and slowly discarding them. Little by little you arrive at the Mozart sonata through your own experiences, performing the miracle of remaining your true self even as you improvise Mozart's own composition! Suppose you play the same sonata a hundred times in your performing career. Every time you land on Mozart's exact spot—and every time you reach it by a different route along the infinite paths. It means the sonata never gets stale.

Liszt championed Wagner's music and conducted his operas extensively. Expressing his reaction to how Liszt performed his music, Wagner hinted at what might become your own attitude toward the composers you perform:

> [At Weimar] I saw Liszt conducting a rehearsal of my *Tannhäuser*, and was astonished at recognizing my second self in his achievement. What I had felt in composing the music, he felt in performing it; what I wanted to express in writing it down, he proclaimed in making it sound.[7]

To "proclaim in sound" what a composer expressed in writing, we'll use an excerpt from Gabriel Fauré's Sicilienne for Cello and Piano, opus 78 in G minor (example 20.8.).

▲ This exercise is illustrated in video clip #69, "Improvising Fauré I: Scales & Arpeggios."

EXAMPLE 20.8. Gabriel Fauré: Sicilienne for Cello and Piano, opus 78 in G Minor

Play scales and arpeggios in the piece's key, following its time signature and tempo indication, and respecting its mood or atmosphere. The Sicilienne is in ⁶₈, andantino, G minor. Play your scales and arpeggios not as mechanical exercises but as musically meaningful versions of the piece—haikus to the piece's sonnet, so to speak. Enter and exit the scales on any degree you want, play less than an octave, change direction in mid-scale, and so on.

The scales' lilting rhythms and colorful sounds awaken your innate creativity, and an improvised composition emerges effortlessly. Your improvisation can sound a bit like the piece, a lot like the piece, or exactly like the piece.

Most pieces in your repertoire use a relatively small number of building blocks. The Sicilienne typically employs a pattern of dotted eighth/sixteenth/eighth. Identify building blocks suitable for improvisation, discerning their rhythmic and melodic shape, implicit or explicit harmonies, and dynamics. Use a building block to improvise a self-contained musical epigram or aphorism. Transform building blocks at will. Play with a building block for a few seconds, and segue into what the composer wrote.

Every technical and musical feature in your pieces can become the subject of a dedicated improvisation. Suppose a passage challenges your coordination in some way. Isolate the passage, diagnose the difficulty, and improvise a solution. I've selected a few passages from the Sicilienne for extra attention.

🔊 These exercises are illustrated in video clip #70, "Improvising Fauré II: Local Techniques." A straightforward performance of the piece is included in video clip #71, "Improvising Fauré III: Performance."

1) There's an awkward region in the cello's fingerboard, halfway between the scroll and the bridge. The left hand feels as if stuck against the side of the cello. The little finger can't reach for its notes, and the cellist has to restrict himself or herself to using the index, middle, and ring fingers. The notes in the second bar of the Sicilienne must be played in this region. Using the Sicilienne's time signature, tempo, and mood, I play the easiest note combinations with the required three fingers until they become comfortable. Not for a second do I think of the procedure as a mechanical, physical, or technical exercise; instead, it's a simple yet delightful improvised composition. Once I find my comfort, I transform my improvisation into the passage from the Sicilienne. Then the problem is no more.

2) The cellist's left hand, in its normal, relaxed state, sounds a semitone in between each finger. To play a whole tone, the index and middle fingers have to stretch outward, potentially causing the hand to stiffen. Let's call the stretch a "problem."

If you simply stretch your hand repeatedly, you're working on the problem, not its solution. You're better off improvising a short passage without stretches; playing it with utmost comfort and musicality; and stretching your fingers opportunistically with well-timed, occasional whole tones, when the hand is having too much fun to tighten up. (Reread the section "The Inner Animal and the Opportunist" in chapter 14.)

3) At the cello, you can't avoid but move your left hand up and down the fingerboard in order to play the required notes. Sometimes the hand moves a few millimeters to cover a semitone; sometimes it jumps a foot or more for a larger interval. Gauging the distances drives most cellists insane, since complete reliability is hard to achieve. I isolate an interval in the Sicilienne that challenges my left hand, and I improvise variations that give me more security than the original interval. Once I find my comfort, I play the provocative interval without being provoked by it.

4) It's easy to get distracted by the left hand and to forget that the right hand is an equal partner in everything that happens at the cello. I bring my attention to the right hand for a while, making it stable and confident over simple passages in which the left hand faces no particular challenges. Bilateral transfer ensures that the right hand's confidence benefits the left hand. Then I go back to playing the passages as written, which the left hand now finds less challenging than before.

You can build your entire technique of playing, singing, or conducting from a never-ending series of improvisations. Reread the section "From Exercise to Improvisation and Composition" in chapter 12.

FINDING THE PRAYER

A scale is a sequence of notes arranged in ascending or descending pitch. The interval between notes may be a semitone, a whole tone, or more. It may also be less than a semitone: a quartertone, for instance. Depending on what pitches and intervals you arrange in sequence, you can construct a major scale, a minor one in several varieties, a whole-tone scale, a chromatic one, a pentatonic one, Church modes, tone rows, and so on. The musical mainstream comprises dozens of scales that are used as building blocks for phrases, sections, and whole pieces.

Ideally played or sung, a scale is impregnated with meaning and beauty. It comes from the musician's core, and it speaks to the listener's core. Such a scale is powerful and compelling, because it hints at a connection with the Divine.

In some ways, the entire body of Western classical music goes back to plainsong, in which speech, song, and prayer came together in a single line sung alone or in unison. Over the centuries this prayer-in-music underwent multiple transformations. A second line was added, at first moving in parallel with the first one. Then the two lines started interacting in more complex ways, creating patterns of consonance and dissonance, tension and release. Rhythms became more varied and agitated. A third line came in, multiplying all the complexities. The evolution has never ceased, going from plainsong to organum, from modal to tonal music, from Palestrina and Monteverdi to Bach and

Handel, Mozart and Haydn, and on to our day. Instrumental music, opera, symphonies, string quartets, and everything else in classical music springs from the same source: the prayer-in-music that was plainsong.

The balance of energies you need to perform a prayer-like scale is delicate. If you attempt to play or sing your scales "technically," the Divine goes missing. Pouring your emotional intensity into the scale also risks chasing away the Divine. Take a few notes from any scale, tonal or otherwise, and spend time exploring its divinity, using your knowledge of the harmonic series, the messa di voce, and prosody, sounding a few notes as if they were words in a psalm resonating in a cathedral. Do the same thing for precisely constructed scales: for instance, two octaves in C major, in $\frac{4}{4}$ time, four quarter notes per bar in andante moderato, ascending and descending.

If a scale uses intervals no bigger than half steps and whole steps, it's called a *step progression*. Besides the obvious scales that we detect upon sight-reading a piece or hearing it for the first time, most compositions—tonal or not—have hidden step progressions. Their component pitches don't necessarily reside side by side as they do in normal scales; instead, they may be interspersed over phrases, passages, and sections. The pitches move by combinations of whole and half steps that can different from ordinary tonal or modal scales, although sometimes they do form ordinary scales. Look at example 20.9. Two scale fragments, underlined by brackets, are perfectly visible and audible. Another scale fragment, less immediately visible, connects four pitches over four bars; in the score its notes are circled and connected.

A good way of learning your pieces consists of isolating these step progressions; performing them as divine, prayerful lines; and improvising upon them, using Borges's "Pierre Menard principle" to transform them back into the very piece you started with. For our purposes, we'll take the first sixteen bars from the Sarabande in J. S. Bach's partita for Solo Flute, BWV 1013, in A minor (example 20.10).

EXAMPLE 20.9. Step progressions

EXAMPLE 20.10. J. S. Bach: Partita for Solo Flute, BWV 1013 in A Minor, Sarabande

● This exercise is illustrated in video clip #72, "Finding the Prayer."

Within these sixteen bars there are a variety of step progressions: some short, others long, some ascending, others descending. At first it may be difficult to determine which scale fragments within your pieces are proper step progressions and how they contribute to the piece's structure. Use what knowledge you have plus a bit of intuition and imagination to work through the step progressions you detect, and let experience lead you toward greater insight and skill.

Heinrich Schenker believed that well-constructed tonal pieces could be distilled into a single scale or scale fragment, and he considered that compositions were "free improvisations" upon these very stretched-out core scales. Schenker called such an improvisation a *prolongation.* You might want to start with my simple procedure regarding step progressions as divine scales and go on to a deeper study of Schenkerian theory and practice, aiming one day to improvise an entire movement as the prolongation of the movement's core.

Step progressions lend coherence to nontonal pieces as well. Example 20.11 is from Ernst Bloch's "Schelomo: A Hebrew Rhapsody" for Cello and Orchestra. It was composed in 1917 in a style that's only intermittently tonal. Playing its underlying step progression and "prolonging" it back to what Bloch wrote is a great way to master the passage technically and musically.

IMPROVISATION AS A JOURNEY

Performing used to be very close to improvising and composing. Average players and singers in the Baroque and Classical eras ornamented passages and transitions, improvised cadenzas and interludes, realized figured basses, and composed quick nothings for specific occasions. Some of these performers may have been lousy improvisers and composers, or plain lousy musicians. Nevertheless, they made music from within (as creators) rather from without (as re-creators). They spoke the musical language as autonomous speakers with minds of their own, rather than parrots who imitate other people's sounds without necessarily understanding the relationship between sound and meaning.

In the early twentieth century, the tradition of performers who composed and composers who performed was still alive and well. The greatest piano virtuoso of the early twentieth century, Ferruccio Busoni (1866–1924), was a visionary composer. George Enescu (1881–1955), a revered violinist, composed deeply felt instrumental and vocal music. Fritz Kreisler (1875–1962), Pablo Casals (1876–1973), Artur Schnabel (1882–1951), Wilhelm Furtwängler (1886–1954), and other performers were trained composers with many works to their credit. Closer to our times, Friedrich Gulda (1930–2000) was as comfortable playing Bach as he was playing his own compositions or jazz improvisations; and Georges Cziffra (1921–1994), an immense Lisztian pianist, was a phenomenal improviser. But by now Gulda and Cziffra were the rare exceptions.

Social, historical, cultural, and economic forces have dissipated the centuries-old tradition of music made from within. The culprits include recording technologies, musicological dogma that has turned the written score into a sort of lifeless recipe, international competitions that prize flashy performances of standardized programs, ignorant teachers, and many others. Ultimately, however, it all comes down to our own choices. You can bang through competition programs for hours and hours every day, or you can spend some (or most) of your time studying the musical language, composing, improvising, and fulfilling your creative potential.

It's possible that you don't have to improvise altogether in your chosen field of music. All the same, you must make music from within, as an autonomous speaker with a mind of your own and a thorough command of the musical language. Improvisation—as a lifestyle, psychophysical attitude, and toolbox—can help you get there.

Perhaps one day you'll perform one or more improvisations in concert. Improvisation would then become both your goal and the means to achieve it. The improvisations I propose in this chapter, however, aren't always goals in themselves, but means to something else. You improvise to solve musical, technical, and psychophysical problems. You improvise to perform any composition in the best possible way, structured yet unbound, coming from within you even though someone else composed it. But mostly you improvise to make yourself whole and healthy, connected to a divine creative impulse that flows freely and yet responds to your direction and control.

You improvise to discover your true voice and become an integrated musician.

CONCLUSION

Music stands at the crossroads of the mundane and the transcendental. A drinking song in triple time, using three chords and a repetitive refrain, is almost too banal to be analyzed. It's a "nothing" bit of music. But how to explain why the song stays in our ears, why we respond to it with amusement or frustration, or why it makes two dozen strangers in a bar feel intimately bonded with one another? If we can't unravel the paradox of a drinking song, our job is infinitely harder in pondering J. S. Bach's cantatas, Mozart's operas, or Beethoven's string quartets.

You wake up in the morning, eat your breakfast, and sit at the piano to start your daily practice. The piano is a machine made of wood, metal, and plastic. It was built in a factory in Japan with tools and techniques not so different from those that are used in manufacturing buses and trucks. Your hands are made of skin, flesh, bones, and blood. In some ways, the pianist in you is an animal not entirely different from a cat or a dog.

What happens when the pianist touches the piano, when the animal touches the machine?

It's impossible to explain the miracle of music. The animal and the machine mate and give birth to the Divine. It doesn't matter how often we meet the Divine, how deeply we feel it—we can never analyze it, explain it, or teach it to others. We can't access it reliably or on command, be it in the mornings while we practice or in the evenings as we perform in public. Hope and faith are as important as the daily scales and arpeggios.

The integrated musician is an expert on everything animal and mechanical. You handle your instrument as if it were part of your own body. In fact you know your body exceedingly well. You never stop considering the laws of movement, balance, energy, tension and release, connection and flow. You know many grids—rhythmic, harmonic, tonal, modal, acoustic—and you know the Grid: the universal organizing principle that opposes order and disorder in dynamic equilibrium. You're part mathematician, athlete, musicologist, psychologist, and physical therapist. *Integrated Practice* lays out some of the things you can do to improve those aspects of your music making.

But what can you do as a musician to summon the Divine? I don't know. I can only suggest that you explore a few possibilities.

If music is a paradoxical meeting of the mundane and the transcendental, the musician's attitude is a paradox too. A scale is a prayer. Or, rather, a scale has the potential to become a prayer depending on how you perform it. Being inattentive is fatal, but being overinvested is another sure way of chasing the Divine away. Hence the paradox: You need to think and yet not think, do and yet not do, observe and yet not observe, control and yet not control. The integrated musician brings all these paradoxes together.

The composer and the improviser are creators, seeking to generate something new. The performer is a re-creator, seeking to give new life to something old. As creators, the composer and the improviser stand just a little closer to the Divine than the performer does as re-creator. It's possible, however, for you to perform any one composition as if improvising and composing it on the spot. This requires that you work on the literature from the inside out, and not from the outside in. It's a practical skill you can exercise daily until it becomes a permanent acquired reflex.

What is rhythm? Nobody can define it in an unequivocal manner. It's too big a concept, too far-reaching—and also too close to the Divine. What makes any one action "right" is its rhythm: the right duration, timing, length, and so on. To be in the moment, fully present in the *here* and *now*, is to find the right rhythm for your actions. Rhythm, then, is a musician's single most important concern. The animal and the machine become divine when their rhythms synchronize. Although we can't define rhythm, we can and must study it, practice it, and live it second by second, using all means at our disposal: prosody, the exercises of Coincidence and Rhythmic Solfège, the superbar structure, moving and dancing, declaiming poetry and scatting silly ditties.

Philosophers and poets might argue that silence is music at its most divine. The rest of us, practicing musicians, depend on sound not only for our livelihood but also for our very existence. And we know from daily experience that sound is divine indeed. One note contains the universe: I sit at the cello and draw my bow across the C string, and what comes out is so complex, so beautiful, and so vibrant that I'd willingly spend my entire life just playing that low C again and again. In fact, the C is not a note but a chord: It contains an infinite number of harmonics, of which the human ear can detect four or five easily and twelve or sixteen with relatively little training. The harmonics give birth to consonance and dissonance, to what we define as beautiful or ugly, to the entire edifice of music. All of it is right there, in that one note!

How you conceive of sound and how you perceive it will affect its divinity. We are all familiar with the story of the disbelieving Saul. On the road to Damascus, where he was planning to hunt down the "disciples of the Lord," he was struck as if by a great light and heard the voice of God, chastising him for his wicked ways. Saul went blind for three days, until Ananias visited him on God's order, laid hands on him, and told him he was going to be okay. "And immediately there fell from his eyes as it had been scales: and he received sight forthwith, and arose, and was baptized" (Acts 9:18).

From then on, he became Paul, a new person who saw every last thing in the world as having been completely changed.

Paul's experience goes to show how important perception and conception are. The ordinary world is limited and harsh. In it you see nothing but struggle and decay. Then something happens that changes your perception of it, and the same place where you dwelled in unhappiness becomes, in your eyes, a place of wonder and fulfillment. Sound is such a world, and your perception of it determines how you live in it. Once you perceive the incredible richness of a single note, your aural experiences—everything you hear, as well as everything that you sing, play, and conduct—become so intense that you might even think that the world itself has changed, not your perception of it.

We opened this book with a public class in which we heard a young pianist who was physically inept and musically incoherent. How to diagnose his problems and how to solve them? *Integrated Practice* lays out a hypothesis. To encapsulate it isn't easy, but I'd like to invoke the concept of Logos. One definition of it is "the divine wisdom of the word of God." Another is "the principle of divine reason and creative order." Etymologically, Logos comes from Greek, where it had several different meanings. One was as an instance of speaking: "sentence, saying, oration." It also meant the inward intention underlying the speech act: "hypothesis, thought, grounds for belief or action." In English, logos also gave us "logic" and "logical," and, more indirectly, "legend."

You become musically incoherent and physically inept when your music making springs from shallow, exterior sources: a desire to impress the audience, for instance, or to imitate famous musicians, or to "do" whatever you feel like doing at whatever cost to music itself. You become an integrated musician when you have something of your own to say, to recount, or to tell, and when an intention or a belief animates your discourse—when your music making springs from the Logos, paradoxically deep inside yourself and yet connected to a force bigger than yourself.

To connect with the Logos is a lifelong pursuit full of risks and dangers, and without guaranteed results. You could lose your sanity in the process, maybe even perish and die.

But it's really worth trying.

APPENDIX

An Overview of the Exercises

This overview encapsulates every exercise described in the book. Some of the exercises are illustrated in video or audio clips, in which case the clip in question is listed next to the exercise. Audio clips are preceded by the letter **A**. Video clips, which are more numerous, are simply listed in the order in which they appear in the book. A handful of exercises aren't described in the book and are bonus video clips, listed here as "web exclusives."

(continued)

Exercise Objective	Video or Audio Clip	Page
Chapter 10, "Patterning and Sequencing"		
Listen to a performance of the piece covered by the chapter.	A 13: J. S. Bach, Presto for Solo Violin	115
Understand the ambiguities of time signatures.	A 14. 𝟔 versus 𝟔	115
Develop interpretive options and the technical tools to perform them.	A 15. ABC, 123	117
Use patterning and sequencing to structure your practice.	A 16. Patterns in Isolation and in Sequence	120
Create intermediate steps to solve a technical problem.	A 17. The Circle of Sevenths	121
Use a passage's underlying structure to improve performance.	A 18. Step Progressions	124
Organize your journey along a musical path.	A 19. 4321	125
Understand the construction of hemiolas.	A 20. The Hemiola in Bars 33 and 34	126
Learn to smooth out the joints between patterns.	A 21. Joinery	127
Learn how to even out your technique.	A 22. Architectural Elements	128
Understand the closing statement in Baroque triple-time pieces.	A 23. The Closing Hemiola	129
Chapter 12, "The Juggler: A Cello Lesson"		
Optimize the sitting position through resistance and mobility.	23. Sitting & Rocking I: The Basics	148
Use the optimized sitting position to free your technique.	24. Sitting & Rocking II: At the Cello	148
Learn to move from side to side without misusing your body.	25. Sitting & Rocking III: From the Side	148
Apply the side-to-side movement in sitting.	26. Sitting & Rocking IV: From the Back	148
Study the relationship between arm rotation and the shoulders.	27. Pronation & Supination I: Shoulders & Arms	150
Study the relationship between arm rotation and hand behavior.	28. Pronation & Supination II: Arms & Hands	150
Discern between two overall patterns of coordination.	29. Pronation & Supination III: Convex/Concave	150
Balance out mobility and resistance throughout the arms.	30. Pronation & Supination IV: Resistance	150
Learn to suffuse your arms with energy.	31. Pronation & Supination V: Direction	150
Study the relationship between movement and energy.	32. Pronation & Supination VI: Movement	150
Apply your study of arm rotation in practice.	33. Pronation & Supination VII: At the Viola	150
Enhance your awareness of coordination in practice.	34. Practice Routines I: Coordination	151
Use your awareness of sound to become focused and centered.	35. Practice Routines II: Sound	152

NOTES

INTRODUCTION

1. Robert D. Levin, *The Syntax and Structure of Tonal Music* (Brooklyn: Author, 1980), 1.
2. Arnold Schoenberg, *Style and Idea: Selected Writings of Arnold Schoenberg*, edited by Leonard Stein, with translation by Leo Black (Berkeley and Los Angeles: University of California Press, 1984), 399.
3. *Tonal Music*, 228.
4. David Robinson, *Chaplin: Sa Vie, Son Art*, translated by Jean-François Chaix (Paris: Editions Ramsey, 1987), 297.

CHAPTER 2

1. Ezra Pound, *ABC of Reading* (New York: New Directions, 1934, 1960), 14.
2. Bernard D. Sherman, *Inside Early Music: Conversations with Performers* (New York: Oxford University Press, 1997), 260.
3. C. S. Lewis, "Mars & Prince Caspian," from *The Planets*, in *Poems* (New York: Harcourt, 1977), 15.
4. Bernard Gavotty, *Les souvenirs de Georges Enesco* (Paris: Flammarion, 1955), 157. My translation.
5. Allen Ginsberg, "τεθνάκην δ ολίγωπιδεύης φαίνομ αλαία," *Collected Poems 1947–1980* (New York: HarperCollins, 1984), 325.
6. Luís de Camões, *Os Lusíadas* (São Paulo: Editora Pensamento-Cultrix, 1999), 21.
7. "Allen Ginsberg (1926–1997)." http://www.poetryfoundation.org/archive/poet.html?id=2547. Accessed June 7, 2009.
8. *Style and Idea*, 414.
9. Ibid., 415.
10. Walt Whitman, "A Song of the Rolling Earth," *Leaves of Grass: The "Death-Bed" Edition*, introduction by William Carlos Williams, notes by Meir Rinde (New York: Modern Library, 2001), 275.
11. "Prosody (linguistics)." http://en.wikipedia.org/wiki/Prosody_%28linguistics%29. Accessed March 29, 2010.
12. *Style and Idea*, 300.

CHAPTER 3

1. William Packard, *The Poet's Dictionary: A Handbook of Prosody and Poetic Devices* (New York: Harper-Collins, 1989), 85.

CHAPTER 8

1. Heinrich Schenker, *Free Composition: Vol. 3 of New Musical Theories and Fantasies,* translated and edited by Ernst Oster (New York: Longman, 1979), 131.

CHAPTER 11

1. *Hamlet* (III, iii, 100–103).
2. Roland Barthes, *The Eiffel Tower and Other Mythologies,* translated by Richard Howard (Berkeley and Los Angeles: University of California Press, 1997), 119.

CHAPTER 13

1. David Yearsley, *Bach and the Meaning of Counterpoint* (New York: Cambridge University Press, 2002), 173.

CHAPTER 14

1. Cornelius L. Reid, *Essays on the Nature of Singing* (Huntsville: Recital, 1992), 168.
2. Frederick Matthias Alexander, *Man's Supreme Inheritance* (Kent: Integral Press, 1957), 188.
3. Ibid., 139.
4. Frederick Mathias Alexander, *Constructive Conscious Control of the Individual* (Downing: Centerline Press, 1985), 201.

CHAPTER 16

1. Ansel Adams (with Mary Street Alinder), *An Autobiography* (New York: Little, Brown, and Company, 1985), 21.

CHAPTER 17

1. Huston Smith, *Music of Tibet.* http://www.gemstone-av.com/mot.htm. Accessed June 6, 2009.

CHAPTER 18

1. "Lettera del defonto Signor Giuseppe Tartini alla Signora Maddalena Lombardini, inserviente. Ad una importante lezione per i suonatori di violino" (Udine, Italy: Pizzicato Edizioni Musicali, 1992), 2–3. Originally published in "Europa Letteraria," Venice, 1770. My translation.
2. *Essays on the Nature of Singing,* 89.
3. In David D. Boyden, *The History of Violin Playing from its Origins to 1761, and Its Relationship to the Violin and Violin Music* (London: Oxford University Press, 1965), 486.
4. Werner Thärichen, *Paukenschläge* (Zurich: Verlag, 1987), 19–20. This passage translated by Alexis Niki and myself.
5. Richard Hudson, *Stolen Time: The History of Tempo Rubato* (Oxford: Clarendon Press, 1994), 210.
6. Ibid.
7. Bertrand Ott, *Lisztian Keyboard Energy: An Essay on the Pianism of Franz Liszt,* translated from the French by Donald H. Windham, with a preface by Norbert Dufourcq (Lewinston, NY; Queenston, Ontario; Lampeter, Wales: Edwin Mellen Press), 2.
8. Sara Chapman Thorp Bull, *Ole Bull: A Memoir* (Boston: Houghton Mifflin, ca. 1882), 369.

9. Ibid., 371.

10. Robert Schumann, *The Musical World of Robert Schumann: A Selection from His Own Writings*, translated, edited, and annotated by Henry Pleasants (London: Victor Gollancz, 1965), 19.

11. Lina Ramann, *Franz Liszt als Kunstler und Mensch* (vol. 1), p. 167. Quoted in *Lisztian Keyboard Energy*, 69.

12. *Lisztian Keyboard Energy*, 4.

13. Ibid., 194.

14. Ibid.

15. Ibid., 144.

16. Heinrich Neuhaus, *The Art of Piano Playing*, translated by K. A. Leibovitch (London: Barrie and Jenkins, 1973), 68.

17. François Couperin, *L'Art de Toucher le Clavecin*, translated by Mevanwy Roberts (Wiesbaden: Breitkopf & Härtel, 1933/1961), 14.

18. Charles Rosen, *The Romantic Generation* (Cambridge, MA: Harvard University Press, 1995), 1.

19. Ibid., 2.

20. *The Art of Piano Playing*, 66.

21. Cornelius L. Reid, *The Free Voice* (New York: Joseph Patelson Music House, 1971), 155.

CHAPTER 19

1. Cornelius L. Reid, *Bel Canto: Principles and Practices* (New York: Joseph Patelson Music House, 1950), 98.

CHAPTER 20

1. Stephen Nachmanovitch, *Free Play: Improvisation in Life and Art* (New York: Jeremy P. Tarcher/Putnam, 1990), 41.

2. Homer, *The Iliad*, translated by Robert Fagles, introduction and notes by Bernard Knox (New York: Penguin Books USA, 1990), 14.

3. Ibid. 16.

4. Jorge Luis Borges, "Pierre Menard, Author of the Quixote," in *Collected Fictions*, translated by Andrew Hurley (New York: Penguin Books, 1999), 91.

5. Ibid.

6. Ibid., 92–93.

7. Sacheverell Sitwell, *Liszt* (New York: Dover, 1967), 196.

BIBLIOGRAPHY

Adams, Ansel. *An Autobiography*. With Mary Street Alinder. New York: Little, Brown, and Company, 1985.

Alexander, Frederick Matthias. *Articles and Lectures: Articles, Published Letters and Lectures on the F. M. Alexander Technique*. London: Mouritz, 1995.

——— . *Man's Supreme Inheritance*. Kent: Integral Press, 1957. First published in 1910.

——— . *Constructive Conscious Control of the Individual*. Downing, CA: Centerline Press, 1985.

Barthes, Roland. *The Eiffel Tower and other Mythologies*, translated by Richard Howard. Berkeley and Los Angeles: University of California Press, 1997.

Borges, Jorge Luis. *Collected Fictions*, translated by Andrew Hurley. New York: Penguin Books, 1999.

Boyden, David D. *The History of Violin Playing from Its Origins to 1761, and Its Relationship to the Violin and Violin Music*. London: Oxford University Press, 1965.

Bull, Sara Chapman Thorp. *Ole Bull: A Memoir*. Boston: Houghton Mifflin, ca. 1882.

Couperin, François. *L'Art de Toucher le Clavecin*, translated by Mevanwy Roberts. Wiesbaden: Breitkopf & Härtel, 1933/1961.

Gavotty, Bernard. *Les souvenirs de Georges Enesco*. Paris: Flammarion, 1955.

Ginsberg, Allen. *Collected Poems 1947–1980*. New York: HarperPerennial, 1988.

Homer. *The Iliad*, translated by Robert Fagles, introduction and notes by Bernard Knox. New York: Penguin Books USA, 1990.

Hudson, Richard. *Stolen Time: The History of Tempo Rubato*. Oxford: Clarendon Press, 1994.

Kennedy, Michael, ed. *Oxford Concise Dictionary of Music*. Oxford: Oxford University Press, 1996.

Levin, Robert D. *The Syntax and Structure of Tonal Music*. Brooklyn: privately printed, 1980.

Lewis, C. S. *Poems*. New York: Harcourt, 1977.

Nachmanovitch, Stephen. *Free Play: Improvisation in Life and Art*. New York: Jeremy P. Tarcher/Putnam, 1990.

Neuhaus, Heinrich. *The Art of Piano Playing*, translated by K. A. Leibovitch. London: Barrie and Jenkins, 1973.

Ott, Bertrand. *Lisztian Keyboard Energy: An Essay on the Pianism of Franz Liszt*, translated from the French by Donald H. Windham, with a preface by Norbert Dufourcq. Lewinston (NY), Queenston (Ontario), Lampeter (Wales): Edwin Mellen Press, 1992.

Packard, William. *The Poet's Dictionary: A Handbook of Prosody and Poetic Devices*. New York: HarperCollins, 1989.

Pound, Ezra. *ABC of Reading*. New York: New Directions, 1934, 1960.

Reid, Cornelius L. *Bel Canto: Principles and Practices*. New York: The Joseph Patelson Music House, 1950.

——— . *Essays on the Nature of Singing*. Huntsville, TX: Recital, 1992.

——— . *The Free Voice*. New York: Joseph Patelson Music House, 1971.

Robinson, David. *Chaplin: Sa Vie, Son Art*, translated by Jean-François Chaix. Paris: Editions Ramsey, 1987.

Rosen, Charles. *The Romantic Generation*. Cambridge, MA: Harvard University Press, 1995.

Schenker, Heinrich. *Free Composition: Vol. 3 of New Musical Theories and Fantasies*, translated and edited by Ernst Oster. New York: Longman, 1979.

Schoenberg, Arnold. *Style and Idea: Selected Writings of Arnold Schoenberg*, edited by Leonard Stein, with translations by Leo Black. Berkeley and Los Angeles: University of California Press, 1984.

Schumann, Robert. *The Musical World of Robert Schumann: A Selection from His Own Writing*, edited by Henry Pleasants. London: Victor Gollancz, 1965.

Sherman, Bernard D. *Inside Early Music: Conversations with Performers*. New York: Oxford University Press, 1997.

Sitwell, Sacheverell. *Liszt*. New York: Dover, 1967.

Smith, Huston. *Music of Tibet*. Online. Available: http://www.gemstone-av.com/mot.htm. June 6, 2009.

Tartini, Giuseppe. "Lettera del defonto Signor Giuseppe Tartini alla Signora Maddalena Lombardini, inserviente. Ad una importante lezione per i suonatori di violino." Udine: Pizzicato Edizioni Musicali, 1992.

Thärichen, Werner. *Paukenschläge*. Zurich: M & T Verlag, 1987.

Whitman, Walt. *Leaves of Grass: The "Death-Bed" Edition*, introduction by William Carlos Williams, notes by Meir Rinde. New York: Modern Library, 2001.

Yearsley, David. *Bach and the Meaning of Counterpoint*. New York: Cambridge University Press, 2002.

INDEX

Bach, Anna Magdalena, 54, 90
Bach, Carl Philipp Emanuel, 246
Bach, Johann Sebastian, 19, 49, 172–175, 235, 246, 259
   and counterpoint, 237
   and physical movement at the instrument, 161
   and punctuation, 32–33
   Works:
      Partita for Solo Flute, BWV 1013 in A Minor, 255
      First Partita for Solo Violin, BWV 1002 in B Minor, 129–130
      Second Partita for Solo Violin, BWV 1004 in D Minor, 129–130
      First Sonata for Solo Violin, BWV 1001 in G Minor, 33, 115–133
      Sonata for Flute, BWV 1030 in B Minor, 158–159, 172–175
      Second Suite for Solo Cello, BWV 1008 in D Minor, 95–96
      Third Suite for Solo Cello, BWV 1009 in C Major, 151
      Sixth Suite for Solo Cello, BWV 1012 in D Major, 74
      Toccata, BWV 914 in E Minor, 36
      "Well-Tempered Clavier," 195
back, 3, 67, 69, 85, 137, 139, 140, 143, 151, 164, 165, 223, 235
   and arms, 149–150, 168, 188–189, 191
   and backache, 158
   and the circuit of connections, 194
   and fingers, 154, 169
   and hands, 169
   and legs, 139, 159–161, 162, 171, 188–189
   and pelvis, 85, 143, 147, 149, 176–178, 180, 188, 191
   and shoulders, 68, 142, 143, 147, 148, 160, 161, 162, 171
   and vocal vibrations, 185
ba-DAM! (exercise), 220–224
balloon, 167, 176, 182–183, 243
bar line, 48–50, 108, 126–127, 130–131
Baroque music, 19–20, 32–33, 80, 88, 121–123, 129, 172, 210, 226
Barthes, Roland, 139–140
Bartók, Béla, 52
Basie, Count, 85
basketball, 150, 164, 193, 227, 237
   See also object wisdom
bass lines, 69, 78, 79, 90
beat, 48, 50
   in rubato, 78–79
   snapping exercise, 68–69

become your text (exercise), 176, 181–182
   See also delayed continuity
Beethoven, Ludwig van, 44, 59, 88, 246, 259
   Works:
      Sonata for Piano #27, opus 90 in D Minor, 232
      Sonata for Piano #32, opus 111 in C Minor, 231–232
      Variations for Piano and Cello on a Theme by Mozart, WoO 46, 57
      Variations for Piano on a Theme by Anton Diabelli, opus 120, 59, 195–198
bel canto, 228–230, 239
Bellini, Vincenzo, 233
Berény, Robert, 147
Bible, 27–28
bilateral transfer, 145, 187–198
   defined, 187
   and prosodic challenges, 195–198
   in string playing, 155–156, 191, 254
   and technical problems, 190, 191–192
   See also quadrilateral transfer
Bloch, Ernst, 256
   Works:, "Schelomo: A Hebraic Rhapsody for Cello and Orchestra," 75, 256
Boccherini, Luigi, 83
   Works:, Sonata for Cello and Piano in A Major, 83
Borges, Jorge Luis, 251–252, 255
bowing, 155–156, 189, 191, 208, 235, 260
   and consonants in articulation, 238
   and health, 14
   and messa di voce, 235–236
Brahms, Johannes, 4, 51, 59, 88, 98
   and hemiolas, 51, 64, 100, 101–102, 103–105, 106, 108
   and the opposition between iambic and trochaic pulls, 107–108
   and phrase structures, 108–109, 111–114
   Works:
      Ballade for Piano, opus 118 #3 in G Minor, 111–114
      Capriccio for Piano, opus 116 #1 in D Minor, 102–107
      Capriccio for Piano, opus 116 #7 in D Minor, 108–111
      Intermezzo for Piano, opus 10 #3 in B Minor, 98–102
      Intermezzo for Piano, opus 116 #5 in E Minor, 107–108
      Sonata for Violin and Piano, opus 78 in G Major, 220
      "St. Anthony Variations" for Orchestra, opus 56a in B-flat Major, 62–64

breath, 45, 54, 94, 178–181, 236
  as aid to awareness, 152
  compressed, 217
  and the cycle of inhalation and exhalation, 180
  and the elastic envelope, 177–178
  linguistic, 180–181
  and messa di voce, 243
  mobility and resistance in, 179–180
  and rhythm, 178, 242
  risks and dangers of, 179
  and walking, 179–180
  See also nonbreathing exercises
broom. *See* object wisdom
Bukowski, Charles, 233
Bull, Ole, 229
Busoni, Ferruccio, 257

Caccini, Giulio, 226
cadence, 55, 87–88, 127
cadenza, 87
caesura, 23
Cage, John, 150
Calloway, Cab, 74
Calvin & Hobbes, 29, *157*
Camões, Luís de, 26
Casals, Pablo, 257
cat's leap (exercise), 138, 152–156
cello, 5, 14, 60–62, 74, 75, 76, 84, 95–96, 145–157,
    171, 218, 235–236, 260
  and bilateral transfer, 155–156, 191
  and friction, 235
  and the harmonic series, 201–202, 211, 212
  left-hand exercise, 152–155
  technical problems solved through improvisation,
    253–254
  technical requirements, 146, 151
center of gravity, 177
Cervantes, Miguel de, 251–252
Chambers, Paul, 79
Chaplin, Charlie, 6
chest voice, 183–185, 217, 222–223, 239–240
"Chinese style," 5
Chopin, Frédéric, 88
  and opera, 228
  and rubato, 79
Christie, William, 19–20, 54, 67, 168
circle of fifths, 44, 46
circle of sevenths, 121, 122
circuit of bodily connections, 142, 162, 168–172,
    177–178, 188–189, 194, 195
Clinton, Hillary, 51–52
coccyx, 142, 148
coincidence (exercise), 65–67, 238, 260

in music making, 66–67
  risks and dangers in, 67
  in speech, 65–66
  using the feet in, 65–66, 67
Coleridge, Samuel Taylor, 13
Coltrane, John, 79, 161
conducting, 11, 99–100, 139, 160, 254
  beats, 68–69
  connected, 138
  and the internalized metric grid, 64, 68
  measures, 69–70
  prosodic impetus, 71–72
  and rubato, 80
  subdivisions, 88
  the superbar structure, 88, 90–93, 97
  See also rhythmic solfège
confidence, 190, 250
  in the work of art, 140, 164
connections, 137–139, 142, 148, 166, 173, 194
  between the back and all limbs, 188–189, 191
  between the back and pelvis, 176, 177, 178
  between the back, shoulders, and arms, 161–163,
    165–166
  with the creative source, 164
  with the Divine, 170, 215, 224, 247, 254–256, 257,
    259–261
  and energy, 193–195
  between the fingers and the rest of the body,
    168–172
  infinite, 176–177
  between intention and gesture in music making,
    119
  and movement, 161
  and opposition, 142–143, 162, 193
  and position, 193
  and pressure, resistance, and release, 148
  and sound, 173, 243–244
  and speech, 178, 179
  and strength, 154–155, 159–160
  and the vocal registers, 185
  and warming up, 251
consequent, 55
coordination
  and body-mind connection, 137–138
  and breathing, 179–181
  and continuity of gestures, 138
  and direction, 141–142
  first principles of, 137–144
  and the grid, 46, 142
  and the messa di voce, 226
  and mobility, 148–149
  and musical energies, 193
  necessary tension in, 147

coordination (*Continued*)
  and non-doing, 140–141, 142
  and the organization of many tasks, 145–147
  and the primary control, 142
  and prosody, 6, 107, 124, 142–144
  and resistance, 147–148
  and rhythm, 11, 65, 107, 142–144, 166, 173
  and the sitting position, 148–149
  and the standing position, 158–161
  using a text as a guide to, 181–182
  using objects to improve, 164–168
  using the tensions of music as an aid to, 125
  of the whole body thanks to vocal harmonies, 218
  and whole-body unity, 137–138
Coro de Iddanoa Monteleone, 161
Corri, Domenico, 227
Cortot, Alfred, 155
counterpoint, 44, 74, 90, 97, 209, 237
Couperin, François, 226, 231, 233
couplet, 22
creative source, 164
cricothyroids, 183
Cziffra, Georges, 257

dactylic, 21, 25, 30, 98, 113, 124
  in a grid, 63
  defined, 13, 29–30
  and hemiolas, 104–106
  illustrated, 16, 52
  impetus in conducting, 72
  in multiple media, 16
  in opposition to amphibrachic, 103–107,
    108–109
  in practice, 117–119
  in walking exercise, 13–14
dancing, 10, 11, 48, 60, 167, 260
  and bilateral and quadrilateral transfer, 188
  and combinations of finger positions, 170
  and the exercise of coincidence, 67
  latent, 68
  and messa di voce, 227
  and object wisdom, 168
  to one's own music making, 158, 161, 163, 173,
    223
  and prosody, 19–20
  and rubato, 79
  and the superbar structure, 54
  See also waltz
Dandelot, Georges, 75–76
dangers. *See* risks and dangers
Davis, Miles, 79
Debussy, Claude, 250
  Works:, "La Fille Aux Cheveux De Lin," 79, 80

delayed continuity, 122, 152, 173–174, 181–182,
  195, 198
dexterity, 57, 145, 146, 168, 229
diacritics, 33–34
diagonal transfer, 188
direction (as psychophysical energy), 141–142, 171,
  189, 193–194
  primary, 148–149, 154, 156, 218
  and the voice, 218
discarding the framework, 157, 224
discourse, 19, 28–29, 66, 140
  and breathing, 178
  and connection, 138, 178
  and improvisation, 174–175
  and the Logos, 261
  and quadrilateral transfer, 192–193
  and vocal energy, 180–182
the Divine, 170, 215, 224, 247, 254–256, 257,
  259–261
Don Quixote (Cervantes), 251–252
drinking song, 259
duple time, 50–51
dynamic accents, 59–60
  in context with other accents, 60–62
  in opposition with other accents, 62–64, 98–114

eight-bar phrases, 36, 54, 74, 88, 90, 95
  in Brahms, 110–114
  and conducting the superbar structure, 90–93
  and improvisation, 250
  and walking the superbar structure, 94–95
  See also four-bar phrases
elastic envelope, 177, 178
elbows, 69, 147, 162, 189
  and "elbows out, wrists in," 150, 193–194, 195
  as prosodists, 107
  reflex movement of in string playing, 154
Ellington, Duke, 69, 250
emotional charge, 45, 168, 190, 211
end-gaining, 139–140
energy
  of accents and stresses in metric music, 56–60
  of arm gestures in conducting, 70, 71
  as bodily directions, 141–142
  of breath, 180–181
  channels of, 141
  compressed and condensed, 194, 217–218, 240
  of consonance and dissonance, 122, 194–195
  of consonants and vowels, 238
  flowing through the body, 169–172
  and the grid, 38
  limbs as channels of, 189
  of the musical text, 138, 230

lips, tongue and jaw, 66, 107, 158
    in ba-DAM! (vocal exercise), 220–221
    in howling (vocal exercise), 216–218
Liszt, Franz, 161, 228–230, 246, 252, 257
locomotion. See walking
Logos, 261
Lombardini, Maddalena, 225, 226
looping circuit, 169
luftpause, 94
lunge, 158–161, 167, 171
    and walking, 160
Lusiadas, Os (Camões), 26

magnetic force in works of art, 90
marching bands, 54, 93
marking up scores, 33–36
mathematics
    and the four-bar phrase, 54–55
    and the grid, 39, 40, 44, 45, 46
    and the harmonic series, 202, 209, 213–214
    and the infinite possibilities of music, 252
    and intonation, 213–214
    and the metric grid, 47–48
    and prosody, 23, 57
    and rhythmic solfège, 71
measure, 26, 221, 250
    and the grid, 45, 230
    and metric accents, 56–57
    and rubato, 79
    and time signatures, 50–51
    See also rhythmic solfège; superbar structures
mechanical advantage, 160
meditation, 65, 118, 161, 162, 171, 208, 237
melisma, 186
melodic accents. See tonal accents
Menard, Pierre, 251–252, 255
messa di voce, 151, 173, 225–233
    and the actor, receptor, and witness, 236–237,
        238
    and breath control, 243
    and consonants and vowels, 238–239
    and coordination, 226
    defined, 172
    defined as a virtuosity of contact, 227–228, 273
    demise and rebirth of, 233
    and friction, 235–236
    and the harmonic series, 240–241
    historical context of, 225–226
    at the keyboard, 226, 228–233
    latent, 227, 238, 242
    as metaphorical intimacy, 243–244
    practicing, 234–244
    and prosody, 230–233

and rhythm, 228, 241–243
tangible, 227
as tension and relaxation, 226, 230
and the vocal registers, 239–240
warming up, 251
Messiaen, Olivier, 25–26
    Works:, "Quatuor pour la fin du temps," 26
meter. See metric grid; time signatures
metric accents, 56–57, 58, 98
metric grid, 47–64
    and the bar line, 48–50
    and coordination, 127–128
    defined, 45
    and energy, 46
    internalized, 46, 64, 68, 75, 99, 100, 102, 103,
        107, 114
    and the interplay of accents and energies, 60–62
    and metric accents, 56–57, 58
    opposing it, 62–64
    and rubato, 80
    and the superbar structure, 53–55, 95, 113–114
    and time signatures, 50–53
metronome, 46, 77–86
    and bodily misuse, 57, 64, 99
    latent, 86
    making friends with, 77–78
    and prosody, 85
    and unreliable sense of timing, 80
    using the foot as, 64, 85
    using the voice as, 81–83
    varieties of, 84–86
mobility, 147–148, 151, 154, 158, 160, 162
    arm, 177
    and connection, 178
    finger, 169–170
    and fixity, 166–167, 179–180, 223
    latent, 69, 145, 146, 148, 149, 151
    tongue, 216
    See also resistance
Möbius strip, 176–178
momentum, 93, 98, 121–122, 145, 166, 231
    See also impetus
Mondrian, Piet, 139
monody, 225–226
mortise and tenon, 87
movement
    needed and unneeded, 158–159
    and personality, 163–164
    potential harm in, 159–161
    See also mobility; momentum; walking
Mozart, Wolfgang Amadeus, 19, 34, 59, 69, 88, 89,
        246, 250, 252, 259
    Works:, Symphony #40, k.550 in G Minor, 35

multiphonic singing, 250
musical language. *See* language
musical notation. *See* notation
musical reverse engineering, 100–102, 108

Nachmanovitch, Stephen, 247
neck. *See* head and neck
Neuhaus, Heinrich, 231, 232
nodding. *See* anti-nodding strategy
nonbreathing exercises, 176, 178–181
non-doing, 140–141, 142, 179
notation, 33, 34, 48–49, 104, 115, 117–118
numerology, 40, 54

object wisdom, 164–168, 171
    and allowing an object to guide your hands,
        164–165
    and the hands' multiple capacities, 164–165
    and using a basketball to work on
        rhythm, 167–168
    and using a broom to work on coordination,
        165–166
    and using a paint brush to work on fixity and
        mobility, 166–167
    and using a tennis ball to sensitize the hands,
        164–165
oboe, 158–159, 168, 172–175
octave (in poetry), 42
octaves (in music), 202, 204, 207, 213
"Oh! Susanna!," 53, 55, 90
Old English, 23–24
opera, 225–226, 228–229
opportunists, 176, 185–186, 223, 254
    See also inner animal
opposition
    between the body and energies passing through it,
        194
    between elbows and wrists, 150, 193
    between fixity and freedom in rubato, 78
    of forces within the body, 85, 142–143, 188
    between the inner animal and the opportunist,
        185–186
    between the limbs and the back, 188
    between the metric grid and agogic, tonal, and
        dynamic accents, 60–64, 98–114
    between mobility and resistance, 223
    between order and disorder, 77, 131, 247
    between thumbs and fingers, 170
    between vocal registers, 186, 222
organ, 67, 107, 178, 207–208
organum, 209
oscillation, 201, 211, 213, 237
Ott, Bertrand, 229, 230–231

overblowing, 208
overtones, 201–203
    defined, 201
    in machines, 204
    and the messa di voce, 241
    at the piano, 191–192
    and the voice, 215

Packard, William, 40
Paganini, Niccolò, 161, 229, 230
paintbrush. *See* object wisdom
paradox, 86, 93, 147, 168, 176, 247, 260
Parker, Charlie, 69, 161
Parry, Milman, 249
patterning, 115–133
    applying prosodic analysis to, 117–119
    interpreting information in, 115–117
    as organized information, 119–121
    and recognizing, isolating, and practicing patterns,
        119–121
    and sequencing, 119–121, 123–129, 131–133
Paul, 260
pedal point, 128
pelvis, 137
    and back, 85, 143, 147, 150, 176–178,
        180, 191
    and breathing, 178–180
    misuse in speaking, 64, 67
    overrelaxed, 162
pendulum, 211
period (phrase structure), 55–56
Petrarch, 42
Petzold, Christian, 90–91
    Works:, Menuet in G Major, BWV anh. 114
        (attributed), 90–91, 94
piano
    as a machine, 259
    as a percussion instrument, 163, 233
    and bilateral transfer, 191–192
    and bodily misuse, 3–4, 164
    and "elbows out, wrists in," 193–194, 195
    fighting against, 102
    and the harmonic series, 191–192, 202–207, 210,
        212–213
    imitating an organ, 208
    and improvisation, 246
    and intonation, 213–214
    keyboard as grid, 44
    and legato, 230, 232
    and messa di voce, 226, 228–233
    posture and energy at, 3, 193–195
    and quadrilateral transfer, 188
    and singing, 218–220

Ramann, Lina, 229–230
Ravel, Maurice, 44
    Works:, "Valses Nobles et Sentimentales" for
        piano, 60
reflex
    acquired, 17, 20, 46, 119, 214, 260
    natural, 85, 154–155
Reid, Cornelius L., 178, 233, 239–240
relaxation. *See* tension and relaxation
release
    described, 11
    See also preparation, stress, release
repentistas, 248–250
resistance, 146, 147–148, 149, 158–161, 162
    and breathing, 179–180
    in fingers, 169–170
    gauging, 162
    latent, 147–148
    and object wisdom, 165–166, 167
    and practicing, 151, 154
    and singing, 223
    and sound production, 240–241
    See also mobility
resonance, 59, 151, 201–202, 237
    and coordination, 148
    defined, 201–202
    and intonation, 214
    and practice, 151
    and prosody, 211
    and vocalizing harmonics, 218
reverse engineering. *See* musical reverse engineering
reverse tonal accent, 58
rhyme. *See* poetry
rhythm
    and breath, 178
    constituting elements of, 10
    and coordination, 11, 65, 107, 142–144, 166, 173
    and the Divine, 260
    as driving force, 20, 24–25, 69, 73–75, 90, 93, 152
    and energy, 10, 95–96, 112–114
    and the grid, 45
    and health, 11, 143–144
    and the inner animal, 51
    in life, 9–11, 201
    as meaning and emotion, 19–20
    and messa di voce, 228, 230, 241–243
    as motor, 223
    nonmetric, 242
    and object wisdom, 167–168
    patterns in multiple media, 11–14
    and personality, 11, 13–14, 163–164
    precision and imprecision, 80–81
    and prosody, 6, 19–36, 249

and slow practice, 119
and sound, 223
and the superbar structure, 53, 88
and technique, 154–155
and walking, 9, 10
See also impetus; metronome; rhythmic solfège;
    rubato
rhythmic solfège, 68–76, 104, 152, 171, 249, 260
    advanced work with, 75–76
    conducting measures in, 69–70
    conducting subdivisions in, 70–71
    conducting the prosodic impetus in, 71–72
    coordination of the body, arm, and hand in, 68–69
    inflection and impetus in, 72
    internalizing the metric grid through, 68, 75
    scatting musical texts in, 73–75
    snapping beats in, 68–69, 249
risks and dangers
    in bilateral transfer, 187
    in breathing, 179
    in connecting with the Logos, 261
    in the exercise of coincidence, 67
    explained, 148
    in externalizing the metric grid, 99
    in improvisation, 246, 249
    in the linguistic layout, 96–97
    in making sustained sounds, 151, 168
    in the Möbius strip, 177, 178
    in object wisdom, 168
    in the plunge, 162
    in practicing a piece always from the
        beginning, 89
    in the quest for precision, 80–81
    in sitting and rocking, 148–149
    in vocal registration, 223
Rosen, Charles, 231
rubato, 46, 77–86, 228
    defined, 78
    desirable and undesirable precision in, 80–83
    experiments in, 79–80
    organic, 80, 84, 86
    and prosody, 80
    three types of, 78–79
    two personalities of, 79
Rubenstein, Arthur, 161

Saint-Saëns, Camille
    Works:
        "Carnival of the Animals," 250–251
        Concerto for Cello and Orchestra, opus 33 in
            A Minor, 58
Sappho, 25
Saul, 260

trochaic (*Continued*)
  defined, 11, 15
  and iambic contrasted, 50
  impetus in Brahms, 107–108
  impetus in conducting, 71–72
  impetus in multiple accents, 58
  impetus in the metric grid, 63, 130–131
  in multiple media, 16
  pattern of downbeats in superbar structure, 55,
    112–114
  stress in English, 33–34
  in walking exercise, 12–14
trombone, 192, 207, 208
twelve-tone music, 37, 44, 45
"Twinkle, Twinkle Little Star," 15

undertone series, 207
upbeats in Baroque music, 121–123

vibration, 176, 207, 213, 244
  of consonance and dissonance, 194
  and friction, 235
  and the harmonic series, 46, 202, 211
  and intonation, 213–214
  and machines, 204
  at the piano, 203–204, 213, 218–220
  primacy of in discourse, 19
  and resonance, 201, 218
  sound as, 182–183, 203–204
  sympathetic, 201, 207, 218–219
  vocal, 86, 181, 183, 185, 217–224
vibrato, 139, 146, 151, 153, 226
  latent, 153, 189
Vienna Philharmonic, 161
Vieuxtemps, Henri, 229
violin
  arm and hand latencies in playing, 189, 190
  circuit of bodily connections in playing, 137,
    189–190
  and the harmonic series, 212, 214, 220
  and intonation, 214
  and the messa di voce, 225, 226, 229, 230, 232
  technical and linguistic challenges, 62–64,
    115–133
Vivaldi, Antonio, 44
vocal registers, 183–185, 217, 222–224, 239
  and the messa di voce, 239–240
  See also chest voice; falsetto

voice, 89, 201
  and the birth of opera, 225–226
  and breath, 178
  and compressed energy, 217–218
  and the harmonic series, 204, 211, 215–224
  and howling, 216–218
  imitating instruments, 73–74
  and improvisation, 246
  and the inner animal, 185–186
  and the messa di voce, 225–226, 227, 233,
    237–241, 242–243, 244
  the Möbius strip, 178
  and prosody, 10–11, 20
  and sympathetic vibrations, 218–219
  and text, 181–182, 192–193
  use of as a metronome, 81–83
  and vibration, 86, 181, 183, 185
  and warming up, 251
  See also vocal registers

Wagner, Richard, 41–42, 227, 228–229, 252
walking, 137, 152, 227
  and breathing, 179–180
  and the connection between the back and pelvis,
    178, 179–180
  and the exercise of coincidence, 65–66
  and friction, 234–235
  and health, 13
  and the inner animal, 47
  and the lunge, 160
  and the primary control, 142
  and prosodic improvisation, 249–250
  and quadrilateral transfer, 192–193
  and rhythm, 9–11, 12–14
  and the superbar structure, 93–95, 97
  and time signatures, 51
  and the use of arms and hands, 167–168
waltz, 51, 60, 67, 79
Webern, Anton, 29, 41–42
Whitman, Walt, 28
  Works:, "A Song of the Rolling Earth," 28
Williams, William Carlos, 27
wrists, 82, 150, 167, 170, 177
  See also elbows

yodeling, 184
YouTube videos, 6, 67, 79, 85, 161, 215, 249
yo-yo, 18, 237

CPSIA information can be obtained
at www.ICGtesting.com
Printed in the USA
BVOW08s0207070318
509786BV00008B/376/P